A Tip A Day

WITH

Ellie Kay

A gift from **WALTON COMMUNITIES**

APARTMENT HOMES

2181 Newmarket Parkway
Marietta, Georgia 30067
Phone: 678-303-4100
www.waltoncommunities.com

Our Mission Statement
We are committed to serving the needs of families with excellence through
the development and ownership of apartment communities.

A Tip A Day

WITH

Ellie Kay

12 MONTHS' WORTH OF
MONEY SAVING IDEAS

Moody Publishers
CHICAGO

Editor: Julie Ieron
Cover: Barb Fisher, LeVan Fisher Design
Cover photo: Jimi Allen
Interior: Julia Ryan | www.DesignByJulia.com
Interior images: © 2007 Jupiterimages Corporation, © 2007 iStockphoto.com

Library of Congress Cataloging-in-Publication Data
Kay, Ellie.
  A tip a day with Ellie Kay : 12 month's worth of money-saving ideas.
     p. cm.
  ISBN-13: 978-0-8024-3433-3
  ISBN-10: 0-8024-3433-9
  1. Home economics. 2. Finance, Personal. I. Title.
TX158.K39 2008
640--dc22

                                   2007034874

We hope you enjoy this book from Moody Publishers. Our goal is to provide high-quality, thought-provoking books and products that connect truth to your real needs and challenges. For more information on other books and products written and produced from a biblical perspective, go to www.moodypublishers.com or write to:

Moody Publishers
820 N. LaSalle Boulevard
Chicago, IL 60610

1 3 5 7 9 10 8 6 4 2

Printed in the United States of America

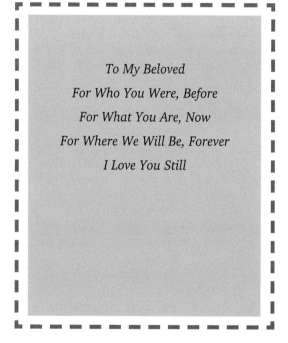

To My Beloved
For Who You Were, Before
For What You Are, Now
For Where We Will Be, Forever
I Love You Still

Table of Contents

Acknowledgments

It may take a village to raise a child, but it takes a family to birth a book—no one can do it alone.

For example, behind every mediocre, ho-hum book, there's one person writing away in solitude—no one to challenge them to excellence and no one to offer tangible help. Behind every good book, there's a team—to help sell, edit, and market the book. This team even has a hand in the practical aspects of writing a book like encouragement and ideas.

I think that behind every great book there's also a village idiot.

The village idiot thinks that a great book can impact the world. This person may or may not have any reason to believe this, but they hold fast to that driving, compelling thought—that if they do their part, the team does their part, then God may step in and something amazing can happen. I guess I'm this character in a lot of ways. It's the village idiot in me that dreams so big.

This big world theory is shared by those on my team; we're like a family that enjoys building each other up, slapping each other down (when needed) and persevering down a path to bring you the book you're reading today. Along those lines, I'd like to thank the people that made this book happen.

Steve Laube is my editor-turned-agent and he still serves in both roles in my life. His editorial eye helps take ideas and turn them into a readable format that eventually becomes a book.

He's had his hand in all my books in one way or another, and I trust his judgment in all things literary. I do not, on the other hand, trust him in all things regarding basketball. He cheers for the Phoenix Suns, for goodness sake! Everyone knows the Mavericks are America's team.

Wendy Wendler is my business manager and friend—she takes care of business details and makes it look easy. She also takes care of me and that's the hard part! I'm so thankful for her efficiency, enthusiasm, and energy. I'm also thankful that she's willing to follow me around the country and the world to bring help to those who need it.

The Moody Publishers team is next on my list of people to thank. The publisher, Greg Thornton, has such integrity and wisdom—he has built a great team of professionals that are delightful to work with. Steve Lyon is the perfect editor-in-chief, and I thank him for his help in the direction of this book. Janis Backing is the publicity manager and does a top-notch job in her role—she's also a fabulous lunch mate. She and her team are tireless and make all the hard work look effortless. Rhonda Elfstrand, the marketing brand manager, is fantastic at her job and helps ideas become reality in the publishing world. Steve Gemeiner, the director of sales, and his entire team have done an amazing job at getting the books into the stores so that people can take them home—I appreciate all your amazing efforts. Dave DeWit, the director of editorial, is such an encouragement and has wonderful ideas that have helped guide these book projects and I'm thankful for Dave's wisdom. Betsey Newenhuyse is a wonderful editorial director, one who intuitively knows what works best in publishing and how to get her team to work together toward that end. I'm pleased to be a part of that top-notch team.

Behind the professional support team, there is a personal support team that I would like to acknowledge. I have a group of friends who have been there for all these years to encourage, exhort, and energize me in the work I have to do in this world of writing. I want to thank Brenda Taylor, Madeline Brazell, Audrey Dick, Terese Wilson, Cheryl Shelton, Julie Barnhill, and Gracie Malone for their prayers, words of wisdom, and encouragement over the years.

Finally, I'd like to thank the foundational element of my team—the people who know me to be the village idiot up close and personal and who have cheered, cried, and cackled at all the right times. My beloved husband, Bob, is the one who takes care of the homefront when I am gone, makes sure my techie stuff is working well, and is there to pray with me when I want to quit. I wouldn't want to do this without you, beloved, and I thank you. My oldest son, Daniel, is following his passion of writing as well and allowed me to publish his tips in order to enhance the section on college savings. Philip, our future general, is such a help at home with a lot of the chores, the puppies, and other details. Bethany has become the errand queen and not only drives her little brothers around, but she does it with a smile on her lips and a song in her heart. Jonathan has become the master chef and that has helped me get the book writing done. I don't cook when I'm on deadline, but I'm glad you do, son, and I thank you. Joshua, well, you are the tender one with a heart that is sensitive to your mama's needs, and I thank you for your prayers and those of your class too. Last, but not least, are Missy, Moran, Oriah, and the new baby, Eden—even though you live far away, your prayers for us have been felt deeply and I thank you.

In closing out this section, I want to give honor to the One who has anointed my pen and redeemed my time—may Your name be glorified for now and forevermore.

Introduction

I'm a Master Tipper. No, I'm not talking about the money I leave on the table after we've enjoyed a good meal at a restaurant. I'd like to think I'm a *good* tipper for waitresses, concierge professionals, and valet attendants. But when it comes to knowing the easiest, fastest, and cheapest way to save money, I'm better than good, I'm a Master Tipper.

In my role as a Master Tipper, I have the privilege to travel the world, experience a few adventures here and there, and, hopefully, improve the quality of lives of families everywhere from Chino, CA, to China! On one trip last year, I was flying Southwest Airlines and something amazingly fun happened. I'd read about this kind of thing in the business book *Nuts: Southwest Airlines' Crazy Recipe for Business and Personal Success*, but I never saw it in person until that day as I was taking a flight from Dallas to Los Angeles. It had been a pretty normal travel day as I was on my way back home from a trip and looking forward to hugging my hubby, kissing my kids, and petting the puppies. We were making our way down the Jetway, standing in line, and waiting to go on board when the woman behind me said, "Excuse me, could you tell me why they didn't let us bring water through security, is something wrong today?" She was in her midtwenties and seemed a bit nervous.

I smiled warmly. "There's nothing wrong. The reason they confiscate water bottles is because there was a security threat involving liquids last year, and they set up these new requirements to protect our safety. It's inconvenient, but it's designed to keep us safe."

She shifted from one foot to another. "I've never flown before and it's been nerve-wracking to try and be sure I do everything right." She smiled weakly and confessed, "Besides that, I'm a little scared."

I looked in her eyes and gently patted her arm. "Why don't we board together? Since I've done this a few times, I'll explain what's happening, so that you can stay calm and enjoy your flight."

When we boarded, all the seats in the front were filled, so I led the way toward the middle of the aircraft. As I reached up to open the closed overhead luggage bin, I reassured my new traveling companion. "It's great weather out there today, so I think we're going to have a very good fli - - FLI- - FLIGHT!!"

I SCREAMED and jumped back from the overhead bin.

In the compartment was a smiling flight attendant who was hiding—part of the "nuts" style of flying that made Southwest Airlines famous.

As the rest of the passengers laughed in hilarity at the sheer surprise of the unexpected, the size-four flight attendant crawled down from the bin. Stunned, I looked over at my new charge. So much for being the calm, cool, and collected flying veteran.

She was frozen to her spot in the aisle and stuttered, "D-d-do they al-always k-k-eep the extra s-s-stewardesses in there?"

There's a huge difference between someone who flies all the

time and someone who is on their first flight. For one thing, those who never fly call the employees "stewardesses," while frequent fliers will call them the more conventional "flight attendants." Some curmudgeonly pilots will use the slang term (which they hate) known as "Stu"—never call them that unless you want to walk from Dallas to Los Angeles.

When it comes to saving money, some of you are frequent fliers or master savers, while others reading this book are beginners, on their first flight out of the airport. There's going to be a great contrast between the veteran who has been shopping for bargains for a decade and the brand-new bride who has new responsibilities for the first time. This book is not meant to exclude either of these groups—we're all on the same plane and the people on row one will arrive to their destination at the same time as the people in row fifty-one. To the veteran, some of these tips may seem like common sense. But to the novice, they've never learned to look at saving money, much less recognize the savings factor the first time down the aisle (so to speak). Conversely, to the novice, some of these tips may be hard to comprehend, so I've marked certain tips "advanced" in order to distinguish the fact that sometimes there's no substitute for experience. While you may not fully grasp the full understanding of a tip that's marked "advanced," just keep shopping and saving and you'll eventually say, "Aha!! THAT'S what the Master Tipper meant in her tips book."

Hopefully, some of you who feel you're only a beginner or intermediate saver will come across some of the advanced tips and think, "Wow! I'm really a better saver than I thought, because I already practice this tip." And finally, there will be a group of Majestic Misers who pride themselves on their saving skills, turn up their aristocratic noses, and say, "These tips aren't really advanced, I learned these when I was still in my teens!" To this last group, I say, "Ah, NUTS!"

It's great to save money and that's the primary focus of this book. But living life is more than saving money. If we can save time while saving a cent, then there's a greater reward for the effort. If we can save a marriage by learning to communicate about money, then we've preserved something priceless. And if we send some of our resources to support a child in a third world country, then we've saved something eternal. So be aware that the tips in this book are not just about money, they are about everything our financial lives touch: the products, the people—and the purpose.

SECTION ONE

The Coupon Queen Rules

*Tips to Save on Groceries,
Cleaners, and Toiletries*

I remember the very first time my eyes locked onto it. In my seven-year-old mind I didn't realize it at the time, but this was love at first sight. Who would have thought that a little piece of paper would one day open the door to a literal, million-dollar life? There was something magical about the script, the numbers, and the pretty picture. It was as if I'd found out the king and queen of Genovia were at the same hospital as my parents when I was born and that I was switched at birth. It was as if the royals took home the wrong baby and I was a princess who went to live with mere commoners. No wonder it was hard for me to keep my room clean. I was destined to have servants! No wonder I didn't like shopping at K-Mart. I was to have a personal seamstress design my clothes! Yes, even as a child, I had the sense that a mere piece of paper could take my common destiny and turn me into a privileged blue blood instead.

What was this precious paper you ask? The paper I fell in love with that day was—a *coupon*.

Coupons made me feel like a queen and ushered in a million-dollar life. I'm such a numbers person that I actually came up with the million-dollar mark. Coupon clipping helped my prince and I get out of $40,000 in consumer debt when we first got married. If we only paid the minimum of $600 per month on that debt (at 18 percent APR), then it would have cost $360,000 and taken 50 years of "indentured servitude" to pay off the credit card companies. Also, by using coupons I saved an average of $8,000 per year for twenty years, which is the equivalent of $13,500 earned on the economy if I were to work outside the home and pay social security, state, and federal taxes. By investing only a portion of that savings each year ($6,000) in an 8 percent mutual fund, we would earn a total of $133,520 after ten years of investing and $280,000 after twenty years of investing! Furthermore, the "Savings Queen" mentality transferred to our children and their desire to pay for college, debt free, with scholarships and work-study programs. Our oldest son, Daniel, garnered a scholarship to the University of Texas at Arlington that is equal to $62,000, and our next son, Philip, just received an appointment to the United States Naval Academy worth $380,000. Add the numbers.

Then, as icing on the cake, my financial habits led to books that expanded on the idea of saving. This led to speaking opportunities and more writing. These led to freelance consumer education spokesperson work for firms like Mastercard, Visa, and Washington Mutual. This brought my coupon-inspired savings lifestyle up to the million dollar mark, and all because at the age of seven, I saw a twenty-cent coupon for a package of Kellogg's Corn Flakes and it changed my life.

But I'm not alone. By learning how to save money in stores for groceries, toiletries, and cleaners, you can also begin your journey to a million dollar life as you also apply the savings tips from other sections in this book and train your children to do the same! The only true failure would be to never start. Here are some tips to save money in the store, whether you're destined to be a Savings Queen or not. If you apply a few of these tips, you could save up to 50 percent and if you apply most of them, you could cut your food bill by as much as 80 percent. Here are some of the best tips to transform you from a coupon commoner to a Coupon Queen.

#1 **TIP OF THE DAY:**
THE LIST: Research indicates if you shop with a list *and stick to it*, you are likely to spend as much as 30 percent *less* than listless (pun intended) shoppers. The exception would be when you can get items for pennies (or free) that are not on your list—get these anyway!

TIP OF THE DAY:

IMPULSE "BUY-BUY" GUYS: Using a list has a second benefit: researchers show that the typical consumer spends almost $100 per hour while shopping in a discount department store, grocery store, or discount club. In other words, the more time you have to window-shop, the more money you'll spend. Just think, spending thirty minutes more in a store can cost you $50! So get in and get out of there as quickly as possible and say bye-bye to impulse buys.

TIP OF THE DAY:

STORE DIRECTORY: Make your list according to aisle order and you'll save even more time and money. By shopping according to aisle order, you won't become a grocery nomad—wandering back and forth while you look for that last item on your list. Go to the customer service desk at the store you frequent and ask them for a map of the store. These are usually called *an aisle order chart, store directory,* or *store map.* **(ADVANCED)**

TIP OF THE DAY:

PRICE COMPING: Many stores, including Wal-Mart Superstores, will match competitors' sale prices. Check and see which stores do this in your area, note the store and sale price on your list, bring those sales circulars with you, and then ask the checker for the lowest price. This tip takes only minutes and saved our family over $3,500 last year because it can also apply to anything in the store (electronics, household goods, etc.). It also saves time and gas.

♛

BEYOND COMPING: As you are taking advantage of

price comping (see previous tip), take it a bit further by making sure you comp the store brand as well. For example, if Safeway offers a sale on their brand bread for only $.49 a loaf, you can substitute the store brand at the price comping store (Wal-Mart would have the Great Value or Sams brands). Sometimes, when these items are on sale in the circular for such a good price, they are gone from the original grocer's shelves, but they are still available (with a wider selection) at the price comping store.

Another advantage has to do with the price comping "limit" per customer. For example, the sale circular may say "limit two per customer," and while you go to the original store and get your two items, you can also get an additional two items at the next store, the store that is price comping those sales. **(ADVANCED)**

TIP OF THE DAY:

TUNE OUT AND CASH IN: Watch fewer television commercials. A recent consumer report indicated that couch potatoes are far more likely to overspend at the store for each one minute commercial they watch due to the marketing effects of this medium—to the tune of an average of $260 per hour! Keep in mind that this dollar figure includes everything from Starbursts and diet Coke to a new car or luxury item.

♛

TIP OF THE DAY:

SAVINGS 101: Buy products when they are on sale. This may sound elementary and it is, but you'd be surprised at how many people do not take advantage of sales. They're "too busy" to shop the sales, or when something goes on sale, they think, *Well, I still have some of that at home, I don't need it now.* Get the sale ads in your weekly paper and make your list according to what is on sale. Be sure and put your list in aisle order and save the sale ads for your price comping trips.

TIP OF THE DAY:

SALE AWARENESS: Don't give in to "impulse buying" for sales. If the discount is only 10 percent, then think twice about giving in to the urge to buy the product simply because it's on sale. The exception would be if the item is needed immediately—in that case, you can be grateful for the fact you've saved 10 percent rather than nothing!

TIP OF THE DAY:

LOSS LEADERS: Shop the loss leaders. These are items in the sale circular that the store is selling for less than their cost in order to get the consumer into the store. If you come in to buy the $.99 chicken breasts, then chances are good you'll go ahead and pick up another thirty to forty items you "need" while you're in the store.

♛

TIP OF THE DAY:

MANUFACTURERS' COUPONS: Use manufacturers' coupons. These are found in a free-standing insert (or FSI) booklet in your Sunday paper. They are also found in magazines, newspapers, product boxes, and mailbox circulars. By organizing these and combining them with other savings factors, a family could save as much as our family did last year—over $13,000. An average family of seven spends $16,000 per year and our family spent only $3,000—and it all began with a manufacturer's coupon!

TIP OF THE DAY:

BUY BRANDS BUT . . . Don't be brand specific. One of the most common misconceptions is that buying the generic brand will save more money than buying a major brand—that's not true! If a shopper buys a major brand on sale and with a coupon or other savings factor, they will repeatedly save more than buying generic.

TIP OF THE DAY:

DOUBLE (OR TRIPLE) THE SAVINGS: Go to a double or triple coupon store. These stores will double the face value of your coupon up to fifty cents or one dollar and they will triple from $.33 to $.50 (depending upon the region and the store). Be aware of the limitations these stores may have in order to maximize your savings. For example, I found Uncle Ben's rice for $1.69 and I had a double coupon worth $.50. This means I would pay $.69 for the rice. But I waited for it to go on sale for $1.09 (another savings factor) and only paid nine cents per box! For a full list of stores that double coupons, go to the links page at www.elliekay.com.

#13 TIP OF THE DAY:
LIVE BEYOND THE LIMIT: If a store has limitations on the sales or use of coupons, then organize your coupons to get the best value each time you run to the store for milk, a newspaper, or coffee (we have a Starbucks in our Vons). For example, if the double coupon policy will only double one coupon per like item, and you can get that item for free or pennies, then paper clip all these freebie coupons together and place them in an envelope in your purse. Each time you run to the store for some unexpected essential (we even have a pharmacy in our store and dry cleaning as well), then use those extra coupons and cash in on the double coupon savings. There's nothing illegal or immoral in making those essential, little trips worth more.

The exception would be if the ad specifies that the sale item is limited to "one item per family" (for example, a coupon for a free turkey during the Thanksgiving sales). In that case, it's important to limit the purchase to only one. **(ADVANCED)**

TIP OF THE DAY:

ONLINE SAVINGS—ESPECIALLY ON ORGANIC: Visit the money savings links at www.elliekay.com on a regular basis. For example, at www.valuepage.com, there's a link for the coupon directory at www.couponDirectory.com. The customer enters her zip code and the site will provide a list of participating stores.

For organic, you can get many USDA-certified staples at www.SunOrganic.com, or you may want to try specialized online grocers. Diamond organics (www.diamondOrganics.com) ships perishables by FedEx, which can be costly but delivery fees are waived on "sampler" boxes. Companies such as Urban Organic (www.urbanorganic.com) and Door to Door Organics (www.doortodoororganics.com) can make weekly deliveries in certain areas.

Organic food is expensive because it's labor-intensive to produce and sell, and without pesticides, farmers lose crops more easily. So, why not head to an organic farm? Local Harvest offers a list of them at www.LocalHarvest.org/organic-farms.

TIP OF THE DAY:

STORE CARDS: Use a store card or "clipless coupon." Some stores offer a discount card that provides additional discounts on selected products. In most cases, about a month after registration, the system will be in place to enter a phone number to access the discount card, and the customer doesn't need to have the actual card with her. Savings on these cards range from 10 percent to 50 percent.

These cards will also track purchases and provide critical marketing information to the store for marketing analysis. Some consumers do not want their actual information (address, name, email address) linked to these cards, so they have the option of getting a card without listing private information. Ask your store manager about this latter option.

TIP OF THE DAY:

STORE CARDS LINKED TO DEBIT CARDS: These store cards should never ask for personal information such as social security numbers. However, some store systems will automatically link to a debit card if the consumer provides this information and expresses a desire for the convenience of having all the information available in one swipe of the card. The customer will still need to access a PIN number. But the consumer needs to also be aware that in this case a swipe of the card will actually access checking account information. Consumers should use extreme caution if they decide to link their debit card to the store card as it has the potential, despite security devices, to compromise checking account information. They might also want to change their PIN number every couple of months. **(ADVANCED)**

TIP OF THE DAY:

ELECTRONIC COUPONS: Use *manufacturers'* electronic coupons. These are available on the shelves in the stores and are ejected from an electronic dispenser (kids love 'em!). But keep in mind that most of these have a notice along the top that states: *May not be doubled.* So if you don't have a coupon and plan to buy that item, then use the electronic coupon. But if you already have a manufacturer's coupon and the double value of that will be greater than the face value of the electronic coupon, then don't use it; just take it, file it in your coupon box for use at a later time.

TIP OF THE DAY:

STORE COUPONS: A *true* store coupon is one that is issued by the store and *not* the manufacturer. Consumers can tell if it's a true store coupon by the redemption address in the coupon's fine print. If it has the manufacturer's name, then it is an in-ad manufacturer's coupon. It's important to read the fine print. If it has the *store's* name and address in the fine print or if there is *no address* and only the store's name, then it is a genuine store coupon. This will be a critical point in the ability to layer savings factors while using a store coupon.

TIP OF THE DAY:

PRICE STORE COUPONS: These are usually store coupons, but sometimes they are manufacturers' coupons. These coupons will give the shopper a product for a specific price and sometimes free. For example, I used a store price coupon last week for Colgate toothpaste, which gave me a price of $.99 (a savings of $2.00 off the regular price).

♛

TIP OF THE DAY:

INSTANT COUPONS: Look for product instant coupons. Sometimes products will have a "Use This Coupon Now" coupon attached that you can tear off and use immediately. Keep in mind that these are always a form of a manufacturer's coupon.

TIP OF THE DAY:

PRODUCT PACKAGING: Look inside the product for more manufacturers' coupons, special offers, or rebates. Sometimes there will be a coupon inside the box for cents off the next purchase or for a rebate or another special offer. I got Kellogg's cereal bowls for a couple of box tops and $2 postage and handling—these were quality bowls that the kids used for several years.

TIP OF THE DAY:

ASSEMBLE A COUPON BOX: Buy a plastic shoe-sized box that has a secure snap-on lid as a central place to store all these coupons. Purchase alphabetical tabs, a highlighter, scissors, pen, and paper (for lists), and you'll have coupon box fit for a Queen!

TIP OF THE DAY:

ORGANIZE COUPONS: Try using an alphabetical approach to organize your coupons rather than a category system. It is more efficient and easier to maintain when you file coupons by the name that is most prominent on the coupon. I've had hundreds of families who have made this switch and testify that it saves time. Highlight expiration dates!

TIP OF THE DAY:

PULL EXPIRED COUPONS: Read through your coupons each month. To keep coupons organized and up-to-date, at the end of each month you will want to sit down with a cup of coffee, some chocolate, and perhaps a new DVD release. While doing this, go through all these coupons, take out the expired ones, and make sure any wayward coupons are re-filed in their proper place.

TIP OF THE DAY:

SHARE EXPIRED COUPONS: Be a Coupon Fairy. If you know a military family stationed *outside* the physical United States, then be a coupon fairy to these special families. Send them any expired coupons because they can use these in military commissaries for up to six months past the expiration date. For a list of current bases, email us at expired@elliekay.com and place "Military Families" in the subject box. We will email a list of overseas bases that will love to get expired coupons. Because of Department of Defense security issues, we cannot list these on our website or print them in this book, but we can email them to you! Be sure to mark "Expired Coupons" on the outside of the package when you send these overseas and fill out a customs form. **(ADVANCED)**

TIP OF THE DAY:

TAKE IT ON THE ROAD: When leaving for a vacation or taking an extended trip to another city to see family, take the coupons with you. This system works anywhere, but the savings factors will range from average to super depending on the offers available at local stores. For example, when our family of seven spent a few days with my sister in Missouri, my husband suggested we pay for a week's worth of groceries for them. My sister bought everything she normally buys and I took my coupon box with me and suggested a different brand every now and then. Her usual total was $300, but with my coupons (at her double coupon store), we only paid $150. It was a win-win situation and one that convinced her she needed to get her coupons organized!

TIP OF THE DAY:

REBATES: Some stores are making rebating very simple, by including them in their sale circulars and advertising campaigns. The consumer buys a product, submits the receipt (or a proof of purchase in some cases), and gets a rebate check in the mail or a coupon for a free product. The key to this tip is to pick and choose offers that are convenient and are not time-consuming. If rebates are part of a sale circular and are outlined and all the customer has to do is turn in the receipt and form, then it is worth the time and postage. A good rule of thumb when considering the price of a postage stamp and envelope and your time is to make sure the rebate is for $5 or more. If you can file them online, it's almost always worth your time.

TIP OF THE DAY:

#29 WEIGH PRODUCE: Not all ten-pound bags of baking potatoes and other produce are created equal. Some bags of oranges, apples, or grapefruit can vary by as much as almost a pound. One five-pound bag may weigh 5.5 pounds and another may weigh 4.6 pounds. Take two minutes to weigh three different bags and get the one that weighs the most.

TIP OF THE DAY:

MAKE FRIENDS WITH A STOCKER: The produce manager or stocker will oftentimes mark down those overly ripe bananas if you ask (and riper bananas make better banana bread anyway!). This also applies to any produce that has a blemish. You can cut a bruise off of an apple while making fruit salad and get a discount for the asking. Follow the same process with the meat, bakery, and dairy departments. Ask the section supervisor for day-old meats or dairy products that are still within the expiration dates but are not fresh enough to be sold at full price.

TIP OF THE DAY:

BE READY IN SEASON AND OUT OF SEASON: Read your local paper daily and ask store personnel for any upcoming bargain days or special values. In California a few months ago, Ralphs and Vons began competing for the market share of grocery shoppers. Vons offered three days of unlimited triple coupons (up to $1). There were loads of things that could be acquired for free with coupons.

The next week, Ralphs followed up with their own offer of three days' worth of unlimited triple coupons. I ran to the store that day, got two carts of groceries, and paid only $5. I took my megareceipt to a PTA meeting that night and showed my girlfriend, who immediately took it to her husband to show him the receipt. Before he even looked at it, he shrugged his shoulders and skeptically said, "It's not in how much you save,

♛

it's in the percentage that you save." She quickly glanced at the bottom line, where the store lists the savings and percentage. "Sweetie, would you say that 99 percent is a good percentage of savings?"

He became a believer right then and there. **(ADVANCED)**

TIP OF THE DAY:

CHEAPER DOES NOT MEAN BETTER: Getting the best value is an important thing to think about when it comes to grocery shopping. For instance, less expensive, bigger bottles of other name-brand products may seem like a better value in the store, but appearance can be deceiving. With a product like Dawn, which has 40 percent less water than the name brands, you're getting what you pay for: more cleaning power, less water, and you are able to wash a sink full of dishes without the water feeling greasy. That's because Dawn contains more cleaning power per drop.

Insurance Assurance

*Tips to Save on Life, Health,
Homeowners, and Auto Insurance*

A while back I got a call in between a phone-in radio interview and an interview for an article in *Family Circle* magazine. My mind was spinning with facts and tips and quotable material when my personal business line rang and Philip, our seventeen-year-old son, said, "Mama, I'm at the Vons intersection and I just had an accident, can you come help me?" Thankfully, the scene of the accident was only one mile from our home and I was there in less than five minutes, only to see my son's Ford Escort completely smashed into the size of a motorcycle and a dazed Philip standing in his junior ROTC uniform on the sidewalk talking to a deputy sheriff. All 6'4" of the boy was towering over the law enforcement officer as he gave his version of what happened.

Philip later said that when he was calling me on the phone, the deputy sheriff mistook him for an enlisted air force member and said, "Sir, you need to get off that phone and give us a report; you can talk later." To which Philip replied, "Sir, I'm only seventeen years old and I want my mama here." While he was stunned and not quite coherent for a while, he was physically unharmed and we were thankful. When Philip realized he had totaled the car, we said, "That's why we have insurance, son."

Insurance is something that almost everyone has and no one wants to use. Most people do not ever anticipate using their insurance, unless it's for something pleasant like a baby (and with the five children I've borne, we've more than gotten our money's worth out of our maternity policy!). But the only thing that would have been worse on the day of Philip's crash would have been if we had been dazed by the idea that we didn't have coverage for his vehicle and/or the other vehicle involved in the accident.

There is a way to save on your insurance without scrimping on the coverage if you know the right questions to ask and the right policy to secure for all your insurance needs. I was an insurance broker for quite a few years, and here is the insider's information on how to have insurance assurance.

TIP OF THE DAY:

LIFE INSURANCE—PROVISION NOT INSURANCE

INVESTMENT: When it comes to life insurance, many people buy a Ford at Rolls Royce prices. But it's important to remember that life insurance is meant to be a *provision* for expenses related to your death (or the death of a family member) and for the life of your beneficiaries after you are gone (children's college, credit bills, living expenses that would be missed if a wage earner dies, etc.). In most cases, life insurance should not be used as a means of saving money or an *investment*. It tends to be one of the most expensive ways to invest for the future, especially when you consider broker commissions. If you look at life insurance as provision rather than investment, then you'll buy a Ford Escort at Ford Escort prices—and invest the difference with one of the investment tools outlined later in this book.

The following tips will help you navigate life insurance policies so that you can buy the policy that is best for you without giving in to the pressure of buying the policy that is best for your insurance broker (and his commissions or his goal to win the trip to Tahiti).

✵

#34 TIP OF THE DAY:
LIFE INSURANCE—LEVEL TERM:
PROS: These include level payments over a specific period, usually five, ten, fifteen, or even twenty years; it may be convertible to a permanent policy. **CONS:** More expensive than an ART (annual renewable term) in the early years; less expensive in the later years.

TIP OF THE DAY:

LIFE INSURANCE—WHOLE LIFE (PERMANENT): PROS:
Fixed premiums; cash value you can borrow against; possible dividends; tax-deferred earnings; guaranteed death benefits. **CONS:** Initially considerably higher premiums than term insurance; little flexibility in premium payments. Oftentimes another investment vehicle will provide better returns at retirement, with or without the tax benefits (IRAs, Health Savings Accounts, CDs, 401Ks, etc.).

TIP OF THE DAY:

LIFE INSURANCE—UNIVERSAL LIFE (PERMANENT): PROS:
Flexible premiums; tax-deferred earnings on cash value; access funds; different options allow cash buildup or insurance protection. **CONS:** If interest rates fall, low cash value buildup may cause policy to lapse unless you add money.

TIP OF THE DAY:

LIFE INSURANCE—VARIABLE LIFE (PERMANENT): PROS:
Fixed, level premiums; guaranteed death benefit; choice of investment options. **CONS:** Premiums start low but rise with each new term; nothing back if you outlive contract.

TIP OF THE DAY:

LIFE INSURANCE—ANNUAL RENEWABLE TERM (ART):
PROS: Usually the most coverage for the least money; protection in increments of one year; can renew yearly up to specified age (usually seventy); may be convertible to permanent policy, accumulates no interest. **CONS:** Premiums can increase considerably each year.

As premiums increase (due to the policyholder's age) the overall need for as much insurance diminishes. At sixty, you will not need to have a policy that will cover putting the children through college, consumer debt, lost wages, because many of those needs have already been taken care of and are no longer an issue.

TIP OF THE DAY:

LIFE INSURANCE—VARIABLE UNIVERSAL LIFE (VUL/ PERMANENT): PROS:
Similar to variable life but with flexible payments. You select the investment vehicle that generates your cash value growth (stocks, bonds, etc.). **CONS:** You are investing your own additional monies beyond the premium payments in order to have cash value growth, and you assume the investment risk, not the insurance company. Nonpayment will lapse the policy. Most VUL policies generate 70 percent in agent commissions the first year.

TIP OF THE DAY:

ONLINE LIFE INSURANCE QUOTES: To compare prices on a variety of term insurance policies, go to www.selectquote.com or call 1-800-343-1985. Always be as accurate and truthful as you can about your health condition and habits (smoking, drinking, prescription drugs, general health, pre-existing conditions, etc.). On the television show *House*, the title physician loves to say, "All patients lie." Well, this is the time to prove Dr. House wrong—be honest on your life (and health) insurance applications! Most policies require a physical evaluation and if the information is not accurate, then the quote will be inaccurate as well.

TIP OF THE DAY:

LIFE INSURANCE FOR KIDS: If the primary purpose of life insurance is *provision* rather than *investment*, then the children's policy should basically be an amount that would cover burial expenses. A child is not a wage earner (unless you're the mom of a Dakota Fanning–type actor) and there will be no income to replace. Therefore, you should never financially benefit from your child's death. Likewise, a child's policy should not be used as a savings vehicle for college expenses. There are far richer options for investment for a child's education found in the section on education.

TIP OF THE DAY:

SAVE ON MEDICATIONS—ASK FOR SAMPLES: If you're on a budget, let your physician know. Many doctors will save certain samples of medications for those who need these.

TIP OF THE DAY:

SAVE ON MEDICATIONS—GO OTC: Over-the-counter medications can be less expensive than their prescription counterparts. Always ask your doctor if there is an OTC equivalent and compare.

TIP OF THE DAY:

SAVE ON MEDICATIONS—GO GENERIC: Many generic drugs are high quality and are still regulated by the FDA (Food and Drug Administration) so you know they are safe. The good news about these prescriptions is that you are not only saving yourself money, you're saving your insurance company some bucks as well.

TIP OF THE DAY:

SAVE ON MEDICATIONS—COMPARE BRANDS: If you don't want to use a generic medication or there isn't one for the prescription you need, be sure to compare different brands— some are priced less expensively than others.

TIP OF THE DAY:

SAVE ON MEDICATIONS—SHAVE AND SAVE: My first book was called *Shop, Save and Share*, and it was kind of hard for radio and television hosts to say when they introduced me. One host welcomed me as the author of *Shop, Shave and Share*! When you are maintaining your health and experiencing a variety of ailments, it's easy for your list of daily (or weekly) medications to grow. Keep a list of these medications and review them with your doctor regularly to see if there are any that can be shaved off the list. Not only can this tip save you money, it could prevent you from continuing to take prescriptions or medications that are no longer necessary for your condition. This could also prevent complications from taking drugs you don't need!

TIP OF THE DAY:

GET FINANCIAL HELP ON PRESCRIPTIONS: You may qualify for financial help for these drugs. Go online to www.pparx.org/about.php, which links you to more than 475 assistance programs and 150 pharmaceutical company programs.

TIP OF THE DAY:

USE STORE COUPONS FOR PRESCRIPTIONS: Pharmacies in grocery stores are becoming the norm and they are a competitive market. Look in the sale ads for transferred or new prescription values. For example, I took two of my children to the doctor for strep throat and needed two prescriptions. Our primary insurance covered the doctor's visit and the secondary covered the co-pay. I took Jonathan's prescription to the Von's pharmacy with a coupon for a "$25 store gift card with a new prescription" and then dropped off Joshua's prescription next door, in the same shopping strip mall, at Rite Aid. This second pharmacy had a "$20 store gift card with a new prescription." This "cost" me about ten minutes out of my day and we came out $45 ahead in store gift cards for our trouble. **(ADVANCED)**

#49 TIP OF THE DAY:
SHOP AROUND: You could save thousands of dollars by getting a second or third opinion on the cost of surgery, hospitals, and anesthesiologists. Make sure the referrals are covered by your primary insurance and that the provider is on the list for approved surgeons. Do your due diligence on the doctor (research on the Internet, get referrals, check with the state medical board for any physician complaints). The Federation of State Medical Boards has a website for this information that patients can access that gives this kind of information on doctors. The address is www.docinfo.org/.

This research should help you select a doctor who meets your medical needs, confidence needs, and financial needs.

❂

TALK TO YOUR PPO OR HMO PROVIDER YOURSELF:

The patient's first line of defense is usually the doctor's office, which will talk with your medical provider to see if a certain procedure or medication is covered under your plan. If your primary physician's office has already talked to your health insurance provider and the claim is denied, then get all your paperwork and make the secondary call yourself. There is usually a little leeway in the approval process in these situations. It's sometimes harder for a live person on the phone to turn down coverage to the patient than it is for the HMO administrator to tell the doctor's office they will not cover it. Before you call, it is essential that you arm yourself with the following:

* Your policy number and rejected claim number

* A copy of the original request from your doctor's office with all codes listed

* A definition of those codes (researched by you and provided by your doctor's office—you have to know what you are talking about!)

* A good understanding of why they are rejecting the claim (talk to the claims administrator at your medical office first). Part of the problem may be in communication and a claim may be accepted because they are operating on a wrong set of information

- Reasons why this medication or procedure is necessary for your situation (quality of life issues involved, ability to do your work, long-term health implications, ability to care for your children)

- Percentage of wages that this claim rejection would cost you (if the surgery costs $15,000 and you make $50,000 per year, that's roughly one-third of your annual salary and almost one-half of your take-home pay that you will have to cover out of pocket)

- This one phone call, if it resulted in a claim being covered, can make the difference in refinancing your home, covering college for your children, and/or having the ability to make ends meet for the next several years. **(ADVANCED)**

TIP OF THE DAY:

HEALTH INSURANCE—BUY WHAT YOU NEED: One of the reasons people cannot afford health insurance is because they don't realize that there are policies out there that are varied and even tailor-made for your health insurance needs. You should never purchase services you will not use. For example, if you will not have any more children, then there's no need to pay for a maternity rider. If your children are toddlers and there is no current need for orthodontics, then do not purchase that on a dental plan—wait to add it until your children are in adolescence. Only buy what you need and make sure you know what kind of riders exist for additional coverage (and additional premiums) so that you do not overpay.

TIP OF THE DAY:

HEALTH INSURANCE—GET FREE MEDICAL SERVICES:
There may be well-baby checkups, shot clinics, and other medical services that are provided in your community at a discount or even for free. For a full list of these medical services and the limitations necessary to qualify for these programs, go to the nonprofit site www.eHealthinsurance.org.

TIP OF THE DAY:

EMPLOYER HEALTH INSURANCE:
It used to be said that the best policy you can get for health insurance is the one offered by your employer. However, that is no longer true. If the employer covers 100 percent of your group policy premiums, then by all means, keep it. But most employers will only cover the employee and not the family. In a growing number of companies, they no longer even offer 100 percent of the premium payment for the employee either! In this case it's a good idea to shop around. For a full menu of companies and a quick online quote (with no sales representatives calling), go to www.eHealthinsurance.com.

TIP OF THE DAY:

SPLIT HEALTH INSURANCE POLICIES:
Group policies are generally a lot more expensive than individual health insurance policies. In some cases, family members may have preexisting

conditions that are best covered under a group policy. If these preexisting cases were to come up on a new individual policy (rather than a group policy), then the health insurance company would have every right, in most states, to deny coverage on that condition. (New York is an exception, where there are notoriously high health insurance rates because no person can be denied full health insurance coverage, no matter what their preexisting condition.)

Consequently, it would be best to have the person with the preexisting condition covered on an employer group plan and have the rest of the family (who is healthy) covered on an individual plan. A case study: Dad is working for Mobil Oil and is completely covered by the group health insurance policy, but has to pay for his wife and three kids to be covered—but one of his daughters has severe asthma. Then he would keep himself and his asthmatic daughter on the group plan, and break out his healthy wife and other two kids into an individual plan. This could save the family several thousand dollars a year in health insurance premiums. **(ADVANCED)**

TIP OF THE DAY:

HEALTH SAVINGS ACCOUNTS OR HSAS: These are tax-favored accounts that are attached to an HSA-compatible health insurance policy, and they usually have a very high deductible but offer very good insurance rates. This is the case of "insuring the big stuff" as we've been doing for twenty years with automobile and homeowners insurance. Case study: With a $2,000 deductible, a family of four (from CA) can pay as little as $172 a month for health insurance instead of $425 per month with the employer group plan. They would then invest the rest of the money that they would normally put toward a higher insurance policy into a Health Savings Account.

These HSAs are funded with tax-favored status and are able to grow like an IRA. If there are medical related expenses such as prescription drugs, orthodontia, over-the-counter drugs, and glasses (to name only a very few), then they are paid for from this tax-favored account with a debit card or checks. For a full explanation of HSAs, go to one of the insurance sites we've already recommended or go to your local bank to see what kind of HSA accounts they offer. Just remember there are two elements to the HSA: an insurance company for the policy and a bank for the HSA fund. **(ADVANCED)**

TIP OF THE DAY:

WEIGHT WATCHERS OR 24-HOUR FITNESS: If your medical doctor says that you are overweight, then you can often write off your membership in a medically approved program, such as Weight Watchers. For some existing health insurance policies, even if you are not overweight, if you can prove that you attend a gym on a regular basis, you can write off a portion of the gym expenses or even get a refund from your health insurance company. This is the health insurance company's way of telling us how important it is to exercise and maintain a healthy weight.

TIP OF THE DAY:

#57 NEVER CANCEL A HEALTH OR LIFE INSURANCE POLICY:

That is, until you have another permanent policy in place (not just a temporary policy that is pending). You are not technically covered until you receive an acceptance letter from the company expressing the permanence of your policy, along with any exclusionary riders. There are all kinds of reasons that a policy may be denied, and when a noninsured trip to the emergency room to cover a child's broken leg now costs an average of $12,000, only one small gap in your coverage could wipe out an entire savings account. In some cases, the existing health or life insurance policy will allow you to cancel the policy retroactively if you can show a copy of the effective dates of your new insurance policy.

TIP OF THE DAY:

THE DOG WHISPERER: While pet insurance is costly and not usually necessary, it is important to get your pet veterinary services. Most local animal shelters will offer shots at a shot clinic, well-puppy checkups, spaying and neutering services, and even electronic chip implantations at prices that are anywhere from 20 percent to 80 percent less than you would pay at a regular veterinarian's office.

In some cases, local community-conscious companies will offer vouchers for gift certificates off the price of sterilization services. Most clinics are as quiet as the Dog Whisperer on these additional benefits and you can understand why. Ask your local vet (whisper quietly) for a list of companies that offer such certificates and call around until you get enough of them to use conjointly and pay for up to 80 percent of the procedure. For example, we could have paid $110 to have our Anastasia dog (a mini schnauzer) spayed, but the certificates we collected only required us to pay $20 out of pocket. **(ADVANCED)**

TIP OF THE DAY:
SAVE THOUSANDS AT THE VET: If you get your pet
sterilized, not only will he live longer and have a better quality of life, but these pets also tend to have fewer medical complications in their aging years. If you exercise your pet every day with a walk or a trip to the puppy park, not only will the Dog Whisperer be proud to call you a friend, but your pet will be happier too. Your checkbook will also look prettier because you will have a healthier pet that requires fewer trips to the vet.

TIP OF THE DAY:
PETS ARE PEOPLE TOO—NOT REALLY!—WATCHING FI-FI'S
WEIGHT: According to my local veterinarian, over 50 percent of the animals he sees are overweight, which results in 60 percent of the health-related ailments he treats. Get your pet weighed twice a year and make sure you are not overfeeding him. Most clinics

will allow free weigh-ins to their regular customers—be sure to ask for this. There's no need to consult a vet for a weigh-in unless your animal is deemed over- or underweight. Never, ever give a pet people food as it can cause long-term health problems and big vet bills. Make sure Fi-Fi has a balanced diet, no matter how much she gives you the sad puppy dog eyes to feed her your table scraps—you're helping her live longer! My vet says that baby carrots make the healthiest snack (but not too many or you'll regret it—enough said).

TIP OF THE DAY:

HOMEOWNERS POLICIES: Do you pay your homeowners policy as part of your monthly mortgage payment? If so, you may be overpaying by several hundreds, if not thousands, of dollars a year! In these cases, the bank automatically pays the homeowners policy's renewal and the customer is sent a copy of the policy that says "not a bill." They know that the bank will cover their premiums and so they don't bother to reevaluate their policy on an annual basis.

Call your bank and ask them for the date that the policy renews (or look at your own copy). About a month before renewal (when you get your copy of the upcoming renewal), call around to check out the prices on various policies and make sure that the other homeowners insurance policy tips we give apply as well. For fast, easy, and free quotes, go to www. NetQuote.com or www.AllQuotesInsurance.com.

Before you switch policies, give your existing insurance

provider a chance to match the competitor's rate and be sure you are comparing all the coverage equally. You want to compare prices on apples with apples, not on apples with kiwis.

TIP OF THE DAY:

HOMEOWNERS—COVER THE HOUSE, NOT THE DIRT!: The actual value of the property

you insure on your homeowners policy should be about 90 percent of the resale value of your home, unless your lot is worth more than 10 percent of the total value of the property. Case Study: If you could sell your home for $200,000, you had it insured for $200,000, and it burned down completely before you could close escrow with a new buyer, you will not get $200,000 for the home because it is not worth that amount. The land the home is on plus the value of the home itself is worth $200,000. Consequently, make sure that you are not overinsuring your property value and overpaying that premium.

TIP OF THE DAY:

FLOOD AND EARTHQUAKES: If you are a first-time homeowner, you may not realize that these two "Acts of God" are not included in a standard homeowners policy but must be purchased separately from the government. Most mortgage companies will not require you to carry flood coverage unless you live in a flood plain. The same applies to earthquakes.

TIP OF THE DAY:

HIGHER HOMEOWNERS DEDUCTIBLES: A $500 or $1000 deductible can make a homeowners policy cost anywhere from 10 percent to 15 percent more than if you had a 1 percent deductible. As in auto and health insurance, the idea is to insure the major losses and take care of the minor losses yourself. If you have a personal articles floater (see next tip), then the deductible is waived for those items specified on the floater (also sometimes called a rider).

TIP OF THE DAY:

PERSONAL ARTICLES FLOATER: My husband has a Russian Samovar that was passed down to the firstborn male in every generation since the Russian Revolution at the turn of the twentieth century. This heirloom is valued at more than $5,000 but would only be covered up to $500 if we did not have it listed on a personal articles rider on our homeowners policy. Case Study: A friend of mine had a family diamond ring appraised at $10,000 and other jewelry that added up to a total of $15,000. Their home was burglarized and she only received $1,000 for all that jewelry because these items were not itemized and they were not covered in a special rider to their policy.

The cost of these floaters vary from state to state and company to company, so be sure to check the prices before you buy the coverage. In this case, it's important to remember that by insuring irreplaceable items, you are protecting yourself (and your material assets) from ruin in the event of a theft or other loss. Most of the riders cover any kind of loss, even if you took a ring off to wash your hands at Marie Callendar's and walked off and left it on the sink! **(ADVANCED)**

TIP OF THE DAY:

HOMEOWNERS REPLACEMENT VALUE: If your hot water heater overflowed and flooded the entire lower lever of your home, causing thousands of dollars in damages, would you be able to repair the damage and replace the carpets with your current policy? If you do not have a "replacement value" clause on your policy, then the damages would be subjected to depreciation and that usually means only 25 percent to 50 percent of the actual damages would be covered. So, a $20,000 job would only get you a $10,000 check (at best) from your insurance company. Making sure that you have the right replacement value coverage could save you a cool $10,000 on a fairly common occurrence.

TIP OF THE DAY:

TENANT POLICIES: If you are a renter, or you are in the military and live in government housing, then your household goods are not covered unless you purchase a tenant policy. Most tenant policies will cover damages caused by fire, natural disasters, and theft (but not earthquake or flood). They even cover personal items stolen from your car or items damaged while in transit on a move. Get a higher deductible for great savings and be sure to purchase replacement value and a personal article floaters as well. Prices for policies can also be researched at the same place you research homeowners policies, www.NetQuote.com or www.AllQuotesInsurance.com.

TIP OF THE DAY:

FICO SCORES SAVE HERE: Throughout this book, you are going to see where a good credit score (Fair Isaac Credit Score) will save you money. In the case of insurance, a good FICO can save you big bucks on your automobile policy and it can make the difference between whether a company will insure you for a tenant policy or whether that coverage is denied. See "FICOS" in section four (Banking, Credit, FICO, and Debt).

TIP OF THE DAY:

COMBINE AUTO AND HOMEOWNERS: Find out if your company offers a discount for having both the auto and homeowners policy with the same provider. If they do, then ask for the discounts. If you're thinking of changing policies, be sure you do not cancel either a homeowners or automobile policy until you have a firm and decided premium price that includes the discounts (a temporary insurance binder is *not* good enough). Sometimes it's cheaper to leave things the way they are—especially if you or family members have one or more tickets or accidents on their record.

☼

TIP OF THE DAY:

#70 BEFORE YOU SWITCH AUTOMOBILE POLICY WARNINGS:

If you are shopping around for a cheaper automobile policy, call your local department of motor vehicles or AAA services to get a copy of your driving report and one for all of those drivers on your policy. More often than not, you will be surprised that a speeding ticket that wasn't suppose to appear (because you took a drivers safety course) or the accident that wasn't your fault (is now rated undetermined, which means you cannot prove no-fault) or the ticket that your teen said they never had suddenly appears on the record. All this information is critical when shopping around for a new policy. You could cancel an existing policy (which will probably not reinstate you at the lower rates) and not realize your driving record hits are on the report. This means you could end up paying hundreds of dollars MORE every year on your policy. So make sure there's a lifeboat down there before you jump ship!

TIP OF THE DAY:

YOUTHFUL DRIVERS: If you have a boy under the age of twenty-one, his insurance premium will be the highest rate possible. To reduce those premiums on all youthful drivers, make sure they are listed as the primary driver on the least expensive vehicle you own. Depending on the state, it might be necessary to put the title in the child's name as well as your name to get this rate. The difference can be anywhere from $300 to $3500 per year savings, depending on the type of vehicles you own. **(ADVANCED)**

TIP OF THE DAY:

DRIVERS SAFETY COURSE: Almost everyone knows to turn in a drivers *training* course certificate for your youthful driver to get as much as 15 percent off the premium. But most people don't realize that adults can also save by turning in the certificate for a drivers safety course they took in order to beat a ticket! Fax this document to your insurance company for significant savings.

TIP OF THE DAY:

KIDS PLAY, KIDS PAY—AUTO INSURANCE: We have a policy in our family with teenage drivers. We will pay their auto insurance until they get a ticket of any kind or are involved in an accident (whether it is their fault or not). From that point on, the child will pay for their own insurance or they will not drive. When we told our oldest son, Daniel, about this policy, he wailed, "You mean if I get only *one* ticket, I'll have to pay my own insurance for the rest of my life?" I laughed out loud. "What do you think, Daniel, that if you don't get a ticket, we'll still be paying your insurance when you're thirty-five years old? You will be paying for your insurance some day, this rule just determines whether it will be sooner or later!"

Make sure your teens know that you mean business on this rule and it will make them more defensive drivers. When Philip totaled his Escort, he became the proud owner of his insurance policy payments. Once Daniel is out of college, he'll be the proud owner of his own policy payments anyway, unless he gets a ticket or has an accident before that; then he'll own his payments sooner than later. **(ADVANCED)**

TIP OF THE DAY:

THE TALK: When I was a broker, one of the services we provided our clients was that of a "youthful driver talk" to new teenage drivers. My colleague, Bob Harper, would look as imposing as he could behind his desk and paint a very ugly, true-life scenario of what premiums cost for kids who don't drive defensively. My job was to try to calm them down after they had the "talk."

If your automobile insurance agent lives in your city, set up a "youthful driver talk" between her and your teenager. Ask the agent to share the necessity of driving safely and have her share some real-life examples of teens who got a couple of tickets and/or an accident and could no longer afford to keep their car because the insurance premiums became higher than the car payments (or similar, scary examples).

This talk could make the difference between your teens driving defensively versus taking risks. If you do not have a local insurance agent because you've moved or you buy online, then ask a friend who might be in car sales to provide the same kind of talk. These professionals work with people on a daily basis whose poor driving history greatly impact their current choice in wheels! **(ADVANCED)**

TIP OF THE DAY:

TAXI MOM SAVINGS: If you have a full-time mom in your home, make sure your insurance company knows about her. The rating for a mom who works outside the home is slightly higher (because of built-in commuting drive time) than a mom who stays home full-time. This is the cheapest rating possible, so try to rate it on your most expensive vehicle. As funny as it sounds, in many states it's considered a "for pleasure only" rating. Yeah, right, like taxi mom drives for her own pleasure—more like the pleasure of her kids and all their activities! **(ADVANCED)**

TIP OF THE DAY:

ANTITHEFT DEVICE: Call your insurance company and ask if they provide discounts for antitheft systems in your car. If it's installed by the dealer or the car manufacturer, you could get a slightly higher discount, so be sure you are specific.

TIP OF THE DAY:

ASSORTED AUTO SAVINGS: While you've got that insurance company representative on the phone, also ask them if they offer good student discounts, multicar discounts, a savings for storing your car in a garage rather than the street or a carport, a nonsmoker or nondrinker discount or a savings for being between the ages of thirty and sixty (the safest age range). There are all kinds of discounts that you may qualify for in your state. You have not because you ask not. **(ADVANCED)**

I Sang on Broadway!

*Tips to Save on Entertainment,
Travel, and Vacations*

I'm a *Wicked* girl sometimes. When I should be writing on a deadline, I'll *Fiddle on the Roof*. Other times I can be found on *42nd Street*. I've even been known to be a *Phantom* when I go to the *Opera*! I like to think I'm a *Beauty* surrounded by *Beasts* and I know that when it comes to writing books and having kids, I'm a *Producer*.

Mama Mia! I'm a theater freak. Every time I'm in New York, I force my poor travel companion (usually my eternally patient business manager, Wendy Wendler) to hike over to Broadway and see what half-price tickets we can get in the Times Square ticket booth. Then, I force them to sing a song with me on Broadway Street so they can also say they've "sung on Broadway." The amazing thing is that I can be standing on a street corner, singing *Oklahoma* quite badly, and in New York, no one notices!

Whether you're on a business trip, a working vacation, or a totally de-li-cious total family vacation, it's important to save money on airfare, hotels, travel expenses, entertainment, and pure family fun. Even if the weather is bad while you're on holiday, if you're saving money, you'll still be *Singing in the Rain*!

TIP OF THE DAY:

REDEFINE ENTERTAINMENT: Life's simple pleasures *truly* are the best. We've been sold a bill of goods advertising expensive entertainment as the ultimate. Americans seem compelled to work themselves silly to afford that dream vacation to the Caribbean—then what? It's never enough. These "things" never truly satisfy until we can learn to enjoy and find our entertainment in the simple things. We can even find enjoyment in productivity. Make a list of what you consider entertainment and try to practice those things on the list that don't cost much but yield high personal satisfaction. Then when you spend the money to take a vacation, you will come back more satisfied, instead of feeling like you have to start planning the next majorly expensive trip to find contentment. **(ADVANCED)**

TIP OF THE DAY:

SET PRIORITIES: Establish some goals for your trip and what you can live with (and what you can't live without). If you want an exotic location, then you may have to settle for fewer days away from home. For example, you might choose a four-day vacation to Hawaii as your only major trip in three years over a week at a nearby resort each year. **(ADVANCED)**

TIP OF THE DAY:

FUTURE VACATIONS—PLAN AHEAD: One of the reasons many families overspend on vacations is because of a failure to plan ahead. They arrive at their destination and decide to take in several unplanned tourist attractions; they eat at specialty restaurants, and buy overpriced souvenirs that will end up in next year's garage sale. This failure to plan ahead costs hundreds, if not thousands, of extra dollars each year.

Set a budget before you pull out of your driveway. Decide what activities take priority and *stay on budget*. Each family member can contribute their ideas and decide on a plan that will accommodate as many interests as possible. For example, your hubby wants to go to the new Wet and Wild Water Park at your selected camping spot—but you want to go to the amusement park. The water park costs just as much as the amusement park and you can't do both. Suggest a trip to the nearby beach on one day (since you have no beaches near your home) and a trip to the amusement park. Which, when questioned further, may satisfy your hubby. A good compromise and you're still within budget.

Estimate the cost of meals, gas, and incidentals. Try planning your vacations during off-seasons, if possible—you'll save significantly on everything from hotel rooms to area attractions.

Select vacation areas in your locale. Since we always moved so much, we tried to see everything there was to see within our area. We made day trips to area sites and saved the cost of a hotel room. We packed our lunch and had a great time relaxing at a roadside picnic table, while the kids ran wild.

TIP OF THE DAY:
TRAVEL OFF-SEASON: By traveling during an off-peak time, you'll not only save money, you won't fight the crowds either. According to Consumer Reports Travel Letter, the optimum time to get the best airline fares is October through early December and January through March. The fares are even better if you stay over a Saturday night.

TIP OF THE DAY:
A STRONG DOLLAR CLOSE TO HOME: If you live near Canada or Mexico, your dollar will go a lot further because of the weak local currencies in these areas. If you use a credit card for the majority of your purchases, you will not pay a fee for converting your dollars into the foreign currency.

TIP OF THE DAY:
VOLUNTEER YOUR WAY TO A CHEAPER VACATION:
Instead of paying $1000 for the week for a family of four to spend

at a gorgeous camp in the Colorado Rockies, you can have a working vacation for free, with plenty of time for family. Some campgrounds offer this kind of a trade-off, but if your family enjoys this kind of environment, it would be worth your time to contact a local retreat center or campground. Go to www.acacamps.org for the American Camping Association. **(ADVANCED)**

 # 84 **TIP OF THE DAY:**
FAMILY HOSTEL: Not all vacation packages are faith-based; some are education-based as well. At Family Hostel, www.learn.unh.edu/familyhostel/index.html, there are trips offered that match families with learning vacations around the world, while Elderhostel offers those fifty-five and older up to 10,000 options starting at as little as $556 for a six-day photography workshop in Massachusetts. **(ADVANCED)**

TIP OF THE DAY:

VOLUNTEER IN THE WILD: Wilderness Volunteers (www.wildernessvolunteers.org) is a nonprofit organization created in 1997 that offers people of any age a chance to help and maintain national parks, forests, and wilderness areas across the United States. Everything from trail maintenance to revegetation projects are on the agenda. Participants provide their own camping gear and share campsite chores. Most Wilderness Volunteer trips last about a week and cost around $219. **(ADVANCED)**

TIP OF THE DAY:

MILITARY FAMILY VACATION: If you are a military family or a veteran, you can save even more through the Armed Forces Vacation Club. You just sign up online at www.AFVclub.com and are allowed to book time-share type condominiums and accommodations for only $250 per week. The club on Oahu, Hawaii was absolutely gorgeous and was located on some of the most expensive real estate in the world, Waikiki Beach! Be sure to book early for popular locations, but if you're prepared to visit less touristy areas, you can book as little as one week in advance! Duluth, Minnesota—here we come!

TIP OF THE DAY:

HOUSES AND CONDOS: Whether you're looking for a cabin in Colorado, an adobe in Arizona, or a lakehouse in Louisiana, you'll find these rental properties at www.vrbo.com (Vacation Rentals by Owners). Unlike a home-swapping situation, you are actually renting someone's vacation home or time-share for the week. This site has photos, rates, and detailed descriptions in all fifty states. If you visit the ski places in the summer and the beach places in the winter, you can save even more. For example, a ski lodge in Park City, Utah, rents a 2100 square foot, two bedroom unit for $1,700 in the winter and only $286 in the summer!

TIP OF THE DAY:

THEME PARK VACATIONS: For tips on theme park vacations, check out www.elliekay.com.

TIP OF THE DAY:

DUDE RANCHES: Think of the movie *City Slickers*, and then expand that idea into the new millennium. These days, dude ranches are all about white-water rafting, big-name chefs, Pilates classes, and yes, horses. You can go to www.Ranchweb.com as your VERY BEST source to find the best value on dude ranches; you can search by location, rates, or activities. There are ranches such as HorseWorks, Wyoming, which offers cattle drives, and places like Montana's Lone Mountain Ranch, where you can do yoga before your morning ride. Elk Mountain Ranch in Colorado is one of the many ranches with extensive programs for young children. Dozens of dude ranches offer fly-fishing and mountain biking, but horsemanship remains the big draw. Some of these even have rock climbing, birding, and environmental lectures. A single price covers all meals, riding, accommodations, and many activities. These start as low as $700 per person per week.

TIP OF THE DAY:

AIRFARES: Check out the fares available on the Internet such as www.travelocity.com, www.webflyer.com, www.orbitz.com, www.bestfares.com, www.expedia.com, www.smartertravel.

com, and www.cheap-tickets.com. Moment's Notice is a booking specialist found at www.moments-notice.com. They charge an annual fee of $25 but boast bargain-basement prices and some of the best values for cruises to Europe, Rio de Janeiro, and certain parts of the Caribbean. Sometimes if you buy a "red-eye" special for substantial savings, you can show up at the ticket counter early and see if they can schedule you out on an earlier flight.

TIP OF THE DAY:

COMPARE WITH THE ORIGINAL: Once you find the best fares at some of these websites, be sure to go back to the original airline's site to check for even better deals. For example, I checked a fare to go to Minneapolis and found a ticket (normally $800) on expedia.com for only $325 on Frontier Airlines. But when I went to the Frontier site, I found an unadvertised fare for only $200. The Expedia fare alerted me to the airline to check for that particular flight. Read on for the details. **(ADVANCED)**

TIP OF THE DAY:

AIRLINE INTERNET SPECIALS: One final air tip is to try the airlines directly for their Internet specials because the previous sites do not track prices for Jet Blue and Southwest—two of the major discount airlines. Most major U.S. carriers offer these weekly specials. I tried Southwest Airlines at www.southwest.com for their Click 'n Save Specials and I just booked two round-trip, nonstop tickets from El Paso to Dallas for a total of $220 (only $110 each). The catch is that you have to buy well in advance and they are nonrefundable and no changes can be made. However, on Southwest, these funds can be reserved toward future flights.

TIP OF THE DAY:

AIRLINE—THE WEDNESDAY FACTOR: Peter Greenberg, of Fodor.com, says that this is the best day to buy airline tickets and the reason is thanks to the small, upstart airlines.[1] In the airline business, fare wars are usually begun by the weakest competitors while the bigger airlines tend to raise fares. Fridays are when these new fare wars usually begin.

When airline "A" decides to raise fares, it usually happens late in the day on Friday. By Saturday, airline A's major competitors will probably match that fare increase (that's why you should never book your tickets over a weekend). But what if the major competitors DO NOT match the higher fares? Then airline "A" drops their fares again by late Sunday or Monday.

On the other hand, let's say that the fare war is going in the downside direction. Airline "B" decides to lower fares and it happens late on a Friday. By Saturday and Sunday, the other major airlines may lower their fares to compete. On Monday, they are seeing how the new fares do in the marketplace. By Tuesday, if the fares are doing well (meaning lots of sales), then airline "C" might jump into the fray with an ever lower fare. Prices may go even lower by Wednesday and that's the day to buy!

By Thursday the fare wars and sales are usually over and it begins all over again on Friday. The best time of the day on Wednesday is 1:00 AM (set the alarm), which is an hour past Tuesday and an hour past midnight, when most airlines usually reload their computers with the newest fares.

TIP OF THE DAY:
ONLINE AUCTIONS AND PRICELINE.COM:
It seems that online auctions on the Internet will survive because of the fact that people are getting good bargains and are willing to continue to use these services in order to get (and sell) the trips they want. Online auction sites for airline tickets and other travel needs tend to be low on service but high on value. Look for established sites such as www.ebay.com, www.priceline.com, www.skyauction.com, or www.bidtripper.com for some good values. You can get half-priced hotels, rental cars, plane tickets, entertainment tickets, etc. You will need to do your research on the balance of a good airfare with a good hotel rate. For example, even though airfare to Chicago can be cheap (they have two major airports, served by dozens of airlines), city hotel costs can be steep. Finding a cheaper hotel at an auction and the airfare at a travel site could be the best value.

TIP OF THE DAY:

PRICELINE.COM is unique from other auction sites because no one bids against you—they just let you know if you can have the price you bid. Some people love Priceline and others are not thrilled. If you're going to use it, you will need to keep the following things in mind:

- Do your research on the lowest fare you can find and plan to bid about 20 percent lower than that fare. If you don't get the bid, you've lost nothing.

- Review their "low price" values at the site for guaranteed low prices on hotels, but don't feel pressured into bidding in that price range—you can still bid lower.

- Have your credit card ready.

- Enter your destination, departing and arrival airports, or dates of departure and arrival for a hotel.

- Enter your price bid.

- Remember these are nonrefundable and you cannot control the departure or arrival times, although you can indicate a preference.

- Usually within twenty-four hours you'll have an acceptance or rejection.

- If you are rejected, *you cannot enter the same information with a higher price*! You will have to change one of the pieces of information listed: departure or arrival airports or travel dates, and then make your bid again with a higher price.

- The catch is to look at all the options of arrivals and departures and bid on the most popular airports, most convenient departure and arrival times first, and save some of the airports in the same vicinity as a backup in case they do not accept your price.

- Remember, once you make a bid and they accept it—there are no refunds or changes! So this system is only good if you have some flexibility in your schedule and know you won't need to make changes.

- Case Study #1: My friend Brenda had to drive fifty miles out of the way, leave on a date she didn't want to leave, and arrive later than expected just to save $50. Since she couldn't use the flight as a frequent flier benefit on her usual airline, she decided it wasn't worth it. You'll have to decide if the savings are worth the inconveniences.

- Case Study #2: On the other hand, our oldest daughter, Missy, booked a flight from California to New York to see some friends for only $150. She booked it six months in advance and it was truly worth the risk since inconvenience was a nonissue in her case. **(ADVANCED)**

TIP OF THE DAY:

HOTEL: You can often find packages for great hotel rates at the airline Internet site when you book travel. You can also find great rates on car rentals when you're booking these other services. I've found that sometimes I'm getting an even better rate at the www.southwest.com site on hotels and rentals than I would get bidding on a room or car at www.priceline.com. Plus, those bookings are reflected on my Southwest miles as well, earning me free trips. So when you're checking the airline fares from the previous paragraph, be sure to check the hotel and rental rates as well.

Besides some of the auction sites we've already mentioned, you can also check hotel sites for their weekly Internet specials, such as www.quickbook.com and www.1800usahotels.com. Try the following for email alerts: Hyatt at www.hyatt.com, Radisson at www.radisson.com/offers, the Holiday Inn at www.basshotels.com/holiday-inn, Best Western at www.bestwestern.com, and the Hilton at www.hilton.com. Don't be put off by the price they list before you look at hotel details. For example, at Hilton.com, I've frequently found the indication "Prices start at $230," only to find that with my AAA and military discounts, I can get the same room for $116 at the Hilton site. Also, those online bookings count toward my frequent stayer points and those translate into free hotel nights.

For last-minute hotel rooms, you could go to the very large TravelWeb site and look for Click-It Weekends! at www.travelweb.com. Each Monday, they post the coming weekend's special offers.

TIP OF THE DAY:

#97 VANTAGE TRAVEL: Not all new travel sites are created equal; some are like homemade cookies in the Kay house—here today and gone tomorrow! That's why it's great to run across a solid site for travel deals. Once you've looked at some of the other sites mentioned earlier, go to Vantage Travel Deals at www.ytb.com to compare your best price with theirs!

TIP OF THE DAY:

HAWAII: I interviewed one woman, who reads my books, who managed to go to Hawaii for $20—the security fees for the airline ticket. She took all her frequent flier miles, all her frequent traveler hotel points and booked them all toward Hawaii!

Bob and I have done Hawaii fairly cheap as well; we booked the tickets and hotel during the off-season (January—due to the rainy season), got some cheap tix out of Los Angeles Airport, and had a wonderful time! If you're thinking about a trip to Hawaii, see my website for *lots* of tips: www.elliekay.com.

TIP OF THE DAY:

PHONE CALLS WHILE TRAVELING ABROAD: Consider signing up for Skype. This is an Internet site (www.skype.com) where you can set up an account and talk over the Internet almost anywhere for about a penny a minute. If you have a webcam or a headset, you can add to the experience. If the people you are calling have Skype, then you talk for free. If not, then you can go on the Skype account and call any number in the world for pennies. We've started using this to talk to friends/family and clients in Israel, China, New Zealand, Australia, and even Hawaii.

TIP OF THE DAY:

CRUISES—NEVER PAY FULL PRICE: Once again the best time to cruise is in off-season. Visitors tend to flock to the Caribbean during the winter months in order to escape the cold. But the summer months usually have milder weather and cheaper prices—plus the water tends to be calmer. Go to www.priceline.com for great prices on last-minute cruises or visit www.11thHourVacations.com and www.LastMinuteTravel.com. These sites sell excess cruise inventory and represent great bargains.

To rate a particular cruise, you can go to www.CruiseCritic.com, which rates the best cruises in several interest groups. This site offers their own database of 12,000 cruise deals and discounts—they offer photos of cabins as well.

TIP OF THE DAY:

CRUISES—SPECIAL GROUPS—BUYER BEWARE: A friend of mine wanted to go on a cruise that was being featured by a radio talk show host. She loved this guy's show and told her husband about it. When they checked out the cruise and booked it, the husband decided to go search for a better deal. He found one—at half price! When he called to cancel the original cruise, he asked why it was twice as much as the same cruise line, the same route, the same everything. They told him that he was paying for the privilege of getting to see the star. No thanks! They could take TWO cruises for the price of seeing the talk show host and they decided it wasn't worth it!

TIP OF THE DAY:

CRUISES—A PERISHABLE PRODUCT: Just remember that the deals on cruises can be so good because it is a perishable product. Hotels can have customers arriving all times of the night, but when a cruise sets sail—that's it. For example, last week I received an email from www.LastMinuteTravel.com offering a seven-day Holland America Alaska cruise starting at $599. This was a fraction of the $1,300 price advertised the same day on Holland America's website. One final website to cruise is www.VacationsToGo.com.

TIP OF THE DAY:

DAY TRIPS: It's been said that "change is as good as rest." So get out your map and look at day trips you can take. You may be surprised at how many fascinating little towns are within a short distance from your home. There will be lots of places you can enjoy going to look at historic buildings, architecture, gardens, or wander around markets and antique stores.

TIP OF THE DAY:

ZOO MEMBERSHIPS: Most zoos are members

of a reciprocal zoo association. This means you pay a fee with the zoo of your choice and get reciprocal privileges in several hundred other zoos, aquariums, and wildlife parks across the country. When we lived in New Mexico, our local zoo in Alamogordo was a small facility and only charged $35 per year for a family membership. However, with our membership card we went to the El Paso Zoo free (it would have cost $28 for the family for the day), the Albuquerque Biological Park (we saved $43 for the day), and the Los Angeles Zoo (we saved $54). As a matter of fact, we maintained our zoo membership when we moved from New Mexico to New York and got to visit zoos in New York for less than the annual membership of our local zoo.

Check out the American Zoo Association at www.aza.org where you can view the several hundred zoos available in this reciprocal zoo program. These memberships can also offer discounts at the bookstore and passes to special exhibits.

For more information, you can contact our zoo at:
Alameda Park Zoo
PO Box 596
Alamogordo, NM 88310
(505) 439-4290

MUSEUM MEMBERSHIPS: Museum memberships work the same way the zoo memberships do with a reciprocal list that can save you locally and when you travel. With our zoo and museum memberships, we are never at a loss for fun, free, and new things to do in another city. We joined the New Mexico Museum of Natural History for only $50 a year and received an ASTC (Association of Science Trade Centers) passport. This passport allowed us access to hundreds even though we only visited a dozen other museums on our trips in the last year; plus our membership included passes to the Dynamax theater.

New Mexico Museum of Natural History
1801 Mountain Road NW
Albuquerque, NM
(505) 841-2869

You can search just about every museum in the country by area if you go to www.astc.org. Something to remember about museums participating in the ASTC Travel Passport Program— they agree to waive general admission fees for one another's members. Fees for planetariums, theaters, and special exhibitions are not waived unless specified.

With this pass, we visit our local space museum where the kids love to operate the new space shuttle simulator. Our friends joined this museum and sent an additional card to their college student daughter in New York City, so she can also have entertainment on a college student's budget.

TIP OF THE DAY:

PARKS AND OPEN SPACES: Few things are more romantic than a picnic in the park. If you have local public gardens or parks, make up a picnic lunch and soak in the scenery. Hiking is also a great way to combine exercise with together time. Discover the countryside around you. You'll be amazed at what's on your doorstep. Search "Hiking Trails" on the Internet for a multitude of ideas. For a complete "what, when, where, and how" of hiking and walking, go to www.teleport.com/~walking/hiking.html. Or for a full listing of national parks go to www.nps.gov/findapark.html/index. If you are a member of AAA, then you must check out www.aaa.com for tried-and-true vacation sites. For state searches of hundreds of leisure activities on federal lands, go to www.recreation.gov.

TIP OF THE DAY:

MAPS: Whether you are taking a major cross-country trip, going to a nearby city, or just looking for that new restaurant across town, print out a free map from the Internet before you hit the road. Click on www.mapquest.com or www.mapblast.com, or for more specific road trips, try www.mapsonus.com and www.interstate4U.com.

The Travel Industry Association at www.tia.org lists state tourism offices with links and lots of pictures.

TIP OF THE DAY:

WEATHER: If you want to check out the weather where you're going, you can look at www.weather.com, www.accuweather.com, or www.worldclimate.com.

#109 **TIP OF THE DAY:**
THE LIBRARY: The local library is a great source of entertainment. You can borrow DVDs, books on tape, CDs, audiocassettes, travel guides, and *Consumer Reports* magazines, besides the ever popular books. Many libraries may offer free classes and guest lectures. Try researching your family tree at a library with a good genealogy reference section.

TIP OF THE DAY:

GAMES—THE GAME OF LIFE: You know all those games you got the kids for Christmas and birthday presents? They're just taking up space on a shelf, when they could be a great source of entertainment for you guys. When surveys tell us the average amount of spouse-to-spouse and parent-to-child time is measured in minutes, we know that game playing isn't the only thing we may be missing in life.

TIP OF THE DAY:

SPORTS AND EXERCISE: Killing two birds with one stone is one of my favorite pastimes. Bob and I like to take a walk and talk at the same time while we are walking the puppies. It accomplishes two important functions—exercise of the legs and jaws for all two-footed and four-footed creatures involved. Basketball, soccer, baseball, and jogging are all inexpensive and fun sports to participate in as a family.

TIP OF THE DAY:

CAMPING—RENT FIRST: According to a recent survey, the most common denominator in individuals who expressed a satisfying childhood is camping. The family that plays together stays together and this is especially true in the great camping adventure. Before you take the big plunge and buy a camper, tent trailer, or motor home, consider renting a camper for a weekend. At www.RVRental.com we found rentals across the country that ranged from $117 to $385 per day. Depending on the owner of the RV, other charges to consider are hospitality kits, kitchen kits, and/or emergency road kits. Cleaning fees will apply if the RV is not returned in the condition in which it was rented. **(ADVANCED)**

TIP OF THE DAY:

CAMPING—PRACTICE FIRST: If you're looking at tent camping and you're not quite sure your family will appreciate it, or if you're just plain chicken to try it out, then practice in your own backyard. Pitch a tent for the kids the first night, letting them have the experience of sleeping in the great outdoors. Buy a mini fire pit and make your own s'mores and tell scary or silly stories. Our family loves to quote one-liners from our favorite movies and the others try to guess which movie they're from.

TIP OF THE DAY:

CAMP WITH FRIENDS AS A BEGINNER: The least expensive way to camp is tent camping and it's truly a family bonding experience. Camping saves money on hotel rooms and food. You may want to consider pooling your equipment with other families to save expenses. For the novice, camping with an experienced camping couple is a must. We learned so many helpful tips while enjoying the great outdoors with the Wendler family, exploring the Cloudcroft mountain area. We forgot the snacks for the outing, but Wendy packed loads for everyone. We missed out on hot chocolate when it was a bit colder than we thought it would be, but Wendy had it piping hot—with marshmallows. The only thing she didn't bring was a port-a-potty, but she did direct us to a nice log.

TIP OF THE DAY:

INEXPENSIVE CAMPING GEAR: Camping equipment can be found at garage sales and thrift shops such as "Play It Again Sports." Make sure the items work and all the parts are there. If you want to invest in camping gear with another family, it would cut costs in half and you would need to alternate camping dates.

TIP OF THE DAY:

FAMILY CAMPS: You can find as much structure or as little as you want for family camps across the country. There's also the full gamut of prices as well. It's a relaxing week where you hunt or fish, sit in a chair reading a book by the lake, and eating popsicles with your kids all day long. The activities for the kids can also allow for some quality couple time during the week.

For options, go to the American Camping Association's website at www.acacamps.org for some 2,300 camps with family programs. YMCA camps are another great resource; just google "YMCA" and your state to find the closest options. The YMCA camps start at $1,000 for a family of four for a week and they even have financial assistance available for families in need. (Can you think of another vacation where someone else will help you pay for it?)

TIP OF THE DAY:

EATING OUT: FSIs—Freestanding inserts are the coupon inserts from your Sunday paper. Mainline restaurants offer great coupon values in FSIs that can add up to 50 percent off the bill, or almost $400 per year!

TIP OF THE DAY:

DINING—NEWSPAPERS: Quickly scan the "Living" or "Entertainment" section of your local paper for weekly restaurant specials on specific days. It may require going out on a Tuesday instead of a Wednesday. What only takes about twenty seconds to check can save you $20 (or more).

TIP OF THE DAY:

DINING—GO TO THE SOURCE: Find your favorite restaurant's website and check out their values. Many sites will offer printable coupons as well as weekly specials. Try looking under www.(favorite restaurant's name).com. For example, www. bennigans.com. On my website at www.elliekay.com, I have links to coupon sources such as www.valpak.com that find local coupon values based on your zip code, or www.coolsavings.com where you are emailed info on great deals.

TIP OF THE DAY:

DINING—GET CASH BACK!: The Rewards Network (www. rewards-network.com) gives you cash back when you eat at a participating restaurant. There are more than 10,000 choices on this card and the cost of it is $49 per year. You register a credit card with the network and then use that card when you dine to get up to 20 percent of the bill credited to your account.

TIP OF THE DAY:

RESTAURANT.COM: There are over 6,000 eateries listed at this site and twenty-five major metropolitan areas. It issues gift certificates and coupons for a fraction of their value in the restaurant. For example, I picked a fave café where I paid $10 at the site for a coupon worth $25 toward my bill—a $15 savings for a restaurant where we were planning to eat anyway.

TIP OF THE DAY:

DINING—TWO FOR ONE/ONE FOR TWO!: If your fave place doesn't offer a "buy one/get one free" special, then why not try the new trend of sharing a meal? This savvy approach is especially smart at a restaurant that's notorious for serving larger portions. You may have to pay a small surcharge for an extra plate, but your wallet (and waistlines) will thank you. Order water and save as much as 25 percent on the bill.

TIP OF THE DAY:

ENTERTAINMENT BOOKS: These coupon books cost around $35 and are used as fund-raisers for a nonprofit organization such as a school. Go to www.entertainment.com to find offers near you. Not only do they feature restaurant coupons, but they also offer great values on a variety of local and national services. But be forewarned: they're not cost-effective if you leave them at home!

TIP OF THE DAY:

SCHOOL/COMMUNITY VALUE CARDS:

Many communities have fund-raiser cards that cost around $10 and are the size of a credit card. It's very easy to put these in your wallet and save with buy one/get one free values, free drinks, desserts, and percentage-off values.

WOO THE ONE YOU LOVE—HAVE FUN: Some of the best dates I've had with Bob have been the simplest ones—when we take time out of a hectic schedule, turn off the radio, television, and computer, and just enjoy each other's company.

Bob and I have discovered that we don't need a trip to Rio, an expensive meal at a posh restaurant, or a big day at a theme park to have genuine, guilt-free fun. Take it from me and my mounds of correspondence from debt-riddled readers who are paying big credit card bills for family fun—accumulating debt *isn't* relaxing.

I thought I'd close this section with several inexpensive ways to woo the one you love—when you're on vacation and even when you're back home again!

- **Beach Time:** When playing in the waves, take time to snuggle your mate in the water.

- **Balcony Dates:** Try to select a room with a view and while the kids are asleep or watching a movie, have coffee on the veranda under the stars.

- **Flowers Anyone?:** Surprise your mate with a bouquet from a street vendor.

- **Sunsets:** Check out the time of sunset at www.weatherchannel.com and then schedule dinner at a local restaurant, asking for a table with a view.

- **Gifts:** Before your vacation, wrap a few inexpensive, yet meaningful gifts for your mate. Place one on his/her pillow each night.

- **Touch:** Meaningful touch can often get lost in the rapid pace of life. Grab your spouse's hand and give him a kiss under the moonlight.

- **Carriage Ride:** Take advantage of the romantic element in family activities. Let your kids ride in the front of a carriage ride while you snuggle in the back.

- **Reflection Time:** Schedule a date at the end of each day to share what you felt was your most romantic moment and why—you may be surprised at what you learn about your mate in the process!

1. Peter Greenberg, Fodors Travel Wire, *"Best Day to Buy Cheap Tix"* (April, 2005).

SECTION FOUR

Moneybags Comes of Age

Tips to Save on Banking, Credit, FICOs, and Debt

When I was in grade school, I was something of a junior entrepeneur.

By the time I was in the fifth grade, I was already on my third successful business venture. During Christmastime, I sold custom-made cards door-to-door and started selling in early November to make sure they got their products on time. My Grandma Laudeman handled the ordering of the cards for me and she did it for free. She also made me lemon meringue pie after a hard day of selling and encouraged me to keep working hard. I even tried to resell my mom's Green Stamp collection, but she caught me and put a stop to that entrepreneurial idea.

I had the ability to see treasure in trash and an uncanny knack for convincing people my product was worth their dollars. When it came to savings, my fifth grade business put me over the top and helped fund a trip to Spain to see my cousins. I learned the miracle of compounding interest, investing in nondepreciating products, and market break-even points—all by the age of twelve. My dad's nickname for me, Moneybags, is one that still fits today as I see ways to save money, invest, and make credit work to my family's advantage.

You may not be a moneybags, but that doesn't mean you have to pay more for financial services than you should. Here are some ways to make smart decisions when it comes to credit, banking, and debt reduction.

TIP OF THE DAY:

KNOW YOUR FICO (FAIR ISAAC CREDIT SCORE): Go to www.myfico.com and get a report on what your FICO score number is. Basically, low is bad and high is good. FICOS range from 500 to 830 and impact several areas of your life, such as insurance premiums (you could pay 20 percent to 50 percent more with a low FICO score), employment opportunities (they may not hire you if your score is spotty), mortgage interest rates, credit card rates, and 0 percent APR loans.

TIP OF THE DAY:

IMPROVE YOUR FICO IN THREE STEPS: Twenty points on your FICO can make the difference between qualifying for a great deal—or not. Case Study: There is the case of a $20,000 0 percent APR car loan versus the standard 7 percent to 8 percent rate on the loan. The qualifying rate is "excellent" (which varies from lender to lender, but it's usually 760 or higher). If you have a 740 rate and do not qualify for the 0 percent APR, the difference is close to $1800 over the course of the loan—all for as little as a twenty point difference! In mortgages, it may mean the ability to qualify for a lower rate and a seventy-nine point spread could mean the difference between an $851 house payment for a $150,000 loan or a payment of $1,157 for the same loan with a lower FICO score.

Improve the FICO score by:

- paying your credit card bills a day early rather than a day late

- paying $5 to $10 more than the minimum payment each month (it shows up on paper as you paying down your debt)

- making sure there is no more than 50 percent of your available credit charged on any given card. For example, if your credit limit is $5,000 on a card, make sure there is no more than $2500 charged on that card, even if you have to transfer the debt to another card to keep the proportion below 50 percent. **(ADVANCED)**

TIP OF THE DAY:

OTHER FICO TIPS: The above three steps are the quick and easy way to improve FICOS, but you can also keep the score looking nice by limiting the number of credit cards you open, avoiding credit inquiries into your account, and paying off existing loans as quickly as possible.

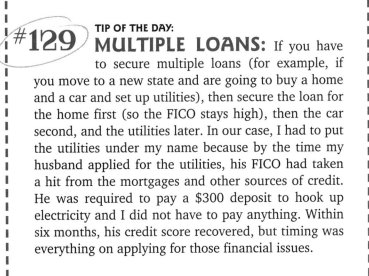

#129 **TIP OF THE DAY:**
MULTIPLE LOANS: If you have to secure multiple loans (for example, if you move to a new state and are going to buy a home and a car and set up utilities), then secure the loan for the home first (so the FICO stays high), then the car second, and the utilities later. In our case, I had to put the utilities under my name because by the time my husband applied for the utilities, his FICO had taken a hit from the mortgages and other sources of credit. He was required to pay a $300 deposit to hook up electricity and I did not have to pay anything. Within six months, his credit score recovered, but timing was everything on applying for those financial issues.

TIP OF THE DAY:

KNOW THE WARNING SIGNS OF CREDIT CARD DISASTER: If any two or more of these factors exist in your situation (or in the case of someone you are trying to help), then you are at risk for a credit meltdown and need to take action immediately. Part of the solution is recognizing the problem:

- Steadily increasing revolving balance on credit cards

- Using credit to buy things that you used to pay for in cash, such as groceries, gasoline, and clothing

- Not paying off the bill for the above point as soon as it arrives

- Using one credit card to pay another

- Paying only the minimum amount due on charge accounts

- Transferring balances to new cards only to run up balances again

Believe it or not, many of the above factors can be tracked by credit card companies, and if they believe you are a credit risk, they can increase your current card's APR, start charging an annual renewal fee (if they don't already), lower your credit line, limit cash advances, or deny credit on future lines of credit.

TIP OF THE DAY:

READ THE FINE PRINT: It might seem like a no-brainer to open a new card with another company who is offering low (or no) interest rates. But once you read the fine print, you may find that not only is there a very short term on the APR, but the lower APR only applies to new debt (and not debt transfers). You also need to know if another credit card company can attach the new card with old card debts that are under seven years old (see the previous tip and next tip). You may find that you open a new card with an instant debt load on it from a ghost from the past.

TIP OF THE DAY:

HOLD TO THE STATUTE OF LIMITATIONS: According to the Fair Credit Reporting Act, a bad debt or bankruptcy is dropped off a credit record after a seven-year state of limitations has been met. Some credit agencies have been known to purchase the bad debt, report them with new dates, and give new life to old debts for another seven years. This is yet another reason to order your three, free credit reports each year, so that you can track this kind of activity as soon as it shows up on your credit report. This kind of "new life to old debt" activity is illegal and worth protesting with the following steps:

- Contact the credit collection agency and protest the falsely dated entry. Tell them if you don't get documentation that it has been fully resolved in thirty days, you will contact the FTC and NACA.

- Contact the NACA (National Association of Consumer Advocates) at www.naca.net and follow their guidelines for recourse.

- At the www.naca.net site, follow up on a list of attorneys who specialize in these kinds of disputes. **(ADVANCED)**

TIP OF THE DAY:

FEE-FEE, THE WONDER DOG OF DOGS: The fees that credit card companies assess and collect have increased four times in the last decade, an increase of $6 billion dollars in fees! They come up with clever ways to add these fees, but you can save money on these if you know how to handle them beforehand and after they arise.

The first step is to set up all your credit cards with an automatic online payment (of the minimum), which would be set to draft the day before the payment is due. If you want to pay more than the minimum, then you can pay it with the copy of the bill that arrives in the mail. But you'll never have a late fee if you set it up this way—ever.

TIP OF THE DAY:

PLATINUM AVOIDANCE: While there are some prestige benefits and other perks in owning a platinum card, there can also be 31 percent above average fees for late payments, going over limits, and taking a cash advance. If your platinum card includes these pricey options, then consider dropping it to a more affordable gold or silver card.

TIP OF THE DAY:

CASH OUT OF CASH ADVANCE: When cash advance services began, there was only a $2 minimum fee with a 2 percent interest fee. Now they cost between $10 and $50 and charge 3 percent interest (or more). Avoid using a credit card for a cash advance.

TIP OF THE DAY:

KNOW YOUR GRACE PERIOD: Some credit cards have gone from a standard thirty-day grace period to a shocking twenty-one-day period, which makes it easier than ever to be late on a payment.

Call your credit card company and ask them how long of a cycle they have and be sure you pay before the end of the grace period.

TIP OF THE DAY:

ASK FOR REDUCED RATES:
If you've gotten your FICO score healthy (675 or higher), then call all your credit card companies and ask them to reduce the interest rate you pay. It would be best if you had your FICO score in hand when you make the request. Many customer service representatives are authorized to make these changes right on the phone! A lower APR can translate into saving hundreds of dollars each year on your credit card balances.

TIP OF THE DAY:

ANNUAL CARD FEES:
About two and a half months before your card renews, call them and ask them to waive the annual fee. If you are a good customer with a solid history, they may want to do this to keep your business. Some companies will never waive the fee, so you should be very judicious about whether you automatically choose not to renew because of the fee. If it is a card that you've held for five years or longer, with a modest APR, then it's best to keep it and pay the fee.

But if the card is less than five years old and you have a few other cards that are older than that, you should consider eliminating the card. If you're new to credit, you want to keep the cards you've held the longest to increase your credit history's longevity and improve your FICO.

TIP OF THE DAY:

ORDER FREE CREDIT REPORTS: You are allowed a copy of your full credit report from each of the three major reporting agencies each year. You can go to www.annualcreditreport.com to order each of these, one at a time, or you can go directly to the credit reporting agency to order it.

Equifax: (800) 685-1111 or www.equifax.com
Experian: (888) 397-3742 or www.experian.com
TransUnion: (800) 888-4213 or www.transunion.com

#141

TIP OF THE DAY:

CHECK THOSE REPORTS: Once you get your free credit report, make sure you close down existing department store accounts that you no longer use. Close any credit card accounts or lines of credit that you have open that you haven't used in the last year. The exception would be a credit card that you've held for a long time (longevity helps your FICO). In that case, hang on to those cards but make sure you have a low interest rate and no annual bank card fees (see previous tips). Also check the amounts that are posted as outstanding debts to make sure they fit your records. These reports are also the first line of defense in detecting and overcoming an identity theft issue.

TIP OF THE DAY:

TAG THE CLOSURES: Whenever you close a credit card account or line of credit account or when you pay off an automobile, be sure you request that the lender tags the account "closed at the customer's request." It looks more favorable on your account when tagged in this way and will help your FICO score. If it doesn't show up this way in your credit report, contact the lender immediately and ask for them to make the change. **(ADVANCED)**

TIP OF THE DAY:

IDENTITY THEFT PROTECTION: Identity thieves stole over 100 million dollars from unsuspecting consumers last year, and there's a lot you can do to prevent it from coming to you.

* First, order those free credit reports and review them to make sure there is no suspicious activity on your record.

* Never put your social security number on a check and never give it over the Internet or from a cell phone.

* Shred all credit card applications and don't just throw them away.

* Only write the last four numbers of your credit card account number on your payment check.

* Never respond to a bank inquiry, credit card inquiry, or other inquiry (PayPal, eBay) via a link in an email account. Always go back to the original website or call them on the phone. Some of these phishing

schemes are getting more and more sophisticated and appear credible.

- Be suspicious of ANY email that has to do with ANYTHING financial—assume it's fraud first and be diligent before responding (see tip below).

- Make sure PIN codes are not based on birth dates, social security numbers, addresses, or other common numbers that may be found in your wallet. One of our favorite TV shows is *Monk* and Mr. Monk always made his passwords something to do with his deceased wife's name, date of birth, or their wedding date. Smart guy, not-smart protection move.

- Make photocopies of every card and ID in your wallet to have in the event it is stolen or lost.

TIP OF THE DAY:

MORE IDENTITY THEFT TIPS: Never give your social security number, account numbers, date of birth, or other personal information via email or on the phone unless you initiated the contact. Most major Internet sites and financial institutions have been targeted, including Citibank, PayPal, eBay, Bank of America, Wells Fargo, the Internal Revenue Service (IRS), and America Online (AOL).

TIP OF THE DAY:

PROTECT YOURSELF FROM EMAIL SCAMS: The Nigerian email scam seeks to obtain your banking information and has been around for years. The message states the sender has millions of dollars and needs help to transfer it out of Nigeria. New scams are emerging all the time, especially those claiming to be a message from the "system administrator", telling you to perform some urgent maintenance on your account or they need your information verification. These can seem to come from reputable sites such as eBay, PayPal, Wells Fargo, and the Internal Revenue Service (IRS). NEVER click onto the email links to verify information. Instead, enter the main website's primary address directly into your browser and go to your account information. For example, go to www.eBay.com or www.wellsfargo.com rather than clicking the hyperlink in the body of the email.

TIP OF THE DAY:

PROTECT YOURSELF FROM AUCTION FRAUD: This was the second most reported consumer fraud complaint to the FTC last year, totaling 51,000 auction complaints in 2006. The fraud is simple—put up a fake ad on eBay, let someone win the bid and send in their money, but never send out the merchandise. Make sure the seller has an established history before you click "buy."

TIP OF THE DAY:

PROTECT YOURSELF FROM CREDIT REPAIR SCAMS: The Federal Trade Commission has warned that some companies that claim to be identity theft prevention companies are scam artists trying to get your driver's license number, mother's maiden name, social security number, and credit and bank account numbers. If you are unsure about a firm, check it out with the Better Business Bureau at www.bbb.org. Even if they are legit, you should not have to pay a private firm to help repair your credit when you can go to the National Foundation for Credit Counseling for free at www.nfcc.org.

TIP OF THE DAY:

PROTECT YOURSELF FROM PRIZE SCAMS: If someone calls you on the telephone and offers you the chance to receive a major prize but insists on gathering personal data first, ask them to send a written application in the mail. If they refuse, then hang up.

TIP OF THE DAY:

SECURE YOUR ONLINE PURCHASES: Never purchase a product or give your social security number on an unsecured site (lock and key icon). Once you do purchase an item, print out the product order and sign off of the account. Do not set up your password to automatically remember the billing information (such as on Amazon, PayPal, some travel sites) because if someone gets into your computer (even your child's friend), they may be able to buy something way too easily.

TIP OF THE DAY:

PASSWORDS FOR CREDIT CARDS: Establish a password for phone inquiries on credit card accounts. Make sure these passwords aren't as easy to decipher as Mr. Monk's (see tip on page 100). **(ADVANCED)**

TIP OF THE DAY:

BUY A BRAND-NAME DEBIT CARD: Make sure you have a Visa or Mastercard logo on your debit card and always choose to use it as a debit (with a PIN number). Those transactions that use a PIN are fifteen times less likely to be compromised, and if a brand-name credit card is stolen (or the number compromised), the consumer will never pay more than $50. If you do not have a brand-name debit card, you will pay $50 for the first two days after the card was stolen. If you do not report the card after two days, you could be liable for up to $500 on the account and if you do not report it for sixty days, you could be liable for the entire amount of fraudulent activity if you do not have a brand-name debit card! **(ADVANCED)**

TIP OF THE DAY:

BANKING CHOICES: Not all banks are created equal. Before opening an account, ask about monthly fees, required minimum balances, charges for stopped payment checks, charges for money orders, etc. For some online banking options, go to www.gomez. com, a service that updates its bank ratings twice a year, and you can tell the search engine the criteria you want (cost, ease of use, saver, borrower, etc.). There is also info at www.bankrate.com or www.ingdirect.com.

TIP OF THE DAY:

INGDIRECT.COM: Some online banks have better rates on basic savings accounts as well as CDs. I bank with IngDirect, and love the fun of watching my money grow as they post their interest savings on a daily basis. It's easy to transfer money from my savings or checking account to IngDirect and it's equally easy to have my money transferred back into my other accounts. It usually takes three days for the money to transfer and all CD, savings, mutual fund purchases can be made online from any computer in the world.

TIP OF THE DAY:

BANKING APRS: The difference in a 5.75 percent mortgage rate and a 5.5 percent mortgage rate can be multiple thousands of dollars over the course of a mortgage loan. Paying attention to the details of banking will save you big bucks as well, whether it's a receipt you get from a teller, or the percentage rate placed on loan paperwork. You must not get complacent in a bank (as most people do), believing they are professionals and cannot make a mistake. It's up to you to guard your financial health.

TIP OF THE DAY:

DEBT REDUCTION PLAN: Go to www.crown.org to find a tool that will help you decide how to pay down existing debt. While there, check out their financial classes in your area to take and learn more about how to manage your money. Many of these classes are free. You might also be able to locate a nonprofit financial counselor in your area as well.

TIP OF THE DAY:

DEBT REDUCTION—PAY THE LEAST FIRST: When it comes to paying off your credit card bills, you can choose one of two routes, depending upon your personality:

1. **Highest Interest Rate**: It makes sense to pay off the card that has the highest interest rate so that you can minimize how much additional debt you are paying due to interest. If you had $5,000 in total debt with $2,000 on a card with 10 percent APR and 18 percent on the card with $1,500 due, while the three final cards had interest rates of 12 percent, you would want to pay down the 18 percent card ($1500) first to avoid those higher interest rates.

2. **Lowest Balance:** However, there are some people who like having only two debts instead of five, and these people will pay off the cards that owe the least amount first in order to get that entire debt swept off the ledger. For example, if you owe $5000 total, with $2,000 to one card, $1500 on another, and three final cards with a $500 or less balance, this kind of personality would want to pay off the three smaller balanced cards and leave only two cards outstanding (with a total of $3500 in debt). It motivates them in a different way that is tied into their money personality. There's no right answer other than responding to the system that will keep you motivated and keep you paying down the debt!

TIP OF THE DAY:

CONSUMER CREDIT COUNSELING SERVICES: If you are having trouble paying your bills and repaying your debts, it might be time to take a visit to your local office. Just go to the yellow pages to find an office in your area. These services are free, but they're fairly restrictive as well. They can help you consolidate loans with the best interest rate, they can negotiate with your credit card companies, and they can create a debt repayment plan to fit your needs. But beware of counterfeit, fee-based companies with similar sounding names. Go to www.nfcc.org to find an office in your city.

TIP OF THE DAY:

ASK YOUR BANK TO WAIVE FEES:
If you've been a good customer and have an occasional overdraft, ask your bank to waive their standard overdraft fees. Also ask them for free stop payment services when you need them (but don't abuse the privilege) and for free money orders. Most tellers are authorized to do these for free for their regular customers and all you have to do is say five words, "May I please have _____."

TIP OF THE DAY:

NONBANKS:
Don't discount the use of nontraditional banks such as credit unions. They oftentimes have better options for checking accounts and fee structures as well as a more personal environment. Go to the Credit Union National Association at www.CUNA.org to find a credit union you may qualify to join.

TIP OF THE DAY:

INVEST IN CDS:
Know your investment options—invest in the traditional certificate of deposit.

- CDs usually **earn more interest** than a savings account and are a very low-risk financial vehicle for retirement savings.

- They are **insured up to $100,000** by the FDIC for all deposits at one institution.

- You agree to **keep your money on deposit** for a fixed period of time and the longer the term, the higher the interest rate.

- There are **penalties for early withdrawal**.

- **Long run:** Good for two to five years, but not good for a long-term investment.

- **Savings available sooner:** The only time you would want to do this is if you have savings you need to use in the next few months or few years; then CDs become a great place to park your money.

- **INGDirect**.com: Easy transfers and **easy savings account** at a higher interest rate.

TIP OF THE DAY:

#162 KNOW YOUR RETIREMENT NEEDS:

To **calculate** what you will need for retirement to fill the gap between social security and pension income, go to any of the following sites and click on "Retirement" for an online calculator: www.crown.org, www.kiplinger.com, www.moneymag.com.

TIP OF THE DAY:

KNOW HOW TO MAKE EASY MONEY—401(K) EMPLOYER RETIREMENT PLAN: A 401(k) can be one of your best tools for creating a secure retirement. It provides you with two important advantages. First, all contributions and earnings to your 401(k) are tax deferred. You only pay taxes on contributions and earnings when the money is withdrawn. Second, many employers provide matching contributions to your 401(k) account, which can go up to 100 percent of your contributions. The combined result is a retirement savings plan you cannot afford to pass up. For a good online 401(k) calculator, go to www.bloomberg.com/invest/calculators/401k.html.

TIP OF THE DAY:

KNOW WHEN YOUR 401(K) PLAN IS VESTED: Be sure you are informed about the vesting situation with your employer. Vesting is very common (about two-thirds of plans work this way). It means that you don't actually *own* your employer's entire contribution right away. There are two basic ways a company's contribution can vest:

1. **Graded Vesting**: An employee will gradually acquire ownership of the employer's contribution over a specified number of years. For instance, if the company's contribution vests over five years (or sixty months), an employee will own 20 percent of the match after one year has elapsed, 40 percent after two years, and so on. If you leave the company after the second year, you walk away from 60 percent of the company's matching contribution. By the way, a company cannot set the vesting period beyond seven years.

2. **Cliff Vesting**: This one is all or nothing. If a company sets the vesting period at five years,

you get 100 percent of the contribution only after the full five years. If you leave the company after four years and eleven months, you won't get any of the matching funds. **(ADVANCED)**

TIP OF THE DAY:

KNOW YOUR IRA INFORMATION AND LIMITS: You can put up to $3,000 a year (pretaxed dollars) into a traditional individual retirement account on a tax-deductible basis if your spouse isn't covered by a retirement plan at work or as long as your combined incomes aren't too high.

You can also put the same amount in for a nonworking spouse—$4,000 if you file your taxes jointly.

Plus, you don't have to fully fund the IRA, you can put in less.

With a Roth IRA, the money you put in is already taxed, but you won't ever pay taxes on the earnings as long as the account is open at least five years.

If you are age fifty and over, you are permitted to make catch-up contributions to your IRA account for years that you did not fully invest. You may contribute an additional $1,000 per year in 2006 and beyond.

As with the 401(k), these are tax deferred and subject to a 10 percent IRS penalty for premature withdrawals (before the age of fifty nine and a half), plus you are taxed on the amount (15 percent to 25 percent) depending upon your tax bracket.

TIP OF THE DAY:

KNOW YOUR US SAVINGS BONDS: Savings bonds are available through www.TreasuryDirect.com and are offered by the federal government.

- They are safe, affordable, and easy to purchase.
- They can be redeemed any time after twelve months.
- They can be purchased at banking institutions such as banks and credit unions.
- They are low risk.
- They are backed by the U.S. government.

TIP OF THE DAY:

KNOW YOUR US SAVINGS BONDS—THE I BOND: The I Bond is purchased at face value and earnings are beyond the face value.

- Offers a real rate of return over the inflation rate
- Exempt from state and federal income taxes
- Funds available after twelve months, but subject to a three-month loss of interest if redeemed before five years

TIP OF THE DAY:

KNOW YOUR US SAVINGS BONDS—SERIES EE BONDS:

- Sold at half the face value (a $50 bond is purchased for only $25)

- Earns 90 percent of market rates on a five-year treasury security

- Exempt from state and federal taxes

- Can be redeemed any time after twelve months, but subject to a three-month loss of interest if redeemed before five years

---

TIP OF THE DAY:

KNOW YOUR OTHER BONDS (NON US):

Similar to CDs in that you can purchase them with a designated maturity date

- For example, a Wal-Mart five-year bond (lending money to Wal-Mart instead of the bank when you buy a CD)

- **You assume the risk:** If Wal-Mart goes bankrupt, you could lose all the investment

- **Usually safe: i**n high quality companies

- **Higher interest:** Because you take the risk, the interest is higher.

- **No FDIC insurance:** in most cases

KNOW YOUR MUTUAL FUNDS: There are a variety of mutual funds that you can invest in. It's important to know the difference in these funds.

- **Stock funds:** If you want your money to grow over a long period of time (and you can handle down as well as up years), choose funds that invest more heavily in stocks.

- **Bond funds:** If you need current income and don't want investments that fluctuate as widely in value as stocks, consider some bond funds.

- **Money market funds:** If you want to be sure that your invested principal does not decline in value because you may need to use your money in the short term, select a money market fund.

BUY "NO-LOAD" FUNDS: Some brokerage firms charge a percentage to purchase your funds for you (from 4 to 8.5 percent). You can find plenty of outstanding no-load funds by going to:

- Vanguard.com
- Troweprice.com
- TDwaterhouse.com
- Scottrade.com   **(ADVANCED)**

4 937900 203229

SECTION FIVE

Life in the Fast Lane
Tips to Save on Transportation

I got my love of life from my mom, as well as her sense of humor. She was a military bride who came over to the United States from Spain and left all of her family behind. She did not know the language well, but she knew how to look at life in a funny way. My mom has always loved to drive Mercedes Benz cars. My dad got them from a friend of his in Germany and would fix them up to sell. Mom got to keep one of her own and it is her pride and joy. It was hard to keep her down and hard to keep her foot off the pedal too.

One day, when my mom was out on a fairly empty desert highway traveling from California cross-country in her Mercedes 280SL convertible, she got pulled over by the highway police in a lonely desert stretch in New Mexico. The officer stuck his head in the window of her car and asked, "Excuse me, ma'am, do you know how fast you were going?"

My mom replied emphatically, "Jes, I go eightee-five."

The officer was solemn. "Yes, ma'am, that's twenty miles over the speed limit."

The little woman was incensed. "No! It is NOT! I saw sign. It say eightee-five, and I no go more than eightee-five! I no should get no ticket because I go what the sign say."

The policeman's face flushed. "Ma'am, that's *highway* 85—the *speed limit* is still sixty-five miles per hour."

My mom suddenly became quiet and replied, "Oh." She paused a moment. "It's a good thing it were not the 101."

She peered at him over her surprised looking eyebrows. "Are chew going to give me a ticket?"

The officer tried to stifle his laughter. "No, ma'am, I'm not, just slow down to sixty-five. You're the best thing that has happened to me today!"

Whether you're driving a Mercedes or you're driving a Ford, we all want to know how to drive a little smarter and cheaper. Here are some tips to save on transportation.

TIP OF THE DAY:

PAY ATTENTION TO THE SIGNS!: If you think the speed limit is eighty five and it's only sixty-five, that ticket is going to cost you more than the price of the fine. It will likely make your insurance premiums rise as well. If you are ticketed, ask if you can take a drivers safety course to have it removed from your record. This course is free and usually lasts a day. The other benefit is that you can turn the certificate into your auto insurance and get an additional discount on your policy.

TIP OF THE DAY:

WHY BUY?: One of the first things we need to ask ourselves before we buy any car is—why? Can the car you have be repaired without major expense? How many miles do you have left on your car? If you have a loan, how much do you still owe the bank on it? Do you really need a new car? Or are you just tired of your present car? The least expensive car you can own is usually the "paid for" car you're driving right now.

TIP OF THE DAY:

USED DOESN'T MEAN ABUSED: The average depreciation of a new car during the first year can be up to 30 percent of the price you paid for it. Incredible!

With most new cars, you lose an average of $6,000 as soon as you drive it off the showroom floor. Let someone else own it for that expensive year! Consider the purchase of a late-model, low-mileage, mechanically sound, and well-maintained used car.

TIP OF THE DAY:

CHECK IT OUT!: If at all possible, try to talk to the previous owner of the used car before you buy it. Be leery of repainted portions of the car—it usually indicates an accident. Look carefully under the car for rust. Try to find the repair history on your vehicle by getting the vehicle identification number and then going to www.dmv.org. This amazing site will give you the following information.

Title Check
- Salvaged
- Rebuilt
- Fire Damage
- Damaged

Odometer Check
- Rolled Back
- Broken Odometer
- Exceeds Limit
- Suspect Miles

Problem Check
- Frame Damage
- Lemon
- Salvage Auction
- Water Damage

Vehicle Information
- Accidents
- Theft
- Police/Taxi Use
- Fleet Car

TIP OF THE DAY:

MINORS ACCEPTED: After you've checked out the major repairs and damages, and know that you do not want to buy those previous troubles, it may be fine to accept minor repairs on a vehicle if the seller will substantially reduce the price. Be prepared to pay for these repairs, and add them to the cost of the car.

Negotiate for a 100 percent short-term guarantee if possible from the seller (at least one week). This guarantee should apply to dealers and individuals. When you drive the car for the first week, you'll find 90 percent of the problems you bought.

TIP OF THE DAY:

NONSMOKERS, PLEASE: If you are purchasing a car from a smoker, remember that cigarette smoke damages seals, glue, and upholstery. Buying a car from a smoker devaluates the car. Be aware of air freshener smells, perfumes, or incense in a car you are test driving; these can be a cover-up for evidence that the car is owned by a smoker.

TIP OF THE DAY:

MAKE A MECHANIC YOUR FRIEND: Take the car to a reliable and trustworthy mechanic—and pay him to look it over. Get an estimate for the once-over before you leave the car with the mechanic. By the way, the best time to find a mechanic is before you need one. Ask your friends, neighbors, or co-workers for a reference. A mechanic's reputation—either good or bad—usually follows him closely. You'll need a friendly mechanic as your advisor and to service your present car.

TIP OF THE DAY:

DON'T BE OVERLY GENEROUS TO YOUR MECHANIC:

When I was looking for a classic Corvette for Bob's fiftieth birthday, I ended up taking two cars to our mechanic and paid $35 for a twenty-five-point inspection; both times the cars had problems and would have been costly to own. He said, "Ellie, if you bought this car, you'd be giving *me* a present instead of Bob." We still don't have that dream car, but we don't have the headaches either!

TIP OF THE DAY:

KNOW THE BLUE BOOK VALUES:
This is the book your bank officer uses to decide how much of a loan to give on your vehicle. It should also be your guide when buying or selling vehicles. It lists the wholesale and retail value of a used car. The price is affected by mileage, wear and tear on the vehicle, and mechanical reliability—among other factors. You can also check the blue book value at www.edmunds.com or www.kbb.com for Kelley's Blue Book online.

TIP OF THE DAY:

SECURE YOUR OWN LOAN:
It's better to secure a loan from your personal lender—negotiating and shopping for the best price. Go to www.bankrate.com for some comparison shopping prices. The exception to this would be if you are getting 0 percent interest financing through the dealership or manufacturer. You can always get the best price from an online source, print it out,

and then take it to your regular banker and ask them to match the deal. Make sure there are no penalties for prepayment.

#182

TIP OF THE DAY:
NEGOTIATE THE CAR PRICE SEPARATE FROM THE LOAN: Know the blue book value of the vehicle and negotiate with the dealership as if you were a cash buyer—you won't be using their banks anyway. Try to never pay more than $100 over the wholesale value of the car and don't be pigeonholed as a "payment buyer," or then the salesman will simply talk in terms of monthly payments instead of overall sales costs.

TIP OF THE DAY:

TRADE-INS: Try to sell your current car privately and don't trade it in. Detail it yourself—wash and wax it to a glorious shine. As you clean and scrub, think of all the extra money you'll make by this minimum effort. You may be able to get $1,000 to $2,000 more for your vehicle! Put an ad in your local paper, and another one on the bulletin board at work, the library, at church, at your kids' school, and tell your friends you're selling your car.

TIP OF THE DAY:

KNOW SALES SPEAK: If you trade in your vehicle to a car dealership, you'll get significantly less for it. It doesn't matter how much the salesman "says" he's giving you on the trade. They'll often inflate the value of the trade, then figure the inflated amount in the negotiated price on the vehicle you purchase. It's not illegal; it's just a card shuffle—to make you buy the vehicle. You don't want to play that game, you want to hold the cards yourself and play your own hand to your own advantage.

TIP OF THE DAY:

CASE STUDY—SALES SPEAK: For example, let's say the sticker price on the new car is $21,500. The blue book value on your used car is $7,000. The dealership says they'll give you $7,500 on your trade. You're ecstatic. Then you negotiate on the sticker price of the car and end up paying $21,000 less your trade, for a total of $13,500.

If you got the normal trade-in value on the car of around $5,500—you could still pay around $13,500 for the car. The sales manager would allow more bargaining room on the sticker price if they had less cash invested in your trade. The difference is that you'd get a $500 discount with a $7,500 trade, and a $3,000 discount with a $5,500 trade. You're better off selling your car on your own and negotiating on the $21,500 sticker price as a cash buyer with no trade. The only exception would be to negotiate the value of the new car separately from the value of the trade-in.

TIP OF THE DAY:

PRACTICE AT HOME: It can be an intimidating process to go to the car dealership and negotiate a deal for what will be the second largest expenditure in your personal finance. So why not practice? It could save you thousands of dollars by taking thirty minutes to work on the techniques and phrases you will use to negotiate the price and trade, knowing that you are going to secure your own financing. Do your homework and practice using the Kelly Blue Book figures so you will build confidence before you walk on the showroom floor.

TIP OF THE DAY:

WHEN YOU NEED NEW: If you must buy new, then try to avoid buying the newest, latest, greatest model—as soon as it comes out. Instead, buy an end-of-the-year clearance model, a demonstrator model, or a rental car. December and January are the best times to get these bargains because that's when dealerships experience their lowest annual sales. Buy a cheaper model of the same vehicle, rather than the luxury model. Buy the least expensive car that will still fit your family's needs.

TIP OF THE DAY:

LEASING A CAR: Generally speaking, the most expensive way to own a car is to lease it. A few of the exceptions are 1) if you use it for business, anticipate extremely high mileage, and there's a substantial tax savings offered. 2) Another

exception might be when the manufacturer is heavily subsidizing the lease (usually by applying large cash-back incentives to the lease). 3) A final exception is if you are looking to avoid maintenance fees on an older vehicle. My son Daniel had this problem at college, and basically it was cheaper for him to lease a vehicle for three years, while building his FICO score, than it was to continue to pay upwards to $4,000/year in repairs on his lemon of a car.

TIP OF THE DAY:

ALTERNATIVE TRANSPORTATION: Since transportation is the moving of goods or persons from one place to another, consider alternative forms of transportation. Some towns we've been assigned to are very small. How small? I'm glad you asked. They were so small that we could get by with one car. In past assignments, Bob got rides to work or rode his bike. Yes, it was inconvenient at times—but it fit our budget and eliminated the financial stress of another vehicle, especially while we were paying down debt.

Car pools, buses, and public transportation are all ways to get your person from one place to another. Even if your alternative transportation is only seasonal, it may help to reassess your genuine need for a vehicle or it might allow you the luxury of time to wait for the perfect deal on the perfect vehicle for you.

TIP OF THE DAY:

GAS MILEAGE: To save on gas, try these tips:

- Remove unnecessary weight from the trunk.

- Gas up at the grocery store; chains such as Albertsons, Vons, and Kroger allow you to get a nice discount when using a store card.

- Avoid quick starts—leave these to teenage boys. Drive smoothly and steadily.

- Check the air in your tires regularly; the wrong amount of air wastes fuel and accelerates tire wear.

- Buy in the cool of the day, when gas is the densest.

- Make sure your wheels are properly aligned and balanced.

- You lose four miles per gallon (mpg) by running the air conditioner, and the same amount by having the windows open on the highway (due to wind drag).

- Drive intelligently—fast starts or speeding can waste gas. Drive smart and save big.

- Tighten the screw cap on the gas lid; otherwise it can quickly evaporate.

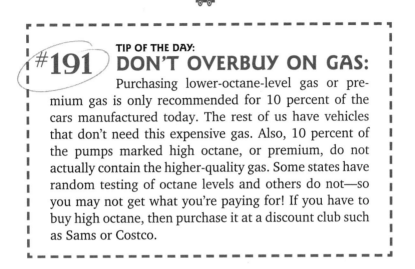

TIP OF THE DAY:

#191 DON'T OVERBUY ON GAS:

Purchasing lower-octane-level gas or premium gas is only recommended for 10 percent of the cars manufactured today. The rest of us have vehicles that don't need this expensive gas. Also, 10 percent of the pumps marked high octane, or premium, do not actually contain the higher-quality gas. Some states have random testing of octane levels and others do not—so you may not get what you're paying for! If you have to buy high octane, then purchase it at a discount club such as Sams or Costco.

TIP OF THE DAY:

CHEAPEST PRICES ON GAS: To find the least expensive prices on gas or to find good values on your next cross-country road trip, go to www.gaspricewatch.com or www.autos.msn.com, click on gas prices, and enter your zip code. These savvy little sites are updated daily and can save you big bucks over the course of a month of driving.

MORE GAS SAVING TIPS:

TAKE CARE: Get a tune-up, change your oil, and you'll save 15 percent a year on gas mileage.

COMBINE ERRANDS: Instead of running errands several days a week, combine and run all of them on the same day.

KEEP SAFE AND SPLURGE: Drive within the speed limit and avoid jackrabbit starts to increase your mpg. Also, the time to splurge is on quality motor oil; it extends the life of the motor and increases mpg.

TIP OF THE DAY:

EBAY: Have you ever thought of eBay as a way to buy and sell vehicles? I sold my 1982 500SL Mercedes Benz on eBay for $500 more than I paid for it when I realized I couldn't keep it due to smog regulations in California.

TIP OF THE DAY:

IMPROVE YOUR FICO AND PAY 0 PERCENT APR: We've all heard of those 0 percent APR car loans, but how feasible are they? If you have a good to excellent credit score (usually between 760–850), then you could probably qualify for this loan. It means that you pay no interest, which can translate to as much as an $1800 savings over the course of a $20,000 loan!

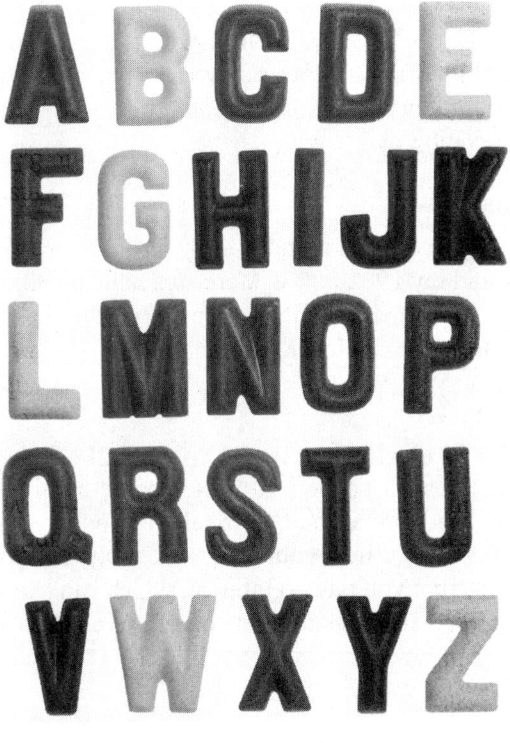
ABCDE
FGHIJK
LMNOP
QRSTU
VWXYZ

Too Cool for School!

Tips to Save on Education

I heard the sound of a child crying. It sounded like it was coming from the back of the house. I walked down the hall and looked in the boys' room. No one was there. I continued to the next room, which was my daughter's. When I opened the door, I found my then five-year-old Bethany sobbing into her pillow. Crying wasn't terribly unusual for our "Bunny," as she could have starred in a movie called *I Was a Preschool Drama Queen*. She was usually laughing and hopping for joy, but she did have an occasional bad day and when she did, we had to watch out!

"What's wrong, Bunny-rabbit?" I asked as I stroked her hair.

"Well . . . it's . . . just." She tried to catch her breath.

". . . it's just. It's just that . . . " Her tiny frame shook as she tried to compose herself.

"I'm going to . . .(whimper) to go away to *college*!" At this, her sobbing started all over again.

Apparently, she had a friend whose much older sibling just graduated from high school and was headed off to college. So Bethany was under the impression that when she "graduated" from kindergarten, we were going to ship her off to school!

College isn't the only expense for children these days. In fact, recent studies say that raising a child born in 2007 will cost over a million dollars to rear (including college). So it's never too early to save on educational costs now and later. Here are some tips that will save you on educational costs from preschool to postgrad.

TIP OF THE DAY:

BACK TO SCHOOL KIDS BUDGETS: Buying back to school equipment and supplies can be a fabulous teaching tool for tots and teens. You can teach them the ability to budget money by establishing a school supply or clothing budget for them. Set a budget per semester to include backpacks, lunch boxes, and all supplies. It's amazing how a child will lose fewer pencils and keep up with their notebook better when they have to pay out of their own budget for these items. You give the child an adequate amount of money for their budget, but they manage it. The fun part is that at the end of the semester, they get to keep what they don't spend. This not only encourages financial independence but it motivates frugality as well. **(ADVANCED)**

TIP OF THE DAY:

#199

WIZER STRATEGIZER: When back-to-school sales are advertised, map your strategy and stick to it. Many specials are loss leaders used to draw you into the store. Establish a budget, decide which sale items you'll take advantage of, and *hold true to that plan*! Be sure to combine store coupons (such as Walgreens or Eckerds) with manufacturers' coupons whenever possible. Many of the tips from section one (shopping, groceries) apply to back-to-school sales.

TIP OF THE DAY:

BE PATIENT OR BE EAGER: There's one thing that is certain: when fall arrives, there are going to be back-to-school sales and you need to either be patient or eager to maximize the values on these kids items. Sometimes the sales start as early as July and we just aren't in the mood to get a discount (we know our kids are certainly not in the mood to think of going back to school), but if we're eager, we can capitalize on those early sales while there's still a great selection.

If we miss the sales on the items we need, then we can be patient and they will go on clearance within two weeks of school starting and you can grab up some bargains, like backpacks for 75 percent off and lunch boxes for the same discount. If your child can start the year with last year's goods, then they'll soon have new stuff at a great price.

TIP OF THE DAY:

WHINERS ANONYMOUS: Before we go shopping, I brief my troops with the same kind of attention to detail that my husband gives before he flies fighter jets. The kids know what we'll buy and how much we'll spend. They understand we're going to be good stewards of our budget. You could spend twice as much by giving in to your child's impulse buys in the store—take care of it *before* you shop.

TIP OF THE DAY:

WIN-WIN FOR EVERYONE!: Why pay *anything* for back-to-school supplies and equipment if you don't need to? A fab website called Freecycle.org is a grassroots, entirely nonprofit movement of people who are giving (and getting) stuff for free in their own towns. Each local group is moderated by a local volunteer and membership is free. The only constraint is that everything posted must be free and for a general audience.

You can find everything from sports equipment to clothes to backpacks!

WEB SAVINGS: Before you go back-to-school shopping at the store, check out additional online savings. Type in the store's name, for example, Staples.com, or use a shopping robot such as MySimon.com or NexTag.com to compare prices. Don't forget eBay either; you can often find lots of back-to-school items such as backpacks, lunch boxes, clothing, and school supplies for up to 75 percent off of retail. If you find an item on sale that is also in the local store, print out the sale item, take the paper into the store, and ask them to match the price.

PRICE COMPING—NOT JUST FOR GROCERIES: I mentioned in section one about certain stores that will match the price of competitors if you bring in the sale ad. There's no need to drive all over town, to all the discount department stores, drugstores, and office supply stores when you can take all these ads into Super Wal-Mart or any other store that matches competitors' ads.

SAVINGS FOR HOMESCHOOLERS—USED CURRICULUM: For seven years, we were a homeschooling family. I found that once you've decided on a curriculum, it's important to ask others in your homeschool group if you can have a used curriculum swap/sale. The best time to do this is in March–April, so that you will have adequate time to order the other materials you couldn't pick up used.

The main thing to keep in mind with used curriculum is if it will work for you. What good is a textbook if the student workbook is out of print and you can't order it? This means you would have to develop your own workbook and we're talking many, many hours to develop this. Homeschooling is a challenge enough without adding these additional chores. You have to carefully consider the financial and time trade-offs when purchasing used curriculum.

TIP OF THE DAY:

NEW CURRICULUM FAIRS: It is very important not to duplicate curriculum or purchase materials that will not work for your homeschool. This is a waste of money and the one area where homeschoolers are likely to blow their budgets.

If you can go to a curriculum fair with several distributors, it would be worth the trip. *Before* the fair, try to get catalogs from the major distributors by calling their toll-free numbers listed on their websites.

Do your homework by looking over the catalogs and writing down the materials you would like to order for the coming year. Pay attention to which textbooks/lesson plans/teacher's guides/ quiz keys you need to look at in person and indicate these on your list with an asterisk.

The reason you want to look at some of these resources is that you may not need to order the lesson plan, if the materials seem to be self-explanatory. If you have a good grasp of mathematics, for example, then you may already know how to teach addition and won't need the teacher guide. I didn't really need these additional resources until my children were in the second and third grades, depending upon the subject.

I learned very quickly, when my oldest was in the third grade, that a mathematics workbook teacher's key was worth $9 a year so I wouldn't have to do each and every fraction and long division problem. By getting organized in terms of your curriculum, you could save several hundred dollars each semester.

#207

TIP OF THE DAY:
FIND MORE TIPS FOR HOMESCHOOLERS
at www.elliekay.com.

TIP OF THE DAY:

HIGH SCHOOL IS THEIR JOB: It's important to teach your children from a young age that they will be responsible for the majority of their college expenses. You do not owe your child a college education. Their job in high school is to get good grades, and/or pursue a passion that can be leveraged into a life after high school, such as athletic scholarships, musical/theater scholarships, and academic scholarships. By training them from a young age, you'll find that this could cut college costs in half as they work hard to do their part.

So far, three out of four of our college bound children have earned scholarships and participated in work-study programs to get through college with minimal or no debt. One child is doing college the hard way, on the high-debt-seven-year plan—but we've given her the freedom to find her own route. There are no guarantees your children will follow your suggestions, all you can do is try! **(ADVANCED)**

TIP OF THE DAY:

NEVER BORROW ON YOUR FUTURE TO PAY THEIRS: In any discussion of college costs, it's important to keep priorities straight. You should never borrow on *your* future in order to pay for *your child's* future. Their education shouldn't cost you your retirement. This means it's not a wise idea to take out a home equity loan, an equity line of credit, or refinance your mortgage in order to pay for school. This would reduce the amount of equity in your home, increase the risk of possible foreclosure, and incur costs in interest charges that may cost more if the term on the new mortgage is greater than the remaining term on the existing mortgage—for example, if you have ten years left on your mortgage and you get a new thirty-year loan. Furthermore, if you pull out enough money in equity for the first year of college, you would need to do it again for the second year. If you pull out enough for four years of college, then you are paying interest on money that you won't need until the upcoming sophomore, junior, and senior years. **(ADVANCED)**

TIP OF THE DAY:

TUITION SAVINGS CALCULATION TOOL: This will allow you to calculate how much you will need for college, based on your child's age and your current savings patterns—www.moneycentral.msn.com/investor/calcs/n_college/main.asp.

TIP OF THE DAY:

PAYING FOR COLLEGE: Go to the parents' page at www.collegeboard.com and learn about college costs, applying for scholarships and other types of financial aid, choosing the best aid package, taking out education loans, and paying the college bill.

TIP OF THE DAY:

SCHOLARSHIP SEARCH WIZARD: There are thousands of scholarships that go unawarded each year because no one applies for them. To research some of the available scholarships, go to FastWeb's scholarship search engine. They will ask for a personal profile and automatically match your student up to the best scholarship applications. Go to www.fastweb.monster.com/cpt and have some fun! FastWeb will even email you with updates as new scholarships become available.

TIP OF THE DAY:

#213 **"THE 100 BEST VALUES IN PUBLIC COLLEGE":** This helpful list can be found at www.kiplinger.com/tools/colleges. You can sort the schools in the survey of public colleges by in-state and out-of-state, overall rank, cost, quality measures, or financial aid measures. Clicking on the college names will take you to each of the individual college's websites.

TIP OF THE DAY:

UGMA—UNIFORMED GIFTS TO MINORS ACT: If you have a young child, start saving now for education but do it the tax-smart way. If you invest in the UGMA in your child's name, then the income is taxed at the child's marginal tax bracket rather than yours. The account must be registered in the child's name. An adult (usually a parent or grandparent) serves as custodian and is responsible for investing and managing the assets. But the child is the "beneficial owner," meaning the assets really belong to the child. At age eighteen (in most states), control of the assets must be turned over to the child (which could be a disadvantage for this plan). All states offer UGMAs, and many have adopted the Uniform Transfers to Minors Act, or UTMA, as well. The former allows children to own stocks, bonds, mutual funds, and other securities; the latter allows the children to also own real estate. Under UTMA, you can delay giving the assets to the child until age twenty-one.

TIP OF THE DAY:

EE US SAVINGS BONDS: If the income from these bonds are used to pay for education expenses, then that interest may be excluded from taxes. But this exclusion is phased out beyond certain income levels.

TIP OF THE DAY:

ZERO-COUPON BONDS: The interest on these bonds is deferred until they mature, when it is paid in a lump sum. You do have to pay income tax on interest as it accrues each year the bond is held. You could "ladder" these bonds in which they mature in every year of the child's college career.

TIP OF THE DAY:

529 PLAN: This is an education savings plan operated by a state or educational institution designed to help families set aside funds for future college costs. As long as the plan satisfies a few basic requirements, the federal tax law provides special tax benefits to you, the plan participant (Section 529 of the Internal Revenue Code). 529 plans are usually categorized as either prepaid or savings, although some have elements of both. Every state now has at least one 529 plan available. It's up to each state to decide whether it will offer a 529 plan (or possibly more than one), and what it will look like. Educational institutions can offer a 529 prepaid plan but not a 529 savings plan (the private-college Independent 529 Plan is the only institution-sponsored 529 plan thus far).

You can invest in any state's plan, no matter where you live and regardless of what plan you choose; your beneficiary can attend any college or university in the country. What's more, grandparents or other benefactors can contribute money to a 529 plan. However, they may crimp financial aid in the future.

TIP OF THE DAY:

COVERDELL EDUCATION SAVINGS ACCOUNTS: This "education IRA" will allow up to $2,000 of pretaxed income to be invested annually. There are limits on how much can be invested based on income, and the funds must be spent before the child turns thirty. This education IRA will not interfere with the parents' ability to invest in a $3,000 tax-deferred annuity in your own retirement account. But it will count heavily against the student when financial aid packages are calculated.

Jay Stillman, a consultant for SavingForCollege.com, says, "Because Coverdell IRA funds can be rolled over into a 529 without penalty, parents can sidestep its principal drawbacks— the age limit and the fact that the IRA counts as the child's asset, which can adversely affect his ability to receive need-based loans." Stillman goes on to say that a Coverdell account may be the best single investment option for parents whose income is below $50,000. The accounts are easier and less expensive to set up than 529 plans, and people in this lower tax bracket aren't usually able to take advantage of the maximum lifetime contributions allowed under a 529, which range from 110K to 305K because they don't pay that much tax in the first place.

FINANCIAL AID OFFICE: The university's financial aid office is a clearinghouse of information. A good financial aid office will not only help students determine what loans they qualify for, but they will steer them to participating lenders who are offering the best terms and service. Parents can do their own assessment at www. collegeboard.com's paying for college calculator.

The FAFSA (Free Application for Student Financial Aid form; fafsa.ed.gov) is the first step in applying for aid that includes: 1) need-based guaranteed loans (Stafford loans are variable and currently at 3.42 percent while Perkins loans are at a fixed 5 percent); 2) Grants—the Pell grant and the federal Supplemental Education Opportunity Grant each provide a gift of up to $4,050 per student per student year; 3) Work-study. Students can receive up to $2,000 per year, 25 percent of it matched by the participating institution, from the federal work-study program.

There are also state loans and grants available and the financial aid office should be able to quickly assess the student's eligibility.

TIP OF THE DAY:

UNIVERSITY'S COUNSELING OFFICE:
Encourage your college student to visit this office before their first year of college and at least twice a year while they are in school. Our son Daniel found that several of the classes he needed for his major were available at a local junior college and fully transferable to his university. The classes are cheaper at the junior college and much to his great pleasure they're easier too.

The counseling office can advise on dozens of other details that may help with college expenses as well—everything from advanced placement tests to community service projects that could count as credit hours. It's worth a trip before each semester.

TIP OF THE DAY:

OTHER OPTIONS TO CONSIDER—ACCEPTANCE:
Just because a high school graduate is accepted to the college of her dreams doesn't mean she is miraculously entitled to go to that school. College should be a matter of what the family can afford, not what kind of school your child can get into. Students and parents need a reality check in this area.

There is an attitude out there that says, "I just figure out what I want and then I try to figure out how to pay for it." The people spouting this kind of dogma are usually the same people who are in debt up to their eyeballs. Unfortunately, this is a destructive philosophy that some parents are passing on to their children. Acceptance into college needs to be balanced with an acceptance of what you can afford without becoming indebted for the next twenty-five years.

TIP OF THE DAY:

GOD'S WILL/GOD'S BILL: We are seeing an alarming number of people who are going to Christian colleges and graduating with $80,000 plus in student loan debt because "God wants me there." Oftentimes, these grads will marry a fellow classmate for a combined student debt load of over $100,000. If they make an excellent living, this kind of debt almost guarantees that both spouses will have to be in full-time employment for a least a decade in order to pay those loans. But the real fact is that many of the graduating students will have professions that are never going to earn more than $50,000 a year. This translates into an entire lifetime of student loan debt and a greatly limited ability to have the freedom to pursue other interests—such as having a full-time parent at home to raise young children.

My feeling is that if it's God's will for you to go to that Christian college, then it's His bill. I don't think part of the master plan is to have the student's parents forced to work into their retirement years to pay for their children's expensive education. I know people in this situation and they admit they made a mistake. I believe you should not graduate with any more than $15,000 to $20,000 in student loans and should adjust your expectations to fit your ability to pay, not your ability to go into debt. **(ADVANCED)**

TIP OF THE DAY:

COMMUNITY COLLEGES: The first two years of basics can be completed at a junior college and then transferred to the university that issues the diploma. The degree doesn't indicate that the graduate paid one quarter the cost of school those first two years. All you have to do is check with the counselor *from the university* to make sure those courses will transfer.

I don't recommend that you get the transfer information from the junior college. It's better to go directly to the source and that would be the university to which your student will transfer to complete their education. Another reason for this is that you not only want to be sure that the courses will transfer, but you want to make sure they will transfer into a specific major. Your student could take two years of junior college classes and have as much as one year's worth of hours not applicable to the major of their choice.

TIP OF THE DAY:

ADVANCED PLACEMENT: This is different from CLEP-ping a course (which we'll talk about later). While a student is still in high school, in the summer before school starts, or even after they have started classes, they can take advanced placement tests. Sometimes these tests are taken after the student has taken an advanced placement course in their high school. The fees on these tests are nominal, but a student can receive credit for a variety of subjects and have those hours apply toward a degree. All it will require are some hours of study and preparation. **(ADVANCED)**

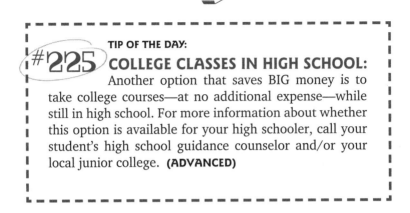

TIP OF THE DAY:

#225 COLLEGE CLASSES IN HIGH SCHOOL: Another option that saves BIG money is to take college courses—at no additional expense—while still in high school. For more information about whether this option is available for your high schooler, call your student's high school guidance counselor and/or your local junior college. **(ADVANCED)**

TIP OF THE DAY:

ROTC: These are programs that offer scholarships to future military officers at a local college. Some ROTC scholarships go unused because of a lack of submissions. There are different levels of scholarships ranging from payment for the last two years of college, all the way to a full ride for four years. As with other military offers, there is a "payback" of five years served in the military as an officer. For more information on these scholarships, go to:

Air Force—www.afrotc.com/scholarships/index.php
Army—www.goarmy.com/rotc/scholarships.jsp
Navy—www.nrotc.navy.mil.
(ADVANCED)

ACTIVE DUTY/RESERVE MILITARY: By joining the military, a young person can learn a trade and earn money for college as well. When I interviewed an army recruiter, the college benefits package was so attractive it made me want to enlist! (But Bob wouldn't let me!)

Basically, a person would take the ASVAB test to determine their aptitude for college and for other enlistment purposes. If an individual scores less than fifty, then they qualify for the Montgomery GI Bill, which is a contributory fund. The soldier would contribute monthly for the first twelve months and would incur a minimal commitment to the army of two years, which would yield close to $16,000 in college funding. Increased commitment would yield up to $20,000 total. However, if they score over fifty, then the army considers them college material and they qualify for the Army College Fund. This fund has the same contributory funds as above but they get anywhere from $27,000 to more than $50,000 for college, depending on whether they sign up for a two-, three-, or four-year term. The air force, navy, and marines offer similar packages, but this gives you an idea of what you can get for your enlistment into the military. The current benefits packages vary, so check with your recruiter. Keep in mind that military living is not just to pay for college; it's not for those who are timid and laid-back. These people literally lay their life on the line to protect our nation's freedoms and the service they provide our nation is more than worth the benefits they receive for college tuition.

TIP OF THE DAY:

WHO WANTS YOU?: Besides Uncle Sam, there may be some other institution that "wants you" for their school. Consider the colleges that are recruiting you first because they are more likely to give you a better financial aid package.

TIP OF THE DAY:

CLEP: The College-Level Examination Program® provides students of any age with the opportunity to demonstrate college-level achievement through a program of exams in undergraduate college courses. There are 2,900 colleges that grant credit and/or advanced standing for CLEP exams. Find out more at www.collegeboard.com. This allows you to save time and money and get credit for what you already know. My oldest son CLEPed out of an entire semester in college, and I CLEPed out of fourteen hours of Spanish when I was in college. Como que no?

TIP OF THE DAY:

JOBS: A summer or part-time job is a great way for students to "own" part of their college education. My oldest stepdaughter, Missy, not only participated in a work-study program at Columbia University, but she also took a year off between her sophomore and junior years to work. She feels very proud of her degree because she *earned* it in every way.

PARENTS CRASH COURSES IN COLLEGE TOO!:

Why should our kids have all the fun of learning? Studies indicate that the most well-balanced, lucid, and healthy older adults are those who keep learning. I recently joined the ranks of student/moms by crashing a couple of courses at our local junior college. All I did was to get enrolled (free) and then get an admittance slip from the office. On the first day of classes, I "crashed" the class (showed up when I wasn't on the rolls) and asked the teacher to sign my acceptance form. Since I'm not taking the class for credit, I can audit it and indicate that it is not for credit. That way, I don't have to pay for the course, but get all the benefits of the class!

I'm currently taking weight lifting and water aerobics. The accountability of the regular attendance and the bonding with fellow students (and a few moms, here and there) is keeping me fit both physically and emotionally. I enjoy hanging with younger people; it makes me think younger as I listen twice as much as I speak. Next semester I plan on taking water aerobics and physical training (running, conditioning, etc.). My daughter Bethany, who is still in high school, will take water aerobics with me, and she'll get high school credit for the summer course and have an easier senior year with fewer credit hours to balance.

Bonus Tips
from Daniel Kay ©2007

COLLEGE STUDENT AT THE UNIVERSITY OF TEXAS AT ARLINGTON

TIP 1: BUY BOOKS ONLINE: It's way cheaper to buy books online instead of used at the bookstore. For example, I got a journalism book that was $30 *used* at a bookstore and I got it online for $1.50. Amazon.com usually has the best deals for books, but www.campusbooks.com compares prices across the Internet and finds the best deals new and used. Just be sure you buy them at least two weeks before classes. (Note: Some books may be cheaper because they are an older version. However, versions tend to change so little that you can simply compare chapter lists between the old and new ones and adjust your assigned readings accordingly.)

TIP 2: AVOID THE MEAL PLANS: First off, college-based meal plans are usually unhealthy (fast food, fried, high calorie, high carbs, etc.). Second, they are way more expensive than just buying your own groceries. Plus, you don't lose out on the days you may not need a meal on your plan because a friend or family bought lunch. If you had the meal plan, you would still have to pay for it. Simply cut a few coupons, and don't buy the expensive brand stuff at grocery stores, and you'll do fine (you can eat fancy later!).

TIP 3: TAKE TESTS!: There are many exams that can be taken for college credit, such as CLEP, SAT II, and more. These tests usually run around $50, but if you pass, it's a lot better than shelling out over a thousand dollars for the course. (I had twenty hours of credit before I even started college, and it only cost around $200 in test fees instead of $5,000 in course fees.)

TIP 4: DON'T BE AFRAID TO LIVE MODESTLY: From apartment furnishings to clothes, you don't have to live flashy in college. Just because other young adults are spending their money foolishly doesn't mean you have to. College is just a step before getting a job where you can earn some real money and buy the little things you want. Ross, T.J. Maxx, and Steve and Barry's are great for clothes (I got four pairs of size fifteen shoes for $50), and there's always great clearance furniture items at stores that will serve your purpose. I bought a nice coffee table for $20, a TV stand for $15, and a new fourteen-inch TV with DVD player for $100.

TIP 5: FIND A ROOMIE: If you're searching for an apartment, it's always better to split the cost with one, two, or more people. Sure, it's always better living by yourself, but you have the rest of your life to do that if you want. (Editorial note from Mama: unless you get married, son, and give us some grandbabies!)

TIP 6: GET A JOB: You can't afford anything if you don't have any money. Use the many campus facilities that help students find jobs, look in the want ads, or work for the campus itself. If need be, just start walking into stores and asking for applications. Even if they aren't hiring, when you turn it in, they will have your application and will know what you look like. After all, you need some sort of experience before you start working full-time. If you can, get a job in your area of interest. I got a part-time job at the *Fort Worth Star Telegram* in the sports department and I love my work!

The Coupon Kids

*Tips to Help Kids Learn
and Save on Kids Stuff*

When our son Joshua was four years old, he began to learn that it is more blessed to give than to receive and we were proud of our youngest child. Although he still resembled the Taz Man at times, he was trying to learn to share. About this time, he started bringing home snacks for Mama and Papa that he saved from his Thursday night kids group at church. One week he brought us watermelon that his teacher helped him wrap in foil. Another week he brought us two pieces of butterscotch candy with the endearing explanation, "You can have dis because I dun't like it much anyway!"

☺

The next week, he came home very excited about sharing his special snack with his "wunnerful" mama and papa. We found ourselves caught up in the whirlwind of bedtime for five children, as I worked down the checklist: "Baths? Brushed teeth? Straightened rooms? Clothes set out for tomorrow? OK! Let's say our prayers and get to bed!" Poor Joshua went to bed still jabbering about the cookies he'd brought home, but I didn't have the chance to get them from him. So he gave them to Papa with the instructions, "You can made sum coffee and hab it affer we all git to bed!"

After the kids were tucked in and all the kisses had been equally dispensed, I asked Bob about Joshua's treat.

"Did you get the cookies that Joshua brought home? I promised him I'd ask you about it."

Bob gave me a wry grin, got up from the couch, and went into the kitchen. He came back with the "treat" wrapped very neatly in a Kleenex tissue. "Here's our special surprise—for us to share."

He unwrapped the two black parts of an Oreo cookie—all that was left of the white filling were two little teeth marks.

Teaching our kids to share, give, save, and work are all part of preparing them for a healthy future when it comes to their financial lives. This is like the cookie part of an Oreo. This training not only helps in the long run, it can help us in the short run—with more money in our pockets! That is the filling!

When kids learn to budget money, to shop smart, to not ask for stuff, and more stuff, then we spend less and save more. It's a great win-win situation for all of us. Here are some tips to help save money on raising your kids and also on how to create financially fit kids.

☺

TIP OF THE DAY:

BABY SAVINGS THROUGH BABY SHOWERS: If you are expecting and haven't had your baby shower yet, then take inventory of what you really need for baby, including the sizes of clothing you still need. When the hostess asks you for a list of items you'd like, be sure to include larger sizes in appropriate seasons. I outfitted our daughter for the first two years of life by doing this for a total savings of $700! Plus, she looked like a doll during those years!

#239

TIP OF THE DAY:

DELAYED GRATIFICATION: When your child wants the latest toy advertised in a commercial, you don't have to run out and buy it. If the neighbors buy their child a new bike, you don't have to buy one for junior. When you're in the store and your little precious sees some cool candy, you don't have to instantly fulfill his every whim! Delayed gratification saves money and teaches our children to develop internal controls, a characteristic that will help them as adults. Give yourself permission to just say, "no!"

TIP OF THE DAY:

STICK TO YOUR GUNS: From the time your kids are toddlers, they will try to overspend you into oblivion. But while they are little (and even when they are teens), it's

☺

important to draw your boundaries before you go into a store as to what they can have or not have, where you will go in the store, and who is in charge. We've had a few times when we left Wal-Mart without buying a thing because the kids violated the boundary. It was so traumatic for them to leave with no one buying anything (not even milk, Mom?) that the temper tantrums soon stopped and there was once again sanity restored while in the store.

TIP OF THE DAY:

GOALS: Larry Burkett said in *Financial Parenting,* "When we teach our children to save to buy something instead of getting it on credit, we teach them two basic financial principles: responsibility and wisdom in stewardship." Some kids will save money to buy a new bike or doll, while others will just save it for the saving's sake. Either way, we need to teach the benefit of balance when it comes to saving. If your child spends his allowance before it can see the inside of a wallet, then he needs to learn the balance in their spending habits and the value of saving money.

While savings goals are important, it's also important to keep some money in savings that will not be spent but will be a long-term investment. This teaches the true value of compounded interest and saving for the long run.

☺

TIP OF THE DAY:

GET SOME MONEY FROM THAT WALL: A few years ago, when we were driving by my husband's favorite ATM haunt, our youngest, who was only four years old, started yelling, "Get some money, Mama!" and pointed. Sometimes kids know that money doesn't grow on trees, but they think it comes out of a wall. Teaching them the concept of the safe and wise use of an ATM is as simple as explaining where the money comes from, who pays it, and why you should never get in the habit of getting money out without marking it toward your monthly budgeted expenses.

TIP OF THE DAY:

ONLINE SAVINGS RESOURCES AND TEACHING TOOLS: There are some great resources online to reinforce the value of saving. At www.JumpStartCoalition.org, there are resources and activities that seek to ensure personal financial literacy in young people from grades K–12. This site lists resources that represent a wide range of formats, including the four main areas of income, money management, saving and investing, and spending. This site will show them how to set up a budget, how the stock market works, the role of insurance, and responsible credit card use. Some other similar sites are www.kidsbank.com and www.younginvestor.com.

TIP OF THE DAY:

THE VALUE OF A DOLLAR: It's important to teach kids to save money on the items they purchase. When you consider what our family saved by using coupons, shopping sales, and buying wisely last year at the grocery store, you can

☺

see where this concept of saving truly adds up. In our first years of couponing, we saved over $8,000, which is the same as $13,500 on the economy by the time you pay state and federal taxes and social security. Show them the value of sales every time they get an item on clearance or with a coupon—it's a dramatic reminder of how fun savings can be. Give them coupons and let them do the buying and paying to teach valuable lessons.

TIP OF THE DAY:

TEACH THEM TO CONQUER A STORE: When you go into a department store, hold your child up and help her try and find the sales signs. Then find the rock-bottom clearance rack and look through it. If there's nothing your family can use, then say, "See, we won't buy anything, because there's nothing here we need. Sometimes saving money means you won't buy it—even if it's on sale—if it won't meet our family's needs. If I bought this shirt" (Pause and pick an awful looking shirt) "just because it's on sale, then it would be a waste of money because I would never wear it." (Then be prepared for your spouse to buy that same shirt for your birthday and be prepared to wear it.)

TIP OF THE DAY:

TEACH THEM TO CONQUER A REAL SALE: Okay, now go back to the previous tip and let's pretend that favor was bestowed on you at the clearance racks that day. You got there just as they brought out a whole slew of gorgeous clothes, all marked 75 percent off, and you had first pick! (Hey! Try praying for this kind of thing—it happens to me all the time!) Then teach

☺

your little girl the JOYS of finding clothes you need, in the right season and style for a bargain that will leave you with enough extra money to go to McDonald's. With each price tag you can say, "Look sweetie, the original price on this leopard skin sweater was $35 and it's 75 percent off and these gray slacks are only $9! I just saved $46.25!"

TIP OF THE DAY:

EQUATE SAVINGS WITH ENTERTAINMENT VALUES:
Sometimes our kids (even teens) understand savings values when associated with the entertainment value of the savings. "Hey, little, precious, sweetie wonderful, 6′5″ son of mine . . . this $30 that you just saved on those jeans is equal to two major league baseball general admission tickets! Now, come over here and let your mama tweak your cheek!"

TIP OF THE DAY:

EQUATE SAVINGS WITH THE LANGUAGE YOUR CHILD UNDERSTANDS: Part of being an effective parent means we become students of our children. It means we learn what makes them tick. In Gary Chapman's best-selling book *The Five Love Languages* (Moody), we learn how to communicate with those we love in a language they will understand. The primary love languages are words of affirmation, gift giving, acts of service, meaningful touch, and quality time. To make your point with a child whose love language is words of affirmation, you'd say, "You know, when you buy wisely and save over

☺

$30 on a single purchase, you are truly on your way to becoming a financial expert! I'm proud of this decision you made!" Continue this technique with each of the different love languages.

TIP OF THE DAY:

THEY VALUE WHAT THEY EARN: Three of my children saved money for new bikes one spring. After they got them, they did not leave these valued bikes out in the rain when they earned a portion of their purchase. When they were saving for their bikes, one of them was helping me cut coupons and found a coupon for bikes ordered through Huffy. They paid a third less than a discount store and the purchase price included delivery. **(ADVANCED)**

TIP OF THE DAY:

THEY PAY FOR UPGRADES: Brand names and kids go together like carrots and peas. We tell our kids we'll pay for the item, and THEY pay for the brand name. I recently told our thirteen-year-old son, Jonathan, I'd pay $25 for his new tennis shoes and if he wanted the $65 Vans brand, he could pay the additional $40. He decided to compromise and found a pair on sale for $40 and paid the additional $15 for the brand he wanted. By the way, he's taken excellent care of those shoes since his recent "investment" and has never forgotten them anywhere! **(ADVANCED)**

☺

TIP OF THE DAY:

ENTERTAINMENT ALTERNATIVES:

The local library offers a lot of inexpensive fun for children. They can borrow DVDs, books on tape, CDs, research material, and books. Many libraries have story time and special summer reading programs for kids.

TIP OF THE DAY:

WORK ETHIC TIPS FOR TODDLERS AGES TWO TO FOUR:

One of the single most important factors in raising kids and saving money in the long run is to teach them certain financially related values from a young age. Here's a guideline as to what they should be doing and when.

* Picks up toys cheerfully

* Obeys parents most of the time

* Is on a schedule

TIP OF THE DAY:

WORK ETHIC TIPS FOR TOTS AGES FOUR TO SIX:

* Makes bed in a basic way (not necessarily neat)

* Picks up room regularly

* Brings clothes to hamper

☺

- Knows how to set and clear the table
- Hangs up clothes and puts them in drawers
- Knows how to take out the trash
- Gives away clothing or toys or money to those in need
- Does work without grumbling
- Does not throw "Wallyworld" tantrums

TIP OF THE DAY:
WORK ETHIC TIPS FOR AGES SEVEN TO TEN:

- Is a master bed maker
- Knows how to sort laundry into colored, whites, and light coloreds
- Can fold laundry and put it in everyone's room
- Is given an allowance
- Has a savings account at home and at a bank
- Regularly tithes from their earnings
- Can load and clear the dishwasher
- Knows how to vacuum and dust
- Manages a fun kid budget (restaurant, zoo, amusement park, etc.)

☺

#255

TIP OF THE DAY:
WORK ETHIC TIPS FOR PRETEENS AGES ELEVEN TO TWELVE:

- Has advanced to "potty training" (they know how to clean a bathroom)

- Begins to do additional jobs for hire within the home and occasionally for friends or family

- Has a savings account with at least $200 to $250 in it

- Manages more advanced budgets such as a semester-long school supply budget

- Is learning the meaning of delayed gratification

- Can save up for half of a larger ticket item they want (bike, skates, video game, etc.)

- Can tell you how many hours it takes to work or save for goods and services

- Knows how to read a savings account statement

- Is regularly contributing to a community organization either through volunteer hours or donating goods (clothing, toys, money)

☺

WORK ETHIC TIPS FOR TEENS AGES THIRTEEN TO FIFTEEN:

- Is regularly sponsoring a third world child or mission

- Can manage and balance their own checkbook with supervision

- Has enough in savings to take out $200 to $300 to start a mutual fund

- Is able to do outside jobs for hire among approved employers in the neighborhood and regular summer jobs (appropriate to age and ability)

- Realizes they will continue to do twice the work if they do not work with a good attitude

- Regularly pays for half of larger ticket items

- Regularly pays for nonfamily outings (movies, theme parks, virtual game centers, restaurants, etc.)

- Is saving for a vehicle

- Is aware of the fact that their grades in high school will impact their ability to get into college and earn scholarships for college

- Understand their primary job in school is to work hard and get the best grades they are capable of making

☺

WORK ETHIC TIPS FOR TEENS AGES SIXTEEN TO EIGHTEEN:

- Has opened a mutual fund and is contributing monthly to the fund

- Can tell you how much money they will earn in their mutual fund if they continue to contribute the minimal amount by the time they are forty-five, fifty-five, and sixty-five.

- Can balance a checkbook without supervision

- Has a debit card and can use it responsibly (follow-up supervision required)

- Have a prepaid credit card as the training for the temptation of plastic in their pocket (close supervision required and minimal prepaid limits on the card come from the child's savings account or earnings—parents do not prepay the card)

- Can manage and balance a clothing budget and personal financial budget

- Regularly goes over their personal financial budget with parents

- Regularly works inside and outside of the home during breaks from school

- Keeps a neat room and car

☺

- Has paid for one-third to one-half of the cost of their car

- Pays insurance if they have a ticket or accident (parents can pay if they keep their driving record spotless)

- Maintains a good GPA (or what they are capable of)

- Has a regular volunteer position (hospital, coaching, church involvement, etc.)

- Has a grip on delayed gratification

TIP OF THE DAY:

TEACHING KIDS TO GIVE—DO THEY GOTTA WANNA?:

It's important to teach our kids to give a portion of their money toward a tithe, meaning they give 10 percent to a nonprofit organization such as their church. Or, they may support a third world child through a nonprofit organization such as Compassion International, Mission of Joy, or World Vision (see section twelve).

Now we get to the question of, do you *force* your little precious ones to tithe, hope they will do it willingly without force, or go into denial and ignore the tithe altogether? We want our kids to give willingly, so we teach them what the tithe is and we tell them they will tithe, but we leave the amount up to the child. So they get into the habit of giving, but they learn to give willingly too.

☺

TIP OF THE DAY:

WILL WORK FOR FOOD: OK, so we're trying to train our children to be generous and giving, but what do we do when we drive by a homeless person on the street corner? Just ignore them and drive on by? Give them a $5 bill? Take another route? Some of the best advice we got on this topic came from a homeless shelter pastor named Rev. Kris King, who ministers to homeless people in a small town in New Mexico. Kris said, "You should never give them money because most of them will spend it on alcohol. Instead, give them canned food or go to your local homeless shelter and ask them for cards from the shelter that you can give to the individuals." These cards are business sized, printed by the shelter, and give the address and phone number of where homeless people can find help (see section twelve).

We carried canned chili and pasta meals in our car as well as the cards from the homeless shelter. If time and safety issues allowed, we had something to offer these people that is better for them than money. We offered the information about a ministry that has helped other homeless people get off the streets, get jobs, and make a significant life change. It's something our kids learned about each week. **(ADVANCED)**

TIP OF THE DAY:

GIVING TOGETHER: If you want to read something amazing in regards to giving, then go to the review page of my book *Half-Price Living*. Even I'm amazed at how many people were able to cut food and other expenses

☺

so dramatically and get free food in the process. Many readers recounted that they were able to donate to homeless shelters, food pantries, crisis pregnancy centers—even the family up the street who just got laid off from work!

Ever since our children were little, we've enlisted their help in gathering toiletries, cleansers, food, and clothing and taking them to all the places listed above. They get to share in the joy of giving. It's important to create a family ministry that your child can participate in. You may give of your time, food, labor, or other resources, but your child needs to learn to be generous and give back to his world through your example. **(ADVANCED)**

TIP OF THE DAY:
DOESN'T EVERY FAMILY GIVE AWAY FOOD, MAMA?:
It's important to create a new kind of normal for your child that includes giving from everything that is yours.

When Daniel was seven, I overheard a conversation he had with our next-door neighbor in Mississippi.

"Hi, can I help you with those groceries?" our thoughtful oldest son asked.

Our neighbor Ralph was surprised. "Well, actually, that was the last bag—we're just about ready to go!" Their family had been planning a fishing trip for some time and were loading up their van before hooking up the boat.

"Who are you giving those to?" Daniel asked out of curiosity.

I peered through the window to catch Ralph's reaction. "Give them to? Well, they're for our fishing trip."

☺

"Oh," Daniel said. "I guess you're going to give away this month's groceries when you get back from your trip, huh?"

"Um . . . yeah, I guess so . . ." He patted Daniel on the head and went back inside to gather the rest of their supplies. Daniel was so used to helping us give away our coupon freebies, that he thought it was a normal part of everyone's life.

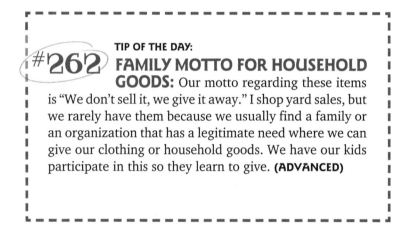

#262

TIP OF THE DAY:
FAMILY MOTTO FOR HOUSEHOLD GOODS: Our motto regarding these items is "We don't sell it, we give it away." I shop yard sales, but we rarely have them because we usually find a family or an organization that has a legitimate need where we can give our clothing or household goods. We have our kids participate in this so they learn to give. **(ADVANCED)**

SECTION EIGHT

Home, Sweet Budget Buster

*Tips to Save at Home
(Utilities, Household Goods, and Gifts)*

I was a fresh-faced, starry-eyed, raven-haired, alabaster-browed new bride, and my dreams of establishing my own home were full of romantic notions. I set up our modest little home with special touches. I had put up curtains and decorated with country cows and I was so proud of how smart and fresh it looked. One day in those early years, I wanted to impress my hubby and make his grandmother's chicken and egg salad sandwiches. My cookbooks were not yet unpacked and were somewhere in boxes in the back of the garage.

I didn't want to call my grandmother-in-law and let her see what a ninny her son had married because I didn't even know how to boil an egg—so I did the next best thing. I called my college girlfriend and asked her. I should have realized that she never cooked in college; we always ate pizza or KFC or Chinese or popcorn and Diet Coke. Why would she know? But when stars are in your eyes, common sense is usually nowhere to be found. So I called Donna.

"Hi Donna! I'm so glad you're home!" I was relieved to get her on the phone.

"How's *married* life, Ellie?" she asked, emphasizing my married status since I was the first member of our gang to take the plunge.

"It's really sweet, Donna, my house is so cute!" I was still feeling that warm, soft rosy hue that came every time I remembered that I was now a married woman. But I also needed to get on to the practical side of life and get my husband's favorite food cooked.

But before I could ask Donna my question, she got on a roll. "I can't believe you're *married*; it just seems like yesterday we were there and you were getting *married*. I mean, it seems like I was just wearing my bridesmaid gown and you were in your lovely dress and you were getting *married*." Donna stopped for a breath.

"Uh, Donna?" I quickly interjected. "It seems like it was yesterday because it was just *last week*. But hey, I've got a question for you: how do you boil an egg?"

"How do you boil an egg?" Donna exclaimed with her typical lilting laugh. "You don't know how to boil an egg?"

I began to feel a little defensive. "Hey! I don't remember you ever boiling an egg in college, so don't think you're the Galloping

Gourmet or something!" I sighed. "So are you going to tell me how to boil an egg or are you just going to laugh at me?"

Donna's answer was simple. "Anyone knows that you just boil it until it floats!" I heard her doorbell ring in the background and she suddenly bubbled, "Hey, that's Rob, I've gotta run now!" She was gone before I could say, "Are you sure?"

So I got out a dozen eggs, put them in a large pot of water, and started boiling them.

And they boiled.

And they boiled.

And they boiled.

And all the water boiled away.

But they never floated.

Do you know what happens to eggs when they boil for seventy minutes and all the water boils out of the pot?

They explode.

– – – – – – – – – – – – – – –

That little incident happened twenty years ago and I'm happy to report that I now know how to boil an egg. I've learned a lot in the last two decades, and with the sixteen moves we've had, I learned how to set up a home in three days as well. There is a lot involved in setting up a home and maintaining it, and all of those little expenses can add up to break your budget if you are not careful. Whether you are setting up your very first home or whether you're a not-so-newlywed, here are some ideas to save on everything related to the home.

TIP OF THE DAY:

CAN THIS MARRIAGE BE SAVED?—
GARAGE SALE: People get rid of new things at

garage sales for all kinds of reasons. I love the newlywed sales. They have wedding gifts (they didn't like or cannot yet appreciate) still in boxes. Or they have duplicate toasters, microwaves, and coffeemakers. These are a great way to decorate your home and save money.

Regularly, we pick up brand-new silver, crystal, and china at newlywed sales and keep them on hand for hospitality gifts, wedding gifts, or even a birthday gift here and there. There's virtually no difference between paying $45 for a coffemaker at Target and paying $8 for the same piece, still in the box, at a yard sale, except $37.

There are also "combining households" garage sales in which two adults are getting married and they no longer need two of everything. These tend to be a good place to find appliances and electronics as well.

If you live near a university that has family housing, you can find some great deals at yard sales. At the end of each semester, especially in the month of May, student families sell off household goods they can't take with them. It's worth a peek!

ESTATE SALES: Estate sales have many of the same bargains as a garage sale, especially on antiques. Check the appliances carefully at these sales, though; they tend to be well-worn, older units. But if you know what you're looking for, you can find a diamond among the coal.

TIPS ON SAVING ON ELECTRICITY AND ENERGY COSTS:

- Check your windows and doors for air leaks. Use sealer tape to seal leaks.

- Clean system filters regularly and maintain heating and air-conditioning units.

- Attic insulation should be at least six inches deep; it will save 10 percent.

- Keep thermostats set at moderate comfort—68° to 70° in winter and 74° to 78° in summer. This can save as much as 40 to 50 percent in hot climates and 12 percent in cooler climates.

- Lower the heating and cooling systems when your home is vacant for more than eight hours.

- Use a clock-operated thermostat.

- Have your local power company perform a free energy survey. Ask them about low-cost community programs to insulate your home.

- Stop the dishwasher after the wash cycle, or use the economy cycle. The warmth from the wash cycle will dry the dishes.

- Change the vacuum cleaner bag to improve efficiency. It saves electric energy—and human energy too.

- Use your main oven for large food items. Bake as many dishes at once as possible.

- Use Crock-Pots and pressure cookers instead of the oven.

- Clean dust from refrigerator and freezer coils.

- Consider the energy guide labels on a new appliance before you purchase it.

- Consider installing storm windows and doors.

- Use blankets for warmth at night. Snuggle your beloved.

- Turn off the TV. Play games with your babies.

- Close the damper on the fireplace when not in use.

- Wear a sweater in winter and wear 100 percent cotton (or high-cotton content) fabrics in the hot months.

- Keep the lint filter clean in your dryer. Use the "manual-operated dryer" outside. Buy extra clothespins.

TIPS TO SAVE ON WATER:

- Set hot water to a moderate setting of around 120 degrees. This keeps the water hot enough to wash clothes but cool enough to keep from badly scalding little hands.

- Wrap the water heater with an insulation kit.

- Buy a water-restricted showerhead to give plenty of water and little waste.

- Periodically drain the water heater from the bottom to remove sediments and allow for more efficient operation.

- Use your dishwasher, clothes washer, and dryer FULL to save water and electricity.

- Use cold water in your laundry. Current soaps on the market will clean your lightly soiled clothing easily without hot water.

- Try using less laundry detergent. Depending upon the water hardness in your area, you could use half the amount you're currently using. The same applies to your dishwasher.

- Use the partial-load water level adjustment on your clothes washer to customize the water to your current need.

- Fix leaky toilets and faucets—especially the hot water faucets. One leaky faucet wastes over 1,300 gallons a year!

- Take a shower instead of a bath. This can save as much as 50 percent of the total hot water in your home. Unless, of course, you tend to take a loooooong shower!

- If you're going to be away from your home for more than three days, turn off the hot water heater.

- Coordinate baths to conserve hot water. It takes 10 percent of the hot water in the tank to heat the lines to the bathroom. If you run the herd in and out of the shower and bath in the same hour, you'll save money.

- Read your utility bills each month and check the meters for accuracy. Water your lawn in the early morning hours and only once a week (if possible).

- Fill a quart-size plastic milk or juice bottle with water. Put it in your toilet tank. This fills up space—you use less water to flush.

TIP OF THE DAY:

NEWER ISN'T NECESSARILY BETTER: Growing up in the United States, we considered an old home anything over fifty years old—then we went to Europe. Fifty years old is new to cultures with thousands of years of history. An old home in that part of the world is three hundred years old!

When it comes to housing, consider the purchase of an older home that you can improve. If you put in your own labor and ask your neighborhood handyman for help, you can increase the value of your home. Older homes oftentimes have better construction, may come with more land, and give you more house than you'd be able to afford otherwise. **(ADVANCED)**

TIP OF THE DAY:

SLAPPING ON PAINT: There are a number of things you can do to improve the value of your home with minimum cost and effort. This is the number one home improvement project that homeowners will try themselves. There are two keys to a good paint job: choosing the paint and prepping the surface. Splurge on a quality paint as well as brushes and rollers. If you're not sure of the color you want, then rent a sample (yes, most full-service hardware stores will let you do this). Prep the surface by cleaning walls, sanding them, and patching holes. This accounts for the majority of the work. This will make your house show better and thereby improve its value.

TIP OF THE DAY:

FINISH THE BASEMENT: A family can add as much as one-third more space to a two-story house for a moderate cost (only a fraction of what it would cost to build one-third on to a home) and recoup as much as 80 percent of the investment upon selling. The first step to success is to determine the basement's condition—primarily waterproofing. If a sheet of plastic wrap is taped to the concrete floor overnight and there are any moisture beads on it the next morning, then a waterproofing company might need to be employed.

It's critical that the basement has a sump pump that is in good working order as well as a backup. It's also important to check with the homeowner insurance provider to see if they fully cover the contents and materials in a flooded basement. Be sure to get an estimate before going forward with the project.

TIP OF THE DAY:

#270 LOSE THE KITCHEN WALL:

Many older homes have a wall that separates the dining room and kitchen. By knocking down the wall, the space is suddenly opened and voila—a new look that can allow you to recover 70 percent to 80 percent of the cost of renovation. The rest of the kitchen will need to be updated as well with wood cabinets, nonlaminate countertops (such as Corian or Wilsonart), and nonvinyl flooring. Additional extras that are popular with homebuyers would be island seating, industrial-look appliances, and heavy-duty drawer hardware. Mitchel Gold, a designer whose work is featured in Pottery Barn and Crate and Barrel stores, said he once bought two stainless steel Fridgedaire stoves for half of what it cost to buy a huge Viking oven and range. The result was that he had two ovens, eight burners, and half the bill.

TIP OF THE DAY:

TRY A LITTLE BATHROOM REMOD: Keep up with today's amenities by updating your bathroom with double sinks, brushed nickel fixtures, powerful, multihead showers, and toilets in their own alcoves. Rather than spending $30,000 on a complete overhaul, you could purchase a new toilet, sink, and fixtures for around $6,000 to $7,000. Consider getting an acrylic mold shaped to the exact curve of your existing tub and slipped over the top. A new drain is then installed and everything is fitted together and given a professional-looking finish. But be sure there is no water damage behind the existing walls before you go with this idea. It can save you several thousand dollars over the price of a new tub unit and space renovation to accommodate the tub. One family from Arizona that I talked to had their porcelain tub refinished nearly eighteen years ago by a professional and it hasn't stained once since then.

TIP OF THE DAY:

WINDOW TREATMENTS: When we purchased our current home, one of the main features that the real estate broker, the seller, and the neighbors kept talking about was the windows. They were double-paned Pellas, which was about as nice an accessory to a home as a Prada handbag would be to a fashion maven. Apparently, name-brand windows can be a huge selling point to potential home buyers. If you don't believe us, just flip though your newspaper's Sunday real estate section. I bet you'll find window brand-names like Andersen, Pella, and Marvin listed by the real estate agents, along with the house's other salient features (pool, hardwood floors, subzero fridge). This investment will pay you back in spades. *Remodeling* magazine predicts a 75 percent recoup upon selling.

TIP OF THE DAY:

HIRING A CONTRACTOR: If you are going to hire a contractor, then contact the National Association of Home Builders and Remodelors™ Council at www.nahb.com.

You can also order a free copy of "How to Find a Professional Remodelor" by sending a self-addressed stamped envelope to:

NAHB Remodelors Council
Dept FT • 1201 15th St, NW
Washington, DC 20005

TIP OF THE DAY:

WHEN YOU BUY A HOME:

* **Don't Pay for Inflated Credit Report and Courier Fees:** Some lenders are charging up to $65 for pulling your credit report. That is unusually high, considering the fact that credit reporting bureaus only charge $6 to $18 per report. Using the same tactics, some lenders charge courier fees for shipping your closing documents for as much as $100, while the majority of overnight express services only charge $22. Tell your lender, up front, that you refuse to pay any more than the going rate for these services. **(ADVANCED)**

- **Don't Pay for Document Prep and Administration Fees:** The origination fee should include these services, so don't pay them! Ask your lender to waive these fees. **(ADVANCED)**

- **Don't Pay for Yield Spread Premiums:** Lenders increase your interest rate slightly to include origination and other fees so you don't have to pay them out-of-pocket at closing, but some lenders and mortgage brokers are double-dipping —by charging both the fees and the higher interest rate. Ask your broker directly if a firm charges you a yield spread premium. If so, you shouldn't pay any additional fees. **(ADVANCED)**

- **Don't Pay for Padded Title Insurance Fees:** When you are shopping for lenders, look for all the above, plus look out for those who don't tack on a lot of extra charges for services such as title search and document preparation. Theses can add hundreds of dollars to your closing costs and they really should be included in the price of title insurance, which depending on where you live, can be as high as $6,000. **(ADVANCED)**

TIP OF THE DAY:

VALUE OF YOUR HOME: If you are looking to see an approximate value of your home, based on the comparison of homes that have sold in your area, go to www.zillow.com and enter your address to get an estimate.

Conquering Saks Fifth Avenue
Tips to Save on Clothing

When our daughter Bethany was two years old, she was the delight of almost everyone she met. Her blonde hair and bonny blue eyes were an irresistible combination, but it was her contagious smile that made for many new friends. Our little "bunny" found that each face was just a territory to be conquered as she smiled, blew kisses, and performed upon command.

There was one thing that Bethany would *not* do, however, and that was to be left behind by her big brothers, Daniel and Philip. If they got some cars, she had to have cars. If they went to Sunday school, she had to leave the nursery and find a Sunday school class to attend. If they got bikes, she had to have a bike. Actually, she didn't get a bike. She got a shoe.

Bethany's riding toy in the shape of a big pink tennis shoe got many miles on it. The shoe fit and she rode it! She loved to ride it round and round the circle in our housing area's driveway. The housing area consisted of a series of circular areas all connected in a horseshoe-shaped main street. We let her ride the circle with supervision, but the main street was off-limits for all the children.

One day I was unloading groceries from our van and ran inside to catch the phone. I must have been inside for about five minutes when I went back out to check on the bunny. She wasn't in the van, she wasn't in the yard, she wasn't riding the circle with the boys, she wasn't *anywhere*!

We were also missing one large, pink shoe.

As I was running from house to house in our cluster of homes, asking if they'd seen a little bunny, a neighbor drove into the circle with a smiling blonde girl and a bright pink shoe in the front seat.

Apparently, as soon as I went in the house to answer the phone, she talked the boys into letting her out of her car seat, then she hopped on her shoe and made tracks. When the neighbor saw her, she was careening down the sidewalk, feet up in the air, blonde curls trailing in the wind and having a joyride to newfound freedom.

Our neighbor recognized Bethany and brought her home to her panic-stricken mother. I thanked God for guardian angels and kind neighbors.

I guess that's just shoe business.

I think we're all a little bit like Bethany at times—we enjoy our freedom. There are many kinds of freedom besides the ability to ride a shoe down the street unencumbered. Financial freedom is something that this book is designed to help you achieve. Part of financial freedom is the ability to recognize a genuine "freebie" and a pseudo-freebie. Clothing is an area where you can get some things free and many items for pennies on the dollar. If you know how to shop, you, too, can enter shoe business.

TIP OF THE DAY:

NEW VERSUS USED CLOTHING: The most obvious way to save money on clothing is to buy it used. Some people get squeamish about germs or think used clothing is dirty. Well, wash it in 120° water, and you'll get rid of any germs and dirt. Do you take your own sheets to hotels? Do you ever try on clothing at a department store? If you don't worry about dirt and germs in those situations, there's no reason to pass up deals on used clothing.

TIP OF THE DAY:

GET BEYOND THE FEEL OF NEW: Some people like the feel of new. Well, if I walked to my closet now, I couldn't tell you which clothes I had purchased new and which were acquired used. They look the same. Who hasn't bought a brand-new article of clothing that puckered or ran after the first couple of washes? Buying clothing new does not guarantee it will wear well.

TIP OF THE DAY:

#278 START BY GIVING IT AWAY: This
may come as a surprise to you—but I don't
conduct a lot of garage sales. As a matter of fact, I've
only had two in the last ten years. "Why?" you ask. I'm
glad you asked that question. It's because our family
prefers to give stuff away. From some of these donation
centers, like the Salvation Army, we get a tax deductible
receipt. From others, we have the satisfaction of giving
our unneeded clothing a good home. It doesn't end
there, either. **(ADVANCED)**

TIP OF THE DAY:

SOWING AND REAPING CLOTHES: For some reason, people
will find that they receive more than they give. I used to wonder
why that was the case. Then I realized a vital truth—the reason
we receive more than we give has to do with the law of sowing
and reaping.

If you sow a turnip seed, you'll harvest a turnip. If you sow a
grain of wheat, you'll grow wheat. If you sow generosity and give
stuff away, you'll reap the generosity of others. The Kay family is
living proof. Here's a peek at the last six months.

We gave away a big garbage bag full of clothes to the
squadron fund-raiser and to the Salvation Army. About a month
later, we got a garbage bag full of clothes for Jonathan and Joshua

—thanks to my friend Edna. Inside were Ralph Lauren and American Eagle brand names—all quality clothing. I also received, thanks to my friend Kelli, a big garbage bag and a half of clothes for little old me! There were a couple of suits, tons of pants, dresses, blouses, a warm-up suit, and lots more. The brand names included LizSport, Calvin Klein, and other quality clothing.

TIP OF THE DAY:

THRIFT SHOPS VERSUS GARAGE SALES: Buying clothes at garage sales is usually the cheapest place you can buy clothing. They are usually half the price of thrift shops.

Although thrift shops may have higher prices than garage sales, they also have a greater selection. Also, most thrift shops have a place to try on clothing, so you can better determine fit and style. Some thrift shops have specials—half-price days or buy-one/get-one free days, among others. Call ahead of time to find out their specials.

TIP OF THE DAY:

VOLUNTEER AT A THRIFT SHOP: Very often, thrift shops are a fund-raising arm for nonprofit organizations, and volunteers at these shops receive (or enjoy) special benefits. I volunteered at the Fort Drum thrift shop, where the proceeds go to pay for college scholarships. (I liked to take Bethany with me so we could do the mother/daughter bonding thing.) One of the benefits for volunteers is a first look at the clothing that comes in. Also, the work we did to maintain the thrift shop required that we go through the clothes on a regular basis. You wouldn't believe the nice things stuck deep inside those racks. Volunteering forced me to find these things and gave me the time to be thorough.

You might even have your teen volunteer for community service hours at a thrift shop. There are scholarships that are based on these hours, so not only is she finding clothes she might like, but she's working toward paying for her college expenses as well. **(ADVANCED)**

TIP OF THE DAY:

CONSIGNMENT SHOPS: These shops have the greatest selection, but the most expensive prices for used clothing. They are often twice as high as a thrift shop (making them four times as high as a garage sale). Some of their prices on children's clothing are as expensive as new clothing purchased on sale at a retail store. However, their prices on designer clothing, coats, formal attire, and business clothing are hard to beat. If you develop a friendship with the store owner, he or she can help you find the kind of clothing you need most.

TIP OF THE DAY:

CONSIGNMENT CREDIT: You cannot only *shop* at consignment stores, but you can get credit there as well! For an easy credit at your local, quality consignment store, gather all your children's outgrown clothing and take it in. Be sure it is clean, buttons are sewn on tightly (and all there), and that it is pressed if necessary—this extra care and effort will garner you a better credit. Then use that credit to purchase your clothing for the current season.

TIP OF THE DAY:

BEFORE YOU SHOP FOR NEW CLOTHES: Look through all your family's closets and take inventory of the present wardrobe. Some of the clothes that haven't been worn may simply need to be altered, repaired, or dry-cleaned—thereby saving a lot of money over buying something new. When taking an inventory of wardrobes, make note of the items that are needed most and their sizes and put them in a small notebook that you carry with you.

TIP OF THE DAY:

TAKE CARE!: Take care of the clothes you have, paying special attention to the care instructions on the label. Teach children to care for and maintain their clothing. Before storing clothes for the season, make sure they are clean. This prevents permanent stains and ensures their usefulness for the next season. Use Woolite for sweaters and lay them out to dry.

TIP OF THE DAY:

SAVE ON DRY CLEANING: Use a coin-operated dry-cleaning machine instead of commercial cleaners to save 75 percent on dry cleaning. Or see if your community has a "$1 Dry Cleaners." There are also home dry-cleaning products on the store shelves; if you buy these on sale and with a coupon, they can be valuable. See if the www.entertainment. com booklet has dry-cleaning coupons for your zip code and be sure to check the local paper for dry-cleaning coupons. Try to use a dry cleaners that offers deals such as "clean four dress shirts, get the fifth free" or percentage off for regulars.

TIP OF THE DAY:

CHANGE!: Change out of church clothes or business clothes before lounging around the house to save wear and tear on your most expensive clothes. If your kids wear a uniform or have nicer clothes for school than for play, have them change when they get home as well.

TIP OF THE DAY:

CLASSIC: Consider buying classic, long-lasting clothes such as the basic black dress, a navy jacket, khaki pants, classic suits, and traditional blue jeans, rather than fads. Also look for classic styles in jewelry and accessories as well.

TIP OF THE DAY:

CREDIT CLOTHES: Perhaps the most important decision you can make when it comes to buying new clothes is to never buy on credit. You only dig a deeper hole and create more financial stress.

TIP OF THE DAY:

INTERNET DEALS: Go to sites such as
www.overstock.com to rack up some real deals, and whenever you buy online, try to find the codes that will give you free shipping, gifts, or percentages off. For these, go to www.dealhunting.com. Look for "lot buy" buys on eBay. Our teenage son helped us find an eBay lot featuring all size twelve boys clothing (both our youngest are in size twelves) and we got ten pairs of jeans (they looked new), five pairs of pants, and fifteen shirts for $80!!

TIP OF THE DAY:

ONLINE COMPARISON SHOPPING: Comparing values online aren't just for electronics and furniture, you can compare the price on brand-name clothing as well by using a shopping robot such as www.mysimon.com or www.nextag.com.

TIP OF THE DAY:

GET IT FREE: Go to www.freecycle.org to find clothing you could get for free! This is a nonprofit website moderated by a volunteer in your community. It's a way to give and get all kinds of free household goods in your area. You just sign up and there's no catch other than if you try to advertise your own business or any .com company, you will automatically be banned from the club.

TIP OF THE DAY:

IN SEASON/OUT OF SEASON: If you buy clothing before the season begins or in season, you'll probably pay top dollar. If you buy your family's clothes at the end-of-the season clearance sales, you'll save top dollar. Buy children's clothing with plenty of growing room for next season. Try to buy quality clothing; check the seams, zippers, buttons, and fabric weight before you buy. Always try to buy machine-washable fabrics for savings on dry cleaning and ironing.

TIP OF THE DAY:

MEN'S SUITS/GARMENT DISTRICT: When purchasing men's suits, stick with conservative styles and dark colors. Select wool or wool blends to extend the life of the suit and increase the wearing opportunity. Always hang up suits after wear, and air them out before putting them in the closet—it helps to minimize dry-cleaning costs.

If you are in business (or on vacation) and travel to a large city, then look up the city's garment district, Chinatown, or Korean section. Oftentimes, there are tailors in these areas who specialize in custom-made suits that look fabulous and only cost $100 or less. When my oldest stepdaughter got married, all the groomsmen ordered suits from a person in the Los Angeles garment district and they only cost $85 each. **(ADVANCED)**

TIP OF THE DAY:

SEWING: My mother was a wonderful seamstress, but one thing she couldn't do was teach me to sew. She even sent me to the professionals to see what they could do with me. There was a sewing class offered at my high school for four months. They couldn't do much with me, either. I tackled a pair of saddle-backed jeans and made one leg so wide that two legs could fit into it, while the other leg was so narrow that one skinny leg wouldn't fit into it.

You can save from 50 to 60 percent off retail prices by sewing your own clothing. These handmade items cost more than garage sales and thrift shops—but the clothing is new and custom-fitted. The savings are conditional upon finding a good price on fabric and notions. Carefully consider the cost of supplies and your time investment before you commit to a project. With the proper planning, you could have a custom-tailored outfit and the satisfaction of making your own clothes. Just don't ask me for help.

For values on supplies, be sure to shop the sales at the fabric stores as well as craft stores. Check the paper for coupons and the store's websites for other values. Never be afraid to ask for 50 percent off the fabric at the end of the bolt.

TIP OF THE DAY:

DISCOUNT OUTLETS: There is a discount outlet mall in every large city and throughout Americana suburbia. Watch these outlets carefully. Just because they are billed as bargain outlets does not mean they are bargain stores. Our family went to a Ralph Lauren outlet store in California and the clothes were marked down a significant percentage. But the discounts were narrow, such as $75 instead of $95 for a casual shirt.

At high-end discount centers such as the Saks Outlet, Nordstrom Rack, Neiman Macus Rack, and Macy's Rack, there are loads of good values to be found. By shopping mid-week at many of these stores, you'll get a better selection and better value. Be sure to ask the manager when the next cycle of discounts are scheduled for the items you are purchasing. If it's the next day, they'll often give you the discount early—however, the employees are not authorized to do this and you'll need to go to the top.

TIP OF THE DAY:

GARAGES SALES—THE WAVE OF THE FUTURE, AND THE PAST: People have garage sales for different reasons. Everything on their tables and hanging in their awnings is there for a reason. Sometimes the reason is—it's damaged.

On the other hand, if repairs are easy (and minor), then buy it. Once Bethany got a beautifully smocked Polly Flinder dress for 15¢—it cost $45 new. It had a tear along the seam that took three minutes to stitch. I'll mend a two-inch seam for $44.85— that's worth my time!

When you go to a garage sale, take your notebook with you that has everyone's size written in it as well as a notation of the kind of clothing they will be needing (jackets for your toddler, soccer shoes for your seven-year-old). Be sure to start out early and hit all the garage sales in one area before moving on. I recommend you leave very young children at home and only take the children that can keep up with the pace as they get older!

Don't be shy about asking for less on anything you are buying—just don't be a nuisance about it. Set a budget for your weekly garage sale shopping and stick to it.

TIP OF THE DAY:

IF IT'S STAINED, LEAVE IT: You can afford to be choosy at a garage sale. If it's dirty, you can wash it. If it's stained or you can't tell—then leave it on the table. Last week you were paying full price at a department store! This week you don't have to settle for a pair of jeans with an oil stain on them. There are quality products for sale at garage sales that are in great shape. Look for clothing with the original sales tags still on them and products in their original packaging.

TIP OF THE DAY:

PAY ATTENTION TO DETAILS: Check the zippers, buttons, and snaps on clothing. Pick and probe purses and jackets to make sure they snap well. Count the buttons on a shirt to make sure they are all there. Look shoes over carefully for nicks, cracks, and dings and feel inside to see if there are any nails or bumps that could cause blisters. Check the knees on jeans to determine wear and tear. Look at the style of a pair of pants to be sure you have a match for a jacket at home. It's not a bargain to buy $5 designer pants when you have to pay $25 for a shirt to match them!

TEEN CLOTHING BUDGETS: When a teen goes shopping, it can get expensive in a hurry. Put your teen on a clothing budget and let them manage their own purchasing. If they run out of money before the end of the term, then they will have to do with what they already have. Guide teens into good purchasing habits and help them learn how to "conquer a store" and find the best values. Also give them the freedom to see what life is like when you fail to live within your means. It's far better for them to fail while in your home, than rack up credit card debt on such consumables as clothing when they are on their own in a few short years.

You may even want to start slow by putting them on a budget for each shopping trip and letting them know when they will be allowed to buy clothes again. For example, I told Jonathan that we were going to buy him some tennis shoes and socks and the budget was $40. If he found those two items, then anything else he could find to come in at that price would be acceptable for purchase that day, but we weren't coming back to buy tennis shoes again for four more months (or when he outgrew them). **(ADVANCED)**

INVESTMENT PURCHASES: For parents of more than one child, buying clothing should be a carefully considered investment. For example, cheaper is not necessarily better for three, four, or more children. If you spend $15 on jeans for Brandon (because they are superior quality) rather than $12 for a cheaper brand, they're going to also last for Brandon's younger brother too. In the long run, higher quality clothing can be passed down the line and will save you from having to spend an additional $12 on another pair of cheap jeans for the next sibling. Consider the quality, durability, and wear of the clothing you buy and consider it an investment.

TIP OF THE DAY:

UNISEX CLOTHING: If your children are different sexes, then it's impossible to pass along clothing, right? Wrong. When you buy jeans for older children, try to get ones that are not gender specific. Do the same thing for coats, plain shirts, T-shirts, belts—even tennis shoes. There should be a few girlie clothes for your girls and manly clothes for your guys—but keep an eye out for as many items that can be used by both sexes as possible.

TIP OF THE DAY:

NEW TO YOU WARDROBE: A very creative approach to clothing your child is to trade out all the clothing you cannot pass to your other children with another family. Look for people in your community or church who have quality clothing and a child who is a year or two older than the child you need to outfit. Then, see if they have a different child that you can outfit from your child's outgrown clothing. Swap your quality clothing for theirs and your child will have a new wardrobe. It's still important to get a few brand-new things for each child, so that they will feel special and won't have to wear hand-me-downs all the time. But the swapped clothing can be especially great for two categories of clothing: 1) play clothes, which are going to be soiled and stained frequently and 2) church clothing, which are usually in better shape to begin with because they're not worn as often. **(ADVANCED)**

Modern-Day Servants

Tips to Save on Furniture, Appliances, Electronics, and eBay

ven though I've got a little pioneer blood running through my veins, if I lived during that time, I think I'd miss my dishwasher too much. When you read accounts of nineteenth- and twentieth-century living, you'll notice that even some middle-class families employed a servant or two (think of Hannah in *Little Women*). These domestic employees often boarded in the home and cooked, cleaned dishes and clothes, purchased food daily, and served the family in their daily life.

Today, we have servants too. They are called "appliances and electronics." They cook our food (oven, stove, microwave, Crock-Pot, toaster oven), preserve our food (refrigerator and freezer), prepare our food (mixer, blender, toaster, juicer), and dispose of our food (garbage disposal, trash compactor). They entertain us (HDTV, stereo, DVD player, video games) and help us do our work (computers, faxes, printers, telephones). These servants clean our dishes (dishwasher, kids in the home), clean and dry our clothes (washer and dryer), and clean our carpets (vacuum cleaner). They take care of our hair (blow-dryers, curlers, and curling irons), pretty up our faces (shavers, makeup mirrors, and electric tweezers), and pamper our bodies (foot massagers—yea!). I'm sure you could add to this list, and I believe you get the point. Appliances are modern-day servants.

These servants make our lives easier on one condition—that we take care of them. For example, if a certain distracted female puts a Tupperware dish in the oven instead of the cupboard, then preheats the oven (some time later) to 375°, said oven will emit an unpleasant odor. It will make the entire house smell like a plastic factory (if you've never smelled a plastic factory, trust me—you don't want to). A clothes dryer works much more efficiently when the absent-minded mama doesn't throw a bag of coffee grounds into it (destined for the garden, but I'm carrying the bag while carrying the dirty clothes) along with the clean load of wet clothes. Yep, that's a clear case of "dryer abuse" that should be reported to the local Appliance Welfare Authority as soon as possible. I've also found, through personal experience, that a curling iron works better on my hair than my hand (ouch!), and an electric shaver should never be used in the bathtub (it could be an electrifying experience).

None of these servants earn their keep if they aren't working, so maintenance is important. Servants not only need to work well, they also vary in cost and effectiveness. The following tips are designed to help you find, buy, maintain, and appreciate the domestic servants you keep at home as well as all those other home-based items such as furniture and electronics!

(#304) TIP OF THE DAY:
TIPS TO SAVING ON FURNITURE AND APPLIANCES—MAINTAIN:

Ben Franklin said, "Beware of little expenses; a small leak will sink a great ship." It's important to take care of those little things in the maintenance of existing units. You could significantly increase the life of the appliance. Throw a nice-looking afghan on the back of your couch or on your recliner to save the upholstery. Use the armchair covers that come with your couches or wing-backed chairs in order to prevent wear on highly used parts of the furniture.

BUYING USED APPLIANCES—FROM INDIVIDUALS: The best bargains on a replacement appliance will be found in the used appliance section of your newspaper.

Due to households breaking up or combining, people transferring to different areas, and families who upgrade, you can find a bargain at a garage sale or in the newspaper. If you buy from a garage sale, you'll need to show up early, as these items go fast. Ask the seller how the unit works, and ask for a written receipt with his name, address, and phone number. List the information regarding the condition of the unit on the receipt. If he says it "works just fine," then you might ask him to sign a receipt and guarantee the information he's given.

If the seller won't back up his word, then buyer beware. If he will, then you'll probably want to take the unit home immediately and hook it up. If it does not work, you'll still have time to return to the sale and renegotiate. Before I put on my traveling shoes, I owned a little house in the woods in Texas. I bought a washer and dryer for $100. The woman signed a receipt, and my units worked well for two years. Then I sold them for the same amount, moved from Texas, and the rest is history.

LAUNDROMATS: One of my readers said that in her early marriage: "We bought a washer from our local Laundromat for $25. My mother covered it with contact paper—as if that would camouflage it. It was ugly, but it sure was cheap, lasted five years, and tons more convenient than hauling baskets of clothes to the Laundromat."

TIP OF THE DAY:

BUYING USED APPLIANCES—FROM A STORE: The next
step up from a garage sale is a thrift shop. There aren't too many
that carry major appliances, but it's worth a few phone calls. Shop
as much from home as you can, rather than wasting gas traveling
from store to store. You may want to try the service repair shops.
Call and ask them if they sell reconditioned appliances.

A used appliance store, or a new appliance store with a
used section, can yield great values. Be sure to negotiate on
these items. Ask for a warranty from your dealer, and ask for
free delivery and setup. They may balk at the latter, but they'll
oftentimes throw it in after you ask the manager.

We bought a Maytag washer and dryer set for $500 from an
appliance store with a used section. They were a year old and still
had a warranty left on them. The previous owners wanted a couple
of extra gadgets on their units and traded these babies in. They
lost big-time. We gained big-time. That was over ten years and
5,200 loads ago. The Maytag man came to our house once—when
the washer was damaged in a move. We haven't seen him since.

TIP OF THE DAY:

BUYING NEW APPLIANCES: Look at discontinued units and
last year's models. Consider buying your purchase on a gold
card that offers double manufacturers' warranties. Then
pay that card off the very next month. Incurring more
debt costs you money. Avoid the deluxe models—they
have too many extra bells and whistles that you don't
need. We bought a small freezer and saved 35 percent

by eliminating two unnecessary features. We decided we had enough noise at our house without the new freezer dinging and whistling. See the other tips below for more information.

TIP OF THE DAY:

STORE DISPLAYS: Every item that is on display is no longer in the box—therefore becoming a store display appliance. By buying the store display and taking advantage of the sale and/or a rebate, you can save major dollars. The guarantee is the same as any other new appliance in a box. Go around to your local dealers in person and ask for these values.

TIP OF THE DAY:

BUYING USED FURNITURE: At a garage sale, furniture and appliances go fast, so shop early. If you hear of a friend who is buying a new bedroom set, and you need one for your teenager—consider asking what they want for their old set. Look in the classifieds, and call before you go by anyone's house to view furniture.

It's important to call on these ads with specifics in mind. If you ask the seller the color, size, shape, condition, and guarantee of his furniture—you can read between the lines and save yourself a lot of time, gas, and energy. It's a good idea to do the same thing with thrift shops, consignment stores, and used furniture stores.

Once you're there, sit on it, step on it, look under it, and turn over the cushions. Check for previous repairs, stains, tears, seams falling apart, and overall condition of the piece. Be prepared to transport your own purchases from garage sales and individual homes. Also, get a guarantee, in writing, that the appliances work and have the seller commit to a refund if they do not.

TIP OF THE DAY:

BUYING NEW FURNITURE—CONSUMER GUIDES: If you do not subscribe to a consumer buying guide (such as *Consumer Reports*), then go to the libaray and look up the information on the items you want before you shop the sales at each furniture store. Once in the store, compare warranties, delivery charges, and features. **(ADVANCED)**

TIP OF THE DAY:

BUYING NEW FURNITURE—MAIL-ORDER COMPARISONS: Consider mail-order houses for furniture. In order to maximize your benefit from mail-order houses, visit a furniture store first and select the brands and styles that best meet your needs and your budget. If you know the brand name and model, you can check the mail-order houses in the back of women's and home magazines to find the contact for manufacturer direct purchases. Go on their websites and then call them to negotiate on the phone for a good price—be sure the bottom line includes shipping and handling. Ask them to email or fax you the paperwork on their quotes. Print out a copy of their best deal and take it with you to compare these prices with what the local stores have to offer. **(ADVANCED)**

TIP OF THE DAY:

BUYING NEW FURNITURE—MATCHING COMPETITORS' PRICES: Once you have the best value from the previous tip and you have the paperwork, take it to your local dealer and ask them to match the price. Throughout the years, I've heard from readers who have consistently saved hundreds and thousands of dollars by using this tip. **(ADVANCED)**

TIP OF THE DAY:

BUYING NEW FURNITURE—TIME YOUR REQUESTS: Once you get a price you can agree on, ask the salesperson for free delivery to be added as well as Scotchgarding (if that applies) and/or setup services (balance a washer/dryer, etc.). Even if the salesperson declines to add these extra values, ask the manager for them and they'll more often than not give you your request. But timing is essential.

TIP OF THE DAY:

BUYING NEW FURNITURE: Look at discontinued pieces of furniture and last year's models. Shop the wholesale stores and take your time. The more you look and watch the advertisements for sales, the more satisfied you'll be with your purchase. Ask the salesman when the item might go on sale. If you just missed a sale by a couple of weeks, ask the manager for the previous sale price.

TIP OF THE DAY:

SMALL APPLIANCES: There was a rhyme from the Depression era that my wonderful great-grandma Laudeman used to recite to me when I was a little girl: "Use it up, wear it out, make do—or do without." I have the same philosophy—with a new attitude. Let's look at each line of this rhyme as it applies to small appliances.

TIP OF THE DAY:

SMALL APPLIANCES—USE IT UP: Let other people get rid of a toaster because it doesn't fit their color scheme. If it still works well, then use it up. You can buy other folks' rejects (in your color scheme) at a garage sale for one-tenth the price.

TIP OF THE DAY:

SMALL APPLIANCES—WEAR IT OUT: This is similar to the above with an exception. In small appliances, you may have to repair a knob or a screw and it will have more life to it. Make sure the thing is really dead before you bury it. If it is still under warranty, then have it repaired (Kirby vaccums have a lifetime warranty). If the cost of a repair is 60 percent or more than the cost of a new item, then do not have it repaired; replace it instead with a new item that has a warranty.

TIP OF THE DAY:

SMALL APPLIANCES—MAKE DO: Okay, you feel deep down in your soul that you can't live without a Black and Decker under-the-cabinet can opener. Those commercials

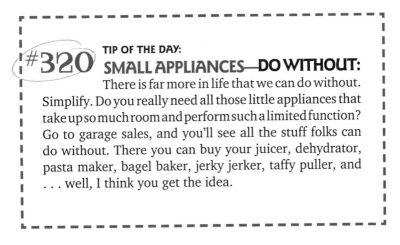

have you convinced! You need the extra space on your counters, and it looks so spiffy under the cabinet. Besides all that, you'll look like the beautiful model in the ad if you buy the product. But your present can opener works great, and it's only a year old. Stop coveting and make do.

#320

TIP OF THE DAY:

SMALL APPLIANCES—DO WITHOUT:
There is far more in life that we can do without. Simplify. Do you really need all those little appliances that take up so much room and perform such a limited function? Go to garage sales, and you'll see all the stuff folks can do without. There you can buy your juicer, dehydrator, pasta maker, bagel baker, jerky jerker, taffy puller, and . . . well, I think you get the idea.

TIP OF THE DAY:

ASK MOM: This is a rather unconventional tip, but why not ask Mom for her rejects? Sometimes other members of our families have that piece of furniture or appliance that we really need just sitting in their storage shed. It's gathering dust and corroding for lack of use. They may feel that it would insult us to offer it, but it could be ours for the asking.

I've also seen items like these, believe it or not, sitting outside by the curb waiting for the trashman. I'm not saying we should start crawling in dumpsters, but bargains are all around us if we have the eyes to see them. Start developing a savings mind-set, and you'll find great deals in the least likely places.

TIP OF THE DAY:

WHEN TO BUY: There is not only a good place to buy, but there's usually a good time to buy just about anything. These values are found during key times due to the model season, marketing season, and inventory season. For example, May is a good time to buy televisions because the new models are coming out and they are clearing out the old models. Also note that there's not necessarily one time to buy. Bargains on washers and dryers can be found in the months of March and July due to seasonal sales and product cycles.

- **Buy in January:** Computers, Small appliances

- **Buy in February:** Floor coverings, Furniture

- **Buy in March:** Air conditioners, Dryers, Washers

- **Buy in April:** Electronics, Kitchen stoves

- **Buy in May:** Radios, Televisions

- **Buy in June:** Floor coverings, Furniture, Refrigerators

- **Buy in July:** Dryers, Washers

- **Buy in August:** Patio and Lawn furniture

- **Buy in September:** Bicycles, Swing sets, Gardening supply clearances

- **Buy in October:** Rugs

- **Buy in November:** Heating devices, Appliances

- **Buy in December:** Electronic Christmas items (after the twenty-fifth, such as lights, house decorations, etc.)

TIP OF THE DAY:

TIPS FOR EBAY BUYERS: Let's face it, some of the best values for household appliances and electronics are found on eBay. But this resource could cost you money rather than save you money if you don't know what you're doing. The following tips are a guide to get you started and help you become a proficient eBay buyer (and seller). The first step is to make sure you have a good printer (that is working) a reliable computer (that won't freeze) and a solid credit card (preferably not a debit card).

- **History:** Check the seller's history before you buy. If others are unhappy with her, then pass. Look for sunglasses or other marks from eBay that indicate caution. Also look at their overall history. If they're just starting out, then don't let them learn on you. Pick a more experienced seller.

- **Final Costs:** If postage, handling, and insurance costs aren't listed, then ask. You want to know the bottom line to make sure it truly is a good value.

- **Research:** Compare prices by finding the same product at www.mysimon.com, www.nextag.com, or www.froogle.com before you bid. Also make sure that the comparison price you get includes taxes and shipping so that you will be comparing oranges with oranges.

- **Experience:** Buy several items to gain experience before you start selling so that you can have high ratings as a buyer and seller. Be sure that you rank the people you've purchased from because they also have the option of ranking you as a buyer.

TIP OF THE DAY:
TIPS FOR EBAY SELLERS:

- **Online Fees:** Figure all fees into your asking price. There's a listing fee, selling fee, and payment fee when you accept an online payment.

- **Turbo Lister:** Use this free eBay software to enhance product listing, layout, titles, image, and fees.

- **Photo:** Invest in (or borrow) a good digital camera. Multiple images are often required to adequately show the item. The better the photograph, the better the price—so that in most cases a camera phone isn't going to hack it if you really want to maximize your selling opportunity.

- **Pricing and Duration:** Decide how long your listing will run, the number of items in your product grouping, and the starting price. Never start the listing price of an item with hopes of getting more.

- **Disclose Flaws:** Be sure to list thorough descriptions including dimensions, etc. The more detailed you are, the more likely you'll have a satisfied buyer.

- **Disclose Fees:** List postage, handling, and insurance fees. Failure to do so can result in a negative review, which would hurt your overall rating.

- **Accepting Payments:** You may accept credit cards through one of the online credit card services by registering at eBay.

- **Feedback:** Cultivate a high seller rating through customer service and adequate descriptions. Always rate the buyer after the transaction is final.

- **Customer Service:** Deliver products on time and follow up after the sale. Determine ahead of time what your policy will be if the product is damaged in shipping. Are you going to cover it, or say "sorry—you didn't buy insurance"?

- **Shipping:** Get free boxes and priority mail packing tape through USPS.com delivered to your door. The catch is that you have to ship the product priority mail, which is good if it's over a pound and under five pounds. If the item is over five pounds, it is better to go with UPS ground or FedEx ground. Or buy boxes or shipping envelopes in bulk at www.usbox.com.

TIP OF THE DAY:

FURNITURE CRAFTSMEN: It may surprise you to find out that *some* craftsmen can build a custom-made dining room set for less than the best sale price of a comparable quality set at a traditional store. When we lived in Columbus, Mississippi, we traded our "early garage sale" motif for 5,000 pounds of custom-made primitive country furniture. Because we bought directly from the craftsman (a dear old man who just loved to make furniture), we paid 30 percent less than *wholesale*!

To locate a craftsman in your city or town, call the local lumberyard, antique store, furniture repair shop, or search the yellow pages and ask if they know of any local craftsmen who build furniture.

Don't waste their time or yours when you call for an estimate. Decide the following before you call: 1) style of furniture and how many pieces; 2) the kind and quality of wood; 3) paint, varnish, or bare wood; 4) fabric design and/or pattern; and 5) your price range. Be flexible in exploring wants versus needs in the pieces you would like to order. Ask the right questions such as:

"Can I see samples of your work and references?"

"Do you guarantee the pieces?"

"What is the estimated delivery time on the work?"

A reputable craftsman will not be offended by these practical questions and should be willing to stand behind their work. The end result could be lovely, custom-made furniture that can be passed on to the next generation. **(ADVANCED)**

TIP OF THE DAY:

MODEL HOME: This is a creative approach that works best in larger towns or cities that are experiencing a boom in business for new homes. Call the local builders, especially those whom you know have model homes and ask the design manager how they liquidate the furniture in their model homes when they've sold the last home in the tract.

Rather than going to the expense of using a liquidation firm to rid themselves of this excess, they are often willing to sell to individuals. You will need to pay cash or check (versus credit) for these items, so be prepared before you make an offer.

Keep in mind that the furniture in model homes is usually much smaller than the furniture you normally buy. Designers will place a full-sized bed in the master bedroom rather than a queen-sized bed in order to create the appearance of more space. The daybeds in these homes will usually accommodate a child rather than an adult, and the dining room sets may only have two to four chairs. This is also a good way to pick up some appliances too—although you may be limited in the color and size of those appliances. **(ADVANCED)**

TIP OF THE DAY:

#327 VINTAGE FURNITURE: This is furniture built several decades ago that isn't old enough to qualify officially as antique. These pieces make for remarkable values because the craftsmanship is often superior to furniture built today. If you adopt the mind-set of a visionary when you go to an estate sale, garage sale, or secondhand furniture store, you could find some lasting values. Before you buy, turn the item over and look at the joints to see if they're in solid shape. If you're looking for a couch, research in advance the cost of reupholstering.

For example, we found fabric at an outlet store for only $3/yd. The same fabric at the furniture store was $26/yd. We also knew the cost of labor to reupholster our couch and love seat and discovered that we saved 40 percent for the style of our choice in this type of approach. You can even find some great upholstery fabric values on the Internet by searching the manufacturer as outlined at the beginning of this section. The advantage of this kind of furniture is that you have quality for less that will last.

TIP OF THE DAY:

COMPUTERS, ELECTRONICS: Many of the previous tips (eBay, Internet shopping, price comping) all apply to any kind of electronic as well, so look to those with your item in mind. One of the best ways to get a good value is to use a shopping robot such as www.mysimon.com, www.nextag.com, and www.froogle.com. As in the previous tips, you can print out the best price, take it into your store, and ask them to match the price—often they will.

TIP OF THE DAY:

COMPUTERS, ELECTRONICS—BEWARE RESTOCK FEES: Be aware of the restock fee policy of any store. For example, Best Buy will charge a 30 percent restock fee in order to issue a refund. If you know this ahead of time, then you'll buy with a mind to keep rather than buying with a "well, if it doesn't fit in the television cabinet, I'll bring it back!"

TIP OF THE DAY:

COMPUTERS, ELECTRONICS—WHOLESALE CLUBS: Wholesale clubs can be a great place to find values on all these items and furniture as well. As we said before, do your price research before you go into the store and be aware of the fact that you'll need to have your own transportation with you to take the item home (as most clubs do not have delivery services unless you order online). Don't forget to go to the club's online store as well to get coupon values and prices.

Before you buy in the store, ask to look at the latest coupon books. There will often be amazing values in there, such as a coupon for $1000 off an HDTV or $1800 off a dining room table set. DO NOT rely on the salesperson's ability to remember if there is a coupon; look through the book yourself. This little tip saved me $800 on some furniture from Costco when the eighteen-year-old clerk said there wasn't a current coupon!

Where's the Money, Honey?

*Tips to Save Relationships
(Money Personalities, Budgeting,
Couples and Money, and Gifts)*

There's nothing that takes its toll on a relationship like having five babies in seven years and moving eleven times in thirteen years while homeschooling all those cute kids. When Bob and I were parents of five very young children, I didn't know what the word "rest" meant because I was always on the go—juggling a variety of hats in the process.

I would awake by 5:30 a.m., put on my mommy hat, and hit the floor running: feeding babies, dressing babies, and loving babies. Next, I put on my maid hat and cleaned the messes babies made. Who had time for rest? I tried to rest during my lunch break with one of six daily glasses of water. Usually, I sat in the living room and ate my meal after the children had their lunches. During that hallowed time, the babies were napping and the older children were having a quiet time in their rooms.

As a special treat, I'd sip a glass of tea while trying to grab a few minutes of relaxation. Eternal vigilance required that I pick up my glass of water or tea afterward, lest the babies awakened and tried to drink it—more likely, spill it.

One day, I put on a lady of leisure hat and rested with a rare glass of tea. I was busy when our three-year-old Jonathan, aka Sweetpea, and one-year-old Conan the Baby Barbarian, aka Joshua, awoke from their naps. Panicked, I remembered my unsupervised tea. Grabbing my emergency hat, I quickly checked it . . . whew! . . . the glass was undisturbed. But it was puzzling to see water in it.

That's funny, I thought I was drinking tea.

There was a vague memory of my pouring water earlier in the day, so I dismissed my confusion as typical forgetfulness (my husband calls it premature senility). That water looked good, so I decided to finish it in a big gulp. Yuk!! This was not the purified water we normally drank! At that moment, confusion reigned because the boys were fighting again, so I put on my referee hat and ran to their room.

After removing Conan the Baby Barbarian's hands from Sweetpea's neck, Jonathan announced, "Mama, I help with your tea . . . I pour it out."

Envisioning tea stains on the bed quilt, I asked, "Where did you pour it out, Sweetpea?"

He squared his shoulders and proudly replied, "In de bafroom."

"Where in the bathroom?" My inquiring mind wanted to know.

His reply brought a sigh of relief as he sweetly answered, "In de sink."

My relief was short-lived, for there was more to his story. "And I get you water," he said, beaming with pride.

Nervously looking at the empty glass on the end table, I asked, "And where did you get the water?"

"In the bafroom," he answered with confidence.

Still hopeful, there was one last question ventured. "Out of the sink?"

"No!" he replied as if he thought I was out of my mind. "Out of de potty, Mama. Der's lots of water in the potty!"

My stomach churned and I momentarily slunk to my knees. I pulled myself together and grabbed a can of Lysol—and freshened my breath. The motto of this anecdote: When at the Kays', DON'T DRINK THE WATER!

Jonathan's "helpfulness" reminded me of how life is when it comes to relationships—things are not always as they appear on the surface. Sometimes couples appear to have their financial lives squared away, but in reality they have trouble communicating. A born saver may appear to have it all under control, but their very money personality may make it hard for them to enjoy life.

The following tips are designed to help couples learn to communicate more effectively about money and fight fair. Other tips will help you understand your money personality and how to keep it in balance. Hopefully, these will help you see that there's another lesson learned from Jonathan's water—there are always a few things about our outlook that we can change in order to improve our relationship with money and with those we love.

♡

TIP OF THE DAY:

COME CLEAN WITH YOUR SPOUSE: Too many couples will not risk full disclosure when it comes to finances and it keeps them in a pit when they could crawl out and find freedom. This is especially true when it comes to couples and their spending habits. Even those who are honest aren't always *completely* honest about *exactly how much* they spent. Some 36 percent of men admit to fudging on the price of an item, while 40 percent of women claim the item cost less than it actually did. So come clean and you'll find your financial situation improve. **(ADVANCED)**

TIP OF THE DAY:

CHOOSE YOUR TIMING: There's a fascinating survey called "Investing in America: Spending Survey" that indicated that most couples discussed their finances under the worst possible conditions—when they were tense and frustrated. It's no huge surprise to realize that most of these "discussions" (we call them fights at our house) were not resolved in a satisfactory manner.

These survey results are not surprising or revelatory, but it is telling. In fact, this survey is the main reason I developed the "Sixty-Minute Money Workout," (below) so that couples can have a purposeful time to discuss money and have an effective tool to maximize the discussion without fighting or wishing you were having a root canal rather than a discussion about money.

TIP OF THE DAY:

TRY THE SIXTY-MINUTE MONEY WORKOUT: Bob and I have experienced the incredible miracle of overcoming seemingly insurmountable debt. As you may already know by now, when we got married, we had $40,000 in consumer debt. We were like many other young people who didn't realize the price we would pay for instant gratification. One of the ways we were able to discuss money without fighting was to work out with the couples money work-out tips below. Try this one-hour workout once a week and you'll be fiscally fit without fighting before you know it! **(ADVANCED)**

TIP OF THE DAY:

TAKE THE FIRST STEP IN THE COUPLES MONEY WORKOUT —MAKE UP YOUR MIND WARM-UP (FIVE MINUTES): In this five-minute warm-up, you decide as a couple to purpose to get out of debt and express a willingness to make immediate changes in your lifestyle to accomplish this. In our case, we also purposed to tithe 10 percent of all we made. We ended up living on less than 25 percent of one income in order to accomplish these goals. Within two and a half years, we were debt free! We made up our minds, prayed to God for His help, and found the strength we needed to make that decision to become debt free. We haven't looked back since.

TIP OF THE DAY:

TAKE THE SECOND STEP IN THE COUPLES MONEY WORKOUT —COUPLE MEETING STRENGTH TRAINING (TEN MINUTES):

It usually takes more than one partner to get a couple into serious debt. Even if one person does most of the spending, the other spouse usually tolerates the destructive behavior in some way. This meeting is a time to write down goals on paper so that you will have a tangible and objective standard to work toward. The goal you set should include: a) how to stop spending more than you make, b) how to pay the interest on the debt you have accumulated, and c) how to retire the debt.

TIP OF THE DAY:

TAKE THE THIRD STEP IN THE COUPLES MONEY WORKOUT—BUDGET BURN (TWENTY MINUTES):

Finalize and agree on your new budget. This may not seem like a lot of time on this topic, but you've already done some legwork earlier in this tips section on your budget.

♡

TIP OF THE DAY:

TAKE THE FOURTH STEP IN THE COUPLES MONEY WORKOUT —TAKING YOUR HEART RATE (TWENTY MINUTES):

This is the point where you get the facts on your credit and debt information so you can decide if you need to go to a professional financial counselor. Check your credit report and order a copy from any of the major credit bureaus: Equifax (1-800-685-1111), Experian (1-888-297-3742), or Trans Union (1-800-888-4213) or as we mentioned earlier, get it free at www.annualcreditreport. com. In the meantime, I would recommend that you cut up all but one or two credit cards and cancel all other open credit accounts. This will help minimize the temptation to impulse buy as well as keep you on track with your goal of no new debt.

TIP OF THE DAY:

TAKE THE FINAL STEP IN THE COUPLES MONEY WORKOUT —CONGRATULATIONS COOL DOWN (FIVE MINUTES):

Sit back and grab a glass of something cool to drink and reflect on all you've accomplished in just one hour! Keep in mind you're building on what you've done so far, and you're in it for the long haul so you can have a checkbook that is at least as buff as your body.

TIP OF THE DAY:

SET A BUDGET: Most people who dig out of significant debt find themselves back in the same amount of debt, if not more, within two years if they do not have a budget. So live on a budget and you'll find yourself twice as likely to avoid significant consumer debt.

TIP OF THE DAY:

CREATE A FLEXIBLE BUDGET PLAN: Fill out the following chart, using the tips that follow as a guide.

BUDGET PAYMENT PER MONTH
Ellie Kay—www.elliekay.com

Account Name	Current Spending	Projected Budget	Difference	Actual Budget
Tithes/ Contributions–10%				
Savings–10%				
Clothing/ Dry Cleaning–5%				
Education/Misc.–5%				
Food–10%				
Housing/Utilities/ Taxes–30%				
Insurance–5%				
Medical/Dental–4%				
Recreation/Vacation/ Gifts/Christmas–6%				
Transportation–15%				
Totals				
Net Income				

TIP OF THE DAY:

ONLINE BUDGET OPTION: If you prefer an online interactive budget rather than the form provided here, go to www.crown. org for a fabulous budget tool.

TIP OF THE DAY:

REMAIN FLEXIBLE: I love the anonymous saying "Blessed are the flexible, for they shall not be broken." Most people fail at budgeting because they are too rigid. Remember that the following tips are guidelines rather than actual rules.

TIP OF THE DAY:

ASSESS CURRENT SPENDING/SAVING: When you are filling out the budget form, be sure to include all debt accumulation, including credit cards and "hidden bills." Make your goal to live *below* your means and allocate money for specific savings areas.

TIP OF THE DAY:

ASSESS NET INCOME: This is the household income *after* state and federal income taxes and social security. Income includes salary, rents, notes, interest, dividends, income tax refund, and other forms of income. Enter the total on the line "net income" on the budget form included in this tips section.

TIP OF THE DAY:

WHERE ARE YOU?: Take your net income and subtract your current spending to establish your overall family spending. Are you spending more (through credit) than you make each month? Are you spending everything you make (with nothing going into savings)? Are there unexplained gaps in your current spending levels? Did you know you were hitting the ATM machine that many times each month? Are you saving as much as you'd like to?

TIP OF THE DAY:

PROJECTED BUDGET: Look on the budget chart and fill in the column "projected budget," according to the percentage given. These percentages are guidelines and will vary according to family size, geographical location, and income.

This column gives a good idea of where to go with your budget. Take the difference between columns one and two to determine if your current spending levels are over or under the projected budget. Compare your current spending column with the projected budget column to determine areas that need the most attention in your family's budget. Write the difference (either in the black or in the red) in column three.

TIP OF THE DAY:

ACTUAL BUDGET: Using the projected budget as a guideline, tailor an actual budget for your family. For example, you might drive a company car, so your automobile expenses would be slightly lower than average. You could take this overage and carry it over to the servicing of consumer debt. Or, you may need to take measures to cut your food budget or shop around on insurance to arrive at a workable budget for your family.

TIP OF THE DAY:

BUDGET VARIABLE: Your expenses may vary according to your geographic location. People living in the north may have higher utility bills due to their harsh winters. People in the south may have a greater electricity bill due to air conditioning in the summer. Our family has higher education costs because of the number of children in our family.

TIP OF THE DAY:

BUDGET COMMITTEE: A "couple meeting" is the best place to establish this budget and make the commitment to stick to it. This meeting can be a fun time for you and your spouse. Make some popcorn, or have dessert and coffee, and approach it from a positive perspective.

TIP OF THE DAY:

HIDDEN BILLS: These are expenses that should be figured into the monthly budget in order to give you an accurate assessment of annual expenses. These include bills that may not come due on a monthly basis. Nevertheless, the budget should provide for the payment of those items. These debts also include insurance premiums, property and other taxes, retail credit, money owed to family and friends, doctor and dentist bills, magazine subscriptions, etc.

STILL MORE HIDDEN BILLS: Each category in our worksheet has hidden expenses you may not have considered. This is a complete, itemized list of costs that should be included in each of these categories.

- **Tithe/Charitable Donations:** Church, civic, community donations

- **Saving:** Savings accounts, savings for hidden debts and unexpected emergencies

- **Clothing/Dry Cleaning:** New clothing and shoes, thrift store bargains, garage sale finds, dry cleaning, alterations, repairs, patterns and sewing supplies

- **Education/Miscellaneous:** Tuition, books, music or other lessons, school supplies, newspaper, miscellaneous expenses. The miscellaneous portion includes all other unbudgeted items and any debt payments.

- **Food:** Groceries and meals eaten outside the home

- **Housing:** Includes mortgage or rent, property taxes, utilities (including phone, gas, water, and electricity), cleaning supplies, labor costs/maid, lawn care, pool care, tools and repair, stationery, postage, household repairs, furniture and bedding, appliances, and garden equipment.

♡

- **Insurance:** The percentage provided assumes some employee insurance benefits. It also includes life, house, and health insurance.

- **Medical/Dental:** Doctor, dentist, eyeglasses, medicines, and vitamins

- **Recreation/Vacation/Gifts and Christmas:** Cameras and film, entertainment, movies, hobbies, pets, television, sporting goods, toys, all gifts, Christmas decorations and gifts, and vacations

- **Transportation:** Airline fares, bus and taxi fares, car payments and insurance, car repairs and licenses, gasoline and oil   **(ADVANCED)**

TIP OF THE DAY:

CREATE GIVEAWAY GIFT BASKETS: Create your own gift baskets by assembling new items you've purchased for less. For example, a baby basket could contain baby wash, baby bath, baby shampoo, and washcloths. A housewarming basket could include sponges, a scrubber, and a bottle of Dawn dishwashing liquid that contains 40 percent more cleaning power per drop, and you can clean a sink full of dishes without greasy water. Your friends will think of you every time they wash dishes!

♡

#354 AVOID BUDGET BUSTERS: There are a few problem areas that can throw a budget off course in a matter of seconds—sending it reeling toward disaster. The use of debt, or credit is the number one budget buster. I suggest you look at making your policy one of cash only. Some couples set up an envelope system for cash. Every two weeks, they place the budgeted amount of cash in envelopes marked, "food," "entertainment," "gas," etc. When the money runs out, you're done until the end of the two-week period. A regular peek at the amount of cash left in each envelope is a vivid reminder of your budget commitments. **(ADVANCED)**

TIP OF THE DAY:

THE THIRTY/SEVEN-DAY PLAN: Impulse buying is a major budget buster and a temptation faced by almost everyone. Whether it's a candy bar or a Corvette—we've all given in to the craving at one time or another. There are ways to short-circuit this tendency within our natures and one of the best ways is the "thirty-day plan." If a moderate to pricey item that is in your budget appears before you, then wait thirty days, thereby delaying the purchase. During that month, find two other items that are similar and compare prices. If it's still available at a good price and it fits the next month's budget, then buy it.

For moderately priced or lesser items that are still not in your budget, apply the same principle but base it on a seven-day waiting period. What I think you'll find is you're buying less stuff because this delay gives you the opportunity to get beyond the impulse. **(ADVANCED)**

TIP OF THE DAY:

BUSTING THE GIFT BUSTER: Avoid the final area that busts budgets—gifts. These items can blow up an entire budget quicker than Bob's jet can go from zero to Mach 1—and that's fast! These include gifts for relatives, baby showers, weddings, birthdays, Valentine's Day, Mother's Day, Father's Day, kids' birthdays, and anniversaries. This doesn't even cover the biggie—Christmas. The first thing we should do is evaluate the "why" of gift giving.

- Do we really have to give a material gift in each circumstance?

- Wouldn't a card work just as well in some cases?

- What about baked goods instead?

- Occasionally, the giving of a gift puts the other person under the sense of obligation. Are you putting more emphasis on the gift rather than the giver?

- Isn't it, after all, the thought that counts?

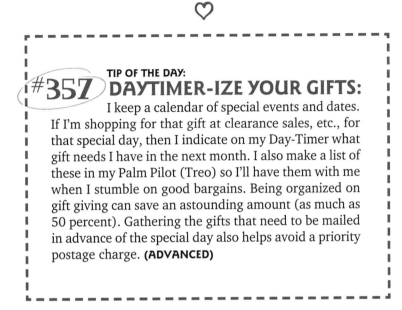

TIP OF THE DAY:

(#357) DAYTIMER-IZE YOUR GIFTS:

I keep a calendar of special events and dates. If I'm shopping for that gift at clearance sales, etc., for that special day, then I indicate on my Day-Timer what gift needs I have in the next month. I also make a list of these in my Palm Pilot (Treo) so I'll have them with me when I stumble on good bargains. Being organized on gift giving can save an astounding amount (as much as 50 percent). Gathering the gifts that need to be mailed in advance of the special day also helps avoid a priority postage charge. **(ADVANCED)**

TIP OF THE DAY:

KNOW YOUR MONEY PERSONALITY: Everyone has a money
personality that dictates the way they relate to financial issues. The following are tips on the different personalities and how to bring each into balance. Know yours and your spouse's and learn how to make it work *for* you and not *against* you. **(ADVANCED)**

TIP OF THE DAY:

ARE YOU A "POWER" PAUL?: Money can be the ultimate strategic pawn in the power game. "He who has the money makes the rules" is the basic philosophy of this personality.

- A man (or woman) who does not produce his own money independently may feel or experience a loss of power with this person.

- If he is the primary breadwinner, he will use this position as a means of control and to "keep his wife in her place."

- He rarely tolerates a wife who makes more money than he does—because she is too much of a threat.

- This personality makes all the financial decisions, does not seek the partner's input, will not allow access to financial information.

- He uses all of these strategies as a means of securing a position of strength in the family.

- Men may comprise the majority for this personality—but they don't own the market on it!

- The primary means of bringing this personality into balance is to stress the value of nonfinancial contributions made by other family members.

- A respected third party is often needed to break through to a Power Paul.

♡

- Both partners can feel more powerful and secure when they share the nonfinancial burdens of the family, including the time demands of household work and child care. In other words, Power Paul needs to change diapers too!

TIP OF THE DAY:

ARE YOU A SECURE SAMANTHA?: Secure Samantha was raised in a family that was one step away from being homeless.

- She is motivated to save money by the powerful emotion of fear.

- She has memories of not knowing where the next meal was coming from and having to move from place to place in order to stay one step ahead of the bill collector.

- She may have vowed, as Scarlett O'Hara once did: "I'll never go hungry again. As God is my witness, neither I nor any of my kin will ever go hungry again."

- Not every Secure Samantha saves money because of a background of poverty; there are a variety of circumstances that birth this personality. But the common characteristic is a basic fear of not having enough for fundamental needs, retirement, the kids' college, a rainy day, etc.

- This personality may marry someone who represents financial security.

- They also tend to be born savers who want to add "just a little more" to their investment programs as they never feel they have quite enough money in savings.

- The loss of financial security is about the worse thing that can happen to Secure Samantha.

- When she says no to a family vacation, even when it has been budgeted—it is her insecurity speaking.

- A possible solution to Sam's tendencies is to reconcile the internal voice that compels her to save with her family's short-term needs.

- Balance for Sam happens when she realizes that God is in control and her financial destiny is not entirely in her own hands.

- When this occurs, she will be in a position to trust a solid budget, with reasonable savings, and can overcome the need to secure her future by compulsively accumulating money.

TIP OF THE DAY:

ARE YOU A TIGHTWAD TILLY?: Born savers have many overlapping traits and may even seem to be identical at first glance. However, there are shades of gray that paint them to be decidedly different. Tightwad Tilly is much like her sister, Secure Samantha, but Tilly doesn't save money based on a fear for security. She does it because she's cheap.

- She has an emotional dread of spending any money for anything (especially on others) and views the accumulation of money as an end in itself.

- The emotional dread is not fear, it is an emotion that is rooted in selfishness.

- There is a difference between being frugal and being tight. The former can still be generous as needs arise (see Balanced Betty), but the latter leaves below-average tips and tries to sell their surplus goods at a garage sale or on eBay first rather than give them away to a family in clear need.

- Could be called Shifty Sheila because there exists a selfish drive to save a buck anywhere and everywhere—even at the expense of others or their own integrity.

- Tightwad Tilly can be brought into balance with concerted effort to give away the little things (bigger tips, unused clothing to Goodwill, food to food pantries).

- The second step to balance Tilly is for her to then transition these conscious acts of generosity into other areas as well (tithes, opening her home, giving her time in volunteer work, etc.).

- A final step for Tilly is to do her giving anonymously.

TIP OF THE DAY:

WORRY WART WANDA: The interesting thing about Worry Wart Wanda is that she can be either a saver or a spender—she's one of the few personalities that can do both.

- Is obsessed with money—she talks about it, thinks about it—and makes decisions based on it.

- She can have too little and worry about how she is going to pay the bills, send her kids to college, and fund her retirement.

- She worries for pleasure, it seems.

- On the other extreme, she can have plenty and worry about a variety of issues such as:

    Do people only like me because of my money?

    Why do people always hit me up for money?

    What do I say to all these family members and friends who ask me for a loan?

    What if I make a bad investment?

    What if I lose my money?

- Can be brought into balance by beginning to shift her focus off of herself and onto God's provision.

- A good exercise for Worry Wart Wanda would be to challenge herself *not* to use the word "money" for one day each week.

- She should keep a notebook for all the ways her worries never transpired and all the ways the opposite was true and she had the provision she needed.

♡

ARE YOU A SPENDTHRIFT STEVE?: Spendthrift Steve never lets his money see the inside of his pocket.

- The spendthrift is greatly distressed by the possession of any money and wants to spend it all as soon as possible.

- Most people have elements of both the tightwad and the spendthrift.

- This personality will oftentimes spend the annual bonus, the inheritance, the birthday money—well before he ever receives it!

- Debt is a major by-product of the spendthrift's makeup and even if he is able to manage his debt load, he doesn't manage to set aside much for a rainy day.

- This personality should not carry credit cards but use a cash-only policy.

- Accountability is a major solution to Spendthrift Steve's money problems.

- He needs to find a financial counselor or trusted friend who is wise with money and will make him accountable to set a budget and stick with it.

- This accountability would be someone from outside of his marital relationship who can view the situation from an impartial standpoint and help him get the assistance he needs to follow through with financial goals.

TIP OF THE DAY:

ARE YOU A FEEL GOOD FRANCINE?: Feel Good Francine
hits the mall whenever she feels sad, lonely, angry, or even when
she feels good and wants to celebrate. In the military, I have
known more than a few "Feel Gooders" who add a new piece of
furniture, a different outfit, or remodel the bathroom when their
spouse is deployed.

- Impulse buying is a common characteristic of someone who buys consumer goods based on emotions.

- The compulsive shopper, who obsessively buys more and more to overcome a negative emotion, is almost always a Feel Good Francine.

- The key to overcoming this personality's overspending habits is to find other alternatives as an emotional outlet (besides overeating!). This person needs to ask herself: "What else makes me feel better when I'm down—besides spending money?"

- If exercise or having lunch with a friend or listening to music in a hot bath makes her feel better, then she should make a list of these activities and check them off each time she's tempted to buy her way out of an emotional black hole.

- Feel Good Francine can break free of this destructive cycle once she faces the decision of "Give me liberty or give me debt" and chooses the former.

♡

ARE YOU A LOVE YA LOUIE?: Uncle Louie may look a lot like his wife, Aunt Feel Good, because they are both very materialistic.

- Uncle Louie uses money to make others feel good about him; however, Francine uses money to feel good about herself.

- His money is a substitute for love and time.

- Louie never knows if people love him for who he is or just because he's buying.

- But in some ways it doesn't matter because he so closely associates love as expressed in the things that he buys for others.

- Power Paul is Louie's dad. His son's behavior is an outgrowth of his father's power and control. His dad controlled him with the use of money so that money became a representation of positive feedback.

- Louie doesn't use money to control people in the same way his dad did—yet he does use money to try and control people's opinions of him.

- In other words, he uses money to get people to like him and have a positive emotional response to him.

- Love Ya Louie's kids will grow up with no knowledge of the value of money. They will be far more likely to misuse their possessions because Dad will always buy them a replacement.

- Love Ya Louie is the big spender and if he doesn't have the money to buy love, then he'll borrow it.

- He can overcome his workaholic tendencies by purposing to spend time rather than money with those he loves.

- Louie can also be brought into balance by realizing the real purpose of money and the value of other things in life like character, selflessness, and anonymous giving.

- If Louie will purpose to focus on things like time with family, training his children, and being loved for who he is, not what he can buy, he will find true wealth and acceptance.

TIP OF THE DAY:

ARE YOU A BALANCED BETTY (OR BOB)?: She's so perfect it makes you feel sick—or convicted!

Balanced Betty has just the right combination of all of these personality profiles.

- She understands what is truly important in life, and she tries to be generous with her resources while still maintaining an aggressive savings style.

- Betty realizes that her kids won't just catch good habits, she has to teach them well. So she administers an allowance while encouraging her children to save, share, and spend wisely.

- She also helps them learn a hearty work ethic through earning their own money for larger items and being responsible for chores.

- Betty is in balance right now, but she wasn't always. She used to have debt problems and even fell prey to some compulsive expenses that nearly ruined the family's budget.

- She also realizes that there are no guarantees that the future will be trouble free—she doesn't have ultimate control.

- She's thankful in her diligence and keeps trying to hold her family's finances in balance in the process. **(ADVANCED)**

TIP OF THE DAY:

CUT YOUR PERSONALITY SOME SLACK!: Keep in mind that all of the money personalities I described are extremes. The final personality is the balance we want to achieve and it is a personality that uses money for good purposes. It's fairly obvious that having financial peace and hope rule our home is better than having our children remember a house full of greed and regret. But just because you are naturally a certain personality does not mean you have to remain in that modality. Anyone is one choice away from finding more balance in their money personality. **(ADVANCED)**

SECTION TWELVE

Here He Comes to Save the Day!

Tips to Make a Difference in the World

(Ways to donate, give back to your community, share with those in need, and use these charitable gifts as a tax deduction)

I long to do something daring, different, and on occasion, dangerous whenever I can. On each business trip, there are usually small (or great) ways to add to the adventure resume—whether it's riding the subway in New York City, getting on a mechanical bull in Fort Worth, or jumping out of an airplane in Atlanta. Recently, when a friend of mine, Julie, had to find an assistant to go with her on a business trip to China, she thought, *Who is crazy enough to go to Beijing with me on short notice?* For some reason, she thought of a whacky mother of many who loves to sing on Broadway and can barely remember the names of all her many children.

When she asked me to go as her assistant, I immediately said "YES!" The only thing that gave me pause was the idea of serving in an assistant role, something I had not done in eight years. Quite frankly, I was used to people assisting me and was afraid I'd be a horrible, no good, very bad assistant. Nonetheless, I knew that going in that capacity would be a boon for my character, not to mention that it would be a big, fat, honkin' adventure. I just prayed that I wouldn't get into a travel mode and start usurping Julie in her business mode. She was eager to help me learn the characteristic of servanthood, and this delightful, comedic speaker graciously said, "Just walk three steps behind me, carry my luggage on your head, and address me as the Honorable Julie."

One of the highlights of the trip hit three birds with one stone: it provided adventure, it clarified my role, and it made for a great opening story to the final chapter of this book! This adventure was the Great Wall of China. I was totally unprepared for the experience of "the wall" at MuTianYu near Beijing. First, we had to get on a rickety ski lift type of gondola that never stopped as you jumped onto the seat. If you were lucky, the workers remembered to pull the safety bar down on your gondola, if not, you rode in the open chair, several hundred feet over a scary canyon on the ascent. Western safety OSHA regulations do not apply in the Far East, you participate at your own risk.

If you survived the gut check of the gondola, then 90 percent of average American tourists would never survive the next step—and the 10,000 steps after that. You see, the wall is filled with *steps* and a series of watchtowers. The only flat place on the wall is the watchtower floor. We went down a hundred steps to the first watchtower and had to descend a twelve-foot steep, narrow ladder that looked as if it were coming loose from the wall. Shelly, our gutsy guide and corporate hostess, went down the ladder first. Then Julie descended, then I followed—carrying Julie's luggage on my head.

It wasn't an ideal day for wall-viewing and consequently, we were the first *and only* customers on the gondola. The good news was: we had the entire wall to ourselves for about two hours. Or at least I *thought* it was good news at the time.

We ascended three hundred narrow steps designed for tiny Chinese feet—not for big fat American shoes. Then we entered another watchtower and saw another staircase, straight up with four hundred more steps—the next had three hundred and the next had five hundred. We treked up the wall, knowing we had to take the same route down on the way back. After the fourth watchtower, breathless, but determined, we came against our next major obstacle: the ancient steps. These were eighteen inches tall, with no guard rails and if possible, they were even narrower than the others. I looked at Julie and Shelley for reassurance. They both said, "If you're game, we are." Armed with determination and a wee bit of a competitive spirit, I bellied up those steps, leading the charge, and forgetting to walk three steps behind the "Honorable Julie." I looked like a toddler taking her first climb up a row of carpeted steps—except for the fact that *these* steps were moss stained and unyielding.

When we made it to the next landing, I looked over the vast distance we had already covered, as well as the wall itself creeping into the distance, across another canyon, and up another steep, craggy mountain. I became eerily aware that we were alone—there were no park rangers, no workers, no one at all to notice if we tumbled down a flight of four hundred steps. It would be hard to go for help if someone got hurt. The creepiest feeling was that we were open prey to anyone who might come along. Worse than that feeling was the feeling that we were being watched—even though there was no one in sight.

After the ancient walls, my suspicions became a reality when a shabbily dressed man suddenly emerged from the shadows of the watchtower. He offered to take our picture with our cameras, but Shelley, who was familiar with the land and customs, didn't feel right about giving him our camera, she had a bad feeling about the situation. She shook her head vigorously and said forcefully, "*Bu! Bu! schee, schee,*" which means "No! No! thank you" and headed up the stairs again. He continued to follow, begging us to buy his postcards and hanging on to my arm as he told me he was from Mongolia and wanted me to buy his wares. We left him behind as the next ascent began. I felt totally on guard and aware of our vulnerability, praying my way up the wall.

As was my usual practice, I took the steps nonstop to the top, breathing hard, but focused on the goal of the ascent. Julie and Shelley were more reasonable, taking their time and resting along the way as they chatted about girl things. When I got to the top of the tallest ascent, I sat and looked down, watching my friends make their way up the wall. I was also looking, on guard, to make sure the shadowy character was not following. As I watched, I thought of the ancient men who were buried by this wall as it is often called "the longest cemetery in the world." When a worker or warrior died, they were simply entombed as the work continued. I pondered that for all our effort we had probably only covered a half mile of the original 4000 miles of this great achievement. It was no wonder that the Great Wall is such a wonder and a tribute to Chinese invention. It is not, however, visible from space—that's urban legend.

The mist was rising from the valley, casting an ethereal presence on the landscape, and I remembered a verse, "I have posted watchmen on your walls . . . they will never be silent day or night" (Isaiah 62:6 NIV). At that moment, this trip to China suddenly came into focus. I realized, with absolute clarity, that my servant role was to be the "watchman on the wall" for Julie as she brought a word of encouragement and life to the ladies at the annual women's retreat. Yes, I was at the top of the wall and yes, I had gotten there first, but it wasn't so much because of my *drive* as it was my sense of *destiny*. I admit that I am driven, but I also believe that God called me to a specific destiny that won't be achieved by taking too many breaks and slowing the ascent. In ancient days, the watchman would sound the alarm at the enemy's approach, but they wouldn't run and hide—they had to be skilled in the use of a spear, shield, and sword. In other words, they were warrior watchmen. I had the same role to play: to go before Julie, taking care of details, removing diversions, and watching for those who would distract her from her purpose. The role of a servant watchman is also a role of a servant warrior.

The women at the retreat knew about adventure and they knew about the role of a servant watchman. Many of these ladies were Americans who served as teachers in communities across China, leaving the luxuries of home trying to live as the locals live and on a Chinese salary (about $150/month). They selflessly taught children in a Communistic land so different from their homes, facing their own battles on a daily basis, and in need of a watchman to guard their walls of destiny and purpose. They looked out for each other. These women were the watchmen on the wall for truth and freedom in this foreign land, and a new admiration grew for them as I sat at the top of the Great Wall of China.

- - - - - - - - - - - - - - -

I think that when it comes to our financial and material resources, we also have to be on guard. If we're not alert, our resources could dwindle away and render us a destiny of obscurity. But if we are wise and watchful, then not only can we save money and help our families, we can also be available to help the quality of life of others in our community, city, country, and even places a world away—like China. The following tips are designed to help you climb your personal and unique steps that will help you make a difference in the world. Hopefully, as you read through them, you'll be able to determine where your watchfulness fits on your own step in the world's wall. Your "step" may be sharing canned corn with the community Boy Scout food drive, or supporting an orphan in a third world country. No matter where you are destined to climb, your time, tithe, and talent can be turned into an adventure by which you make the world wonder.

TIP OF THE DAY:

#368 SHARE MORE THAN A MILLIONAIRE!:

Overall, Americans are among the most generous in the world, sharing an average of 3 percent of their annual income. Even millionaires only share that percentage. So if you share 4 percent or more of your earnings with nonprofit organizations, you are more generous than a millionaire! Most financial experts agree that those individuals and families who share the most tend to maintain the best financial health—whether they make $3,000 per year or three million. **(ADVANCED)**

GIVING TAX SMART: The most obvious value of sharing with others is the fact that you are making a difference in the world. But that doesn't mean you can't benefit financially from your own generosity. When you give, do it strategically with the following five tax-smart tips and be part of a gift that keeps on giving. **(ADVANCED)**

SMART TAX TIP # 1—DOUBLE UP: What if you're just getting started in the area of giving a percentage of your income and don't think you'll have enough deductions to itemize on your income tax return? You could double up on your giving by deferring your normal year-end gifts from December to January. Then give your regular gifts that December of the same year. This doubling up will likely give you the amount you need to itemize.

SMART TAX TIP #2—DON'T FUND OVERHEAD OR FUND -RAISING: You don't want your dollars going to pay fat salaries, fancy overhead, or excessive fund-raising expenses. The Better Business Bureau's (BBB) Wise Giving Alliance offers guidance to donors on making informed giving decisions through their charity evaluations, various "tips" publications, and the quarterly *Better Business Bureau Wise Giving Guide*. You can access this information by calling 703-276-0100, going to www.give.org or writing them for free publications at:

BBB Wise Giving Alliance
4200 Wilson Blvd., Suite 800
Arlington, VA 22203

TIP OF THE DAY:

SMART TAX TIP #3—SAVE RECEIPTS: You should save all receipts for donations of $250 or more if you itemize. If you give away more than $250 worth of clothing throughout the year, you should have saved all the receipts that will add up to that amount. You must donate these goods to a nonprofit organization, or have that organization donate it to another needy individual. The money you donate directly to a needy person is not deductible. It would be better to donate the amount, anonymously, to your church and have them send the donation to the family in need. Check with your tax specialist every year for the latest tax laws.

TIP OF THE DAY:

SMART TAX TIP #4—START YOUR OWN FOUNDATION: If you are fortunate enough to be sitting on a large gain from a stock or mutual fund that you have held for over a year, consider using it to become what is essentially your own "foundation." For example, if you own $10,000 worth of stock that you bought years ago for only $3,000, then you can donate the stock by setting up a Fidelity Charitable Gift Fund account (call 1-800-682-4438 or go to www.charitablegift.org). By doing this, you get an immediate $10,000 tax deduction and save having to pay taxes on the $7,000 gain. In the

years to come, as that $10,000 grows, you get to instruct the company that manages your "foundation" where to donate the proceeds. Besides Fidelity, there are also charitable gift funds available through Vanguard at 1-888-383-4483 or www.vanguardcharitable.org, or Schwab at 1-800-746-6216 or www.schwabcharitable.org. It is a convenient tax-savvy way to give.

TIP OF THE DAY:

SHARE WITH HOMELESS SHELTERS/SOUP KITCHENS: Toiletries are a much requested item among homeless shelters. You often get these items for pennies or even free with coupons. You can also share the travel-sized hotel toiletries that you do not use. Soup kitchens not only need food, but they need dishwashing liquid as well. Our family donated a case of Dawn to our local shelter, and because each drop of Dawn has 40 percent more cleaning ingredients, they were able to serve seven meals a week and have that soap wash dishes for a full year!

TIP OF THE DAY:

SMART TAX TIP #5—KID PHILANTHROPISTS: Around November, let your children know that you will allow them to manage a donation in a predetermined amount ($25, $50, or whatever you have budgeted). They get to research a variety of nonprofit organizations and decide which one will receive their donation. Then donate the amount in your child's name. You get the tax benefit, your child gets the thank-you note, and you both feel good about giving.

TIP OF THE DAY:

SHARE WITH WOMEN'S SHELTERS: Women and children
who seek these shelters often arrive with only the clothes on
their backs. These shelters especially need trial-size toiletries, as
their occupants may stay for a day or for several months, as well
as children's and women's clothing. Look in the yellow pages
under "Spouse Abuse" for the phone number. Don't be surprised
if you are asked to drop off these donations at a downtown office
rather than the home itself—confidentiality is necessary for the
protection of these clients.

During a six-month period, I got thirty-five bottles of hair
coloring free with my couponing. These were donated to this
shelter with the understanding that the women could exchange
them in the local grocery store for the right shade. Sometimes it's
the little things that make the difference in a difficult situation.

SHARE WITH POSTAL WORKERS FOOD DRIVE: Every year postal workers collect millions of pounds of nonperishable food for people in need. In addition, there are Boy Scout/Girl Scout food drives and others throughout the community. Your child's school or your church may also have occasional food drives to stock community food pantries. Take some of the groceries you got from section one that you got for pennies (or free) and spread the wealth!

SHARE WITH SALVATION ARMY AND GOODWILL (www.salvationArmyUSA.org and www.goodwill.org): These nonprofit groups help support disabled Americans through the provision of jobs. Be sure to drop off your donations during business hours so you can secure a tax-deductible receipt. They also help provide clothing to third world organizations. The amount of clothing they've sent overseas in the last twenty years could fill 30,000 Sams stores! That's a good amount of cotton.

REACH THE WORLD: Now that you've shared with those in your community and state, expand your vision to the world. When I was ten years old, I began to support an international organization called EEBM that helped feed children. As I reached my thirteenth birthday, I sent more and more until I graduated from college. Now, well, we're involved with organizations that are making the life-and-death difference to literally millions of people around the world. This isn't because I'm a wonderful person, but it's because giving was part of my destiny from the time I was seven. Here is a partial list of the worldwide organizations we've sponsored, to get you started on your own destiny to reach the world. **(ADVANCED)**

TIP OF THE DAY:

SHARE WITH HOPE FOR ISRAEL (www.hope4israel.org): This nonprofit organization was started by our very own son-in-law, Moran Rosenblit. My husband jokes that he is the man who got his daughter pregnant (after a year of marriage), but since the result was the world's greatest grandson—we forgave him. Missy and her family live in Jerusalem where this organization operates a soup kitchen, offers youth programs, and stresses reconciliation between Jews and Muslims.

> Hope for Israel
> PO Box 385
> Redondo Beach, CA 90277

TIP OF THE DAY:

SHARE WITH COMPASSION INTERNATIONAL (www. compassion.com): This is an organization that is tuned in to crises and special needs as well as the general monthly needs of children around the world. They encourage communication with your child and you have the chance to see photos and read about how your child is doing in school. It's a great project for your family.

> Compassion International
> Colorado Springs, CO 80997-0001

TIP OF THE DAY:

SHARE WITH WORLD VISION (www.worldvision.org): On their "ways to give" link, you can choose where you want your dollars to go. They help children in the United States as well as around the world. Go to their website or call 1-888-511-6598.

TIP OF THE DAY:

#384 SHARE WITH MISSION OF JOY (INDIA) (www.missionOfJoy.org): This is a lesser known organization that was started by two Air Force captains when they saw the needs in India. Almost 97 percent of the monthly contributions go directly to India because the ministry uses volunteer help and has very little overhead.

Mission of Joy
PO Box 64914
Tacoma, Washington 98464
253-983-9743

TIP OF THE DAY:

SHARE WITH HOUSE OF PRAYER MISSION (NEW MEXICO HOMELESS SHELTER) (www.alamohop.com): Kris King has worked with the homeless in New Mexico for over twenty years. She is familiar with those who "fly a sign" that usually says, "Will work for food." She told us emphatically, "You should never give these people money because 90 percent of them will use it to buy alcohol. Instead, donate to a local homeless shelter and give them a card with the shelter's address where they can get a shower, a bed, and a hot meal." We've supported Kris's work for the better part of a decade. For more information, contact:

Rev. Kris King
House of Prayer Mission
601 Delaware
Alamogordo, NM 88310
505-437-7880

TIP OF THE DAY:

SHARE WITH MILITARY MINISTRIES (www.milmin.org): It is said "there are no atheists in foxholes." Whether in peace or in war, American troops (soldiers, sailors, airmen, marines, coast guardsmen) need faith to anchor their souls. Those on the homefront need the same anchor as they wait in fear and uncertainty. Ellie Kay and Company, LLC, has partnered with Military Ministries and Life Today (see below) to provide free copies of my bestselling book, *Heroes at Home,* to military families around the world. This book helps to equip military families with the top ten most important characteristics of those who await their military member at home. To sponsor this ongoing goal, contact:

Military Ministries
6060 Jefferson Ave, Suite 6012
Newport News, VA 23605-3006
1-800-444-6006

TIP OF THE DAY:

SHARE WITH LIFE OUTREACH INTERNATIONAL

(www.lifetoday.org): When my first book *Shop, Save and Share* was released in 1998, the founder of this dynamic organization, James Robison, caught the vision of the "share" aspect of the book. During their annual hunger drive, we partnered with them for a week's worth of television shows and we were able to raise enough funds to provide food for over one million people in third world countries.

Furthermore, James Robison recently wanted to do something for military families and he partnered with Ellie Kay and Company, LLC, and with Military Ministries to provide free copies of my book *Heroes at Home* to every military family around the world. For more information, contact:

LIFE Outreach International
P.O. Box 982000
Fort Worth, TX 76182-8000
1-800-947-LIFE

TIP OF THE DAY:

SHARE WITH MOODY BIBLE INSTITUTE (www.moody.edu): Founded in 1886 by Dwight L. Moody, this huge organization has been committed to training young men and women in all kinds of skills that will be used on the mission field around the world. Their main areas of ministry include education, broadcasting, and publishing. In fact, you are already supporting this organization by the fact that you bought this book.

> Moody Bible Institute
> 820 N. LaSalle Blvd
> Chicago, IL 60610
> 1-800-356-6639

TIP OF THE DAY:

SHARE WITH CROWN FINANCIAL (www.crown.org): Ellie Kay and Company, LLC, has partnered with Crown since 1999. Crown's goal is to equip people worldwide to learn, apply, and teach God's financial principles. They have helped countless families learn to get back on the right track financially and have wonderful online tools such as the one-income calculator, budgetometer, credit card payment, mortgage prepayment, and others. Their radio show, *Money Matters*, is available in all fifty states, around the world, and via XM Satellite Radio and SIRIUS satellite radio.

> Crown Financial Ministries
> P.O. Box 100
> Gainesville, GA 30503-0100
> 1-800-722-1976

TIP OF THE DAY:

SHARE WITH TAKE IT TO HEART MINISTRIES (www. TakeItToHeartRadio.com): This ministry has produced some radio shows that have so inspired me and thousands of others around the world. *Take It To Heart!* is hosted by author and conference speaker Christin Ditchfield. Using real-life stories, rich word pictures, biblical illustrations, and touches of humor, Christin calls listeners to enthusiastically seek after God, giving them practical tools to help deepen their personal relationship with Christ.

Take It To Heart Radio
P.O. Box 1000
Osprey, FL 34229
1-800-478-4178

TIP OF THE DAY:

JOIN YOUR LOCAL CHURCH AND SHARE!: If you are not a part of a local church, then you and your family are missing out on some incredible opportunities. According to Barna Research Online (www. barna.org), Americans believe in the power and impact of prayer: more than four out of five adults (82 percent) pray during a typical week. Four out of five (82 percent) believe that "prayer can change what happens in a person's life." Nine out of ten adults (89 percent) agree, "there is a God who watches over you and answers your prayers." Almost nine out of ten people (87 percent) say that the universe was originally created by God. Clearly, most Americans are open to the idea of God. Are you? Then why not find a church that meets your family's unique spiritual needs. Once you find your fit, then partner with them financially so that you can reach your community with God's love.

TIP OF THE DAY:

TWENTY FREE GIFTS YOU CAN GIVE: There are certain gifts that may not be tax deductible, but their benefits are eternal and the best part is that they don't cost you anything to give. Pick one different thing from this list and "gift" it each day. By the end of the month, your attitude toward giving and toward life will be markedly different for the better. Test me and see if I'm right! **(ADVANCED)**

- Fix broken fences by mending a quarrel.

- Seek out a friend whom you haven't seen in awhile or who has been forgotten.

- Hug someone and whisper, "I love you so."

- Forgive an enemy and pray for him.

- Be patient with an angry person.

- Express gratitude to someone in your world.

- Make a child smile.

- Find the time to keep a promise.

- Make or bake something for someone else—anonymously.

- Speak kindly to a stranger and tell them a joke.

- Enter into another's sorrows and cut the pain in half.

- Smile. Laugh a little. Laugh a lot.

- Take a walk with a friend.

- Kneel down and pat a dog.

- Lessen your expectation of others.

- Apologize if you were wrong.

- Encourage an older person.

- Turn off the television and talk.

- Pray for someone who helped you when you hurt.

- Give a soft answer even though you feel strongly.

Five Bonus Tips

Tips From Down Home

I'm in my forties now. I was a sweet, little, shy Texas girl in my youth. I've been the dutiful military wife for the better part of two decades. And I've worked hard at influencing the lives of five natural children, two stepchildren, and two stepgrandbabies. If I were to express my life philosophy in five tips, here is what I would say:

LIFE IS TOO SHORT TO DRINK BAD COFFEE: Scrimp on canned corn and cars but don't scrimp on coffee. (Besides, if you like Starbucks Fraps with a shot of espresso, then order the espresso frap instead of ordering a shot in the drink, you'll save $.55 per coffee.)

THE SWEETEST DOLLAR IS THE ONE YOU CAN GIVE AWAY: If you've never learned to be a cheerful giver, then you've never learned to enjoy one of the greatest pleasures in life.

LIFE IS TOO SHORT FOR HIGH MAINTENANCE RELATIONSHIPS: You can't control who you are related to, but you can control who you choose to hang out with. Give your friends and extended family the best of who you are. If they continue to give you the worst of who they are, then emotionally move out and move on. Sometimes we have to put all of our energies into our nuclear family and its relationships, and we don't always have time for superfluous, high maintenance relationships.

 BECAUSE I'M A TEXAS WOMAN, THAT'S WHY!: Okay, so I do try to hide my accent when I'm giving financial advice on CNN. I mean, no one wants to hear some Southern gal on television, saying, "Well, ya just need ta get yerself some of them there mootual funds and maybe get yerself an IRA or two."

On the other hand, I am who God made me to be in this world and I *am* a Southern girl—and proud of it! You are who He made you to be—today. Be who you are and make peace with your God, your body, your accent, your upbringing, and basically—yourself. This doesn't mean we have license to be a toad, but we *do* have the freedom to pursue life as we were created to do without listening to the voices of those who never made peace with themselves. Be the best "you" that you can be—you'll never regret it.

 IF YOU AIM AT NOTHING, YOU'LL HIT IT EVERY TIME: Successful people don't just "happen" on to good things. They don't "happen" to raise quality kids. They don't "happen" to have good marriages. They don't "happen" to make a significant living. Instead, these people listen, learn, and live well. They have a plan. They follow that plan and when they mess up, they don't give up and beat themselves about the head and shoulders. They get up, dust themselves off, ask for forgiveness if necessary, and get back on track with the plan. Hitting the target means there are plans in regards to business, goals, and education. But the plan doesn't stop there: successful people have a plan for parenting and relationships. They have a plan for their health and their soul's deepest longings.

The only true failure is the failure to get started—it's not too late. I think the best plans invite the God factor into the process, and then the temporal becomes eternal. The little becomes much and the meaningless takes on significance. How do I know this to be true? Because I'm a Texas woman, that's why!

High in the blue above
Swifts whirl and call—
We are down a-dabbling,
Up tails all!

"I don't know that I think so *very* much of that little song, Rat," observed the Mole cautiously. He was no poet himself and didn't care who knew it; and he had a candid nature.

"Nor don't the ducks neither," replied the Rat cheerfully. "They say, '*Why* can't fellows be allowed to do what they like *when* they like and *as* they like, instead of other fellows sitting on banks and watching them all the time and making remarks and poetry and things about them? What *nonsense* it all is!' That's what the ducks say."

"So it is, so it is," said the Mole, with great heartiness.

"No, it isn't!" cried the Rat indignantly.

"Well then, it isn't, it isn't," replied the Mole soothingly. "But what I wanted to ask you was, won't you take me to call on Mr Toad? I've heard so much about him, and I do so want to make his acquaintance."

"Why, certainly," said the good-natured Rat, jumping to his feet and dismissing poetry from his up *long* ago. Sheer waste of time, that's what it makes me downright sorry to see you fellows, ought to know better, spending all your ener- in that aimless manner. No, I've discovered the thing, the only genuine occupation for a life- . I propose to devote the remainder of mine to nd can only regret the wasted years that lie nd me, squandered in trivialities. Come with dear Ratty, and your amiable friend also, if he be so very good, just as far as the stable-yard, you shall see what you shall see!"

e led the way to the stable-yard accordingly, the following with a most mistrustful expression; there, drawn out of the coach-house into the n, they saw a gipsy caravan, shining with vness, painted a canary-yellow picked out with en and red wheels.

There you are!" cried the Toad, straddling and anding himself "There's real life for you, bodied in that little cart. The open road, the sty highway, the heath, the common, the dgerows, the rolling downs! Camps, villages, wns, cities! Here to-day, up and off to somewhere e to-morrow! Travel, change, interest, excite- nt! The whole world before you, and a horizon

mind for the day. "Get the boat out, and we'll paddle up there at once. It's never the wrong time to call on Toad. Early or late he's always the same fellow. Always good-tempered, always glad to see you, always sorry when you go!"

"He must be a very nice animal," observed the Mole, as he got into the boat and took the sculls, while the Rat settled himself comfortably in the stern.

"He is indeed the best of animals," replied Rat. "So simple, so good-natured, and so affectionate. Perhaps he's not very clever—we can't all be geniuses; and it may be that he is both boastful and conceited. But he has got some great qualities, has Toady."

Rounding a bend in the river, they came in sight of a handsome, dignified old house of mellowed red brick, with well-kept lawns reaching down to the water's edge.

"There's Toad Hall," said the Rat; "and that creek on the left, where the notice-board says 'Private. No landing allowed', leads to his boat-house, where we'll leave the boat. The stables are over there to the right. That's the banqueting-hall you're looking at now—very old, that is. Toad is rather rich, you know, and this is really one of the nicest houses in these parts, though we never admit as much to Toad."

They glided up the creek, and the Mole shipped his sculls as they passed into the shadow of a large boat-house. Here they saw many handsome boats, slung from the cross-beams or hauled up on a slip, but none in the water; and the place had an unused and a deserted air.

The Rat looked around him. "I understand," said he. "Boating is played out. He's tired of it, and done with it. I wonder what new fad he has taken up now? Come along and let's look him up. We shall hear all about it quite soon enough."

They disembarked, and strolled across the gay flower-decked lawns in search of Toad, whom they presently happened upon resting in a wicker garden-chair, with a preoccupied expression of face, and a large map spread out on his knees.

"Hooray," he cried, jumping up on seeing them, "this is splendid!" He shook the paws of both of them warmly, never waiting for an introduction to the Mole. "How *kind* of you!" he went on, dancing round them. "I was just going to send a boat down the river for you, Ratty, with strict orders that you were to be fetched up here at once, whatever you

were doing. I want you badly—
what will you take? Come insid
thing! You don't know how luck
up just now!"

"Let's sit quiet a bit, Toad
throwing himself into an easy cha
took another by the side of him an
remark about Toad's "delightful r

"Finest house on the whole ri
boisterously. "Or anywhere else,
he could not help adding.

Here the Rat nudged the Mole. U
Toad saw him do it, and turned ver
a moment's painful silence. Then
laughing. "All right, Ratty," he sai
way, you know. And it's not such a
is it? You know you rather like it you
here. Let's be sensible. You are the
wanted. You've got to help me. It's m

"It's about your rowing, I suppose
with an innocent air. "You're getting
though you splash a good bit still. Witl
patience, and any quantity of coaching

"O, pooh! boating?" interrupted
great disgust. "Silly boyish amuseme

that
is. It
who
gies
real
time
it, a
beh
me,
will
and

Rat
and
op
ne
gre

exp
em
du
he
to
els
m

that's always changing! And mind, this is the very finest cart of its sort that was ever built, without exception. Come inside and look at the arrangements. Planned 'em all myself, I did!"

The Mole was tremendously interested and excited, and followed him eagerly up the steps and into the interior of the caravan. The Rat only snorted and thrust his hands deep into his pockets, remaining where he was.

It was indeed very compact and comfortable. Little sleeping-bunks—a little table that folded up against the wall—a cooking-stove, lockers, book-shelves, a bird cage with a bird in it; and pots, pans, jugs and kettles of every size and variety.

"All complete!" said the Toad triumphantly, pulling open a locker. "You see—biscuits, potted lobster, sardines—everything you can possibly want. Soda-water here—baccy there—letter-paper, bacon, jam, cards and dominoes—you'll find," he continued, as they descended the steps again, "you'll find that nothing whatever has been forgotten, when we make our start this afternoon."

"I beg your pardon," said the Rat slowly, as he chewed a straw, "but did I overhear you say something about '*we*', and '*start*', and '*this afternoon*'?"

"Now, you dear good old Ratty," said Toad imploringly, "don't begin talking in that stiff and sniffy sort of way, because you know you've *got* to come. I can't possibly manage without you, so please consider it settled, and don't argue—it's the one thing I can't stand. You surely don't mean to stick to your dull fusty old river all your life, and just live in a hole in a bank, and *boat*? I want to show you the world! I'm going to make an *animal* of you, my boy!"

"I don't care," said the Rat doggedly. "I'm not coming, and that's flat. And I *am* going to stick to my old river, *and* live in a hole, *and* boat, as I've always done. And what's more, Mole's going to stick to me and do as I do, aren't you, Mole?"

"Of course I am," said the Mole loyally. "I'll always stick to you, Rat, and what you say is to be— has got to be. All the same, it sounds as if it might have been—well, rather fun, you know!" he added wistfully. Poor Mole! The Life Adventurous was so new a thing to him and so thrilling; and this fresh aspect of it was so tempting; and he had fallen in love at first sight with the canary-coloured cart and all its little fitments.

The Rat saw what was passing in his mind, and wavered. He hated disappointing people, and he was fond of the Mole, and would do almost anything to oblige him. Toad was watching both of them closely.

"Come along in and have some lunch," he said diplomatically, "and we'll talk it over. We needn't decide anything in a hurry. Of course, *I* don't really care. I only want to give pleasure to you fellows. 'Live for others!' That's my motto in life."

During luncheon—which was excellent, of course, as everything at Toad Hall always was—the Toad simply let himself go. Disregarding the Rat, he proceeded to play upon the inexperienced Mole as on a harp. Naturally a voluble animal, and always mastered by his imagination, he painted the prospects of the trip and the joys of the open life and the road-side in such glowing colours that the Mole could hardly sit in his chair for excitement. Somehow, it soon seemed taken for granted by all three of them that the trip was a settled thing; and the Rat, though still unconvinced in his mind, allowed his good-nature to over-ride his personal objections. He could not bear to disappoint his two friends, who were already deep in schemes and anticipations, planning out each day's separate occupation for several weeks ahead.

When they were quite ready, the now triumphant Toad led his companions to the paddock and set them to capture the old grey horse, who, without having been consulted, and to his own extreme annoyance, had been told off by Toad for the dustiest job in this dusty expedition. He frankly preferred the paddock, and took a deal of catching. Meantime Toad packed the lockers still tighter with necessaries, and hung nose-bags, nets of onions, bundles of hay, and baskets from the bottom of the cart. At last the horse was caught and harnessed, and they set off, all talking at once, each animal either trudging by the side of the cart or sitting on the shaft, as the humour took him. It was a golden

afternoon. The smell of the dust they kicked up was rich and satisfying; out of thick orchards on either side of the road, birds called and whistled to them cheerily; good-natured wayfarers, passing them, gave them "Good day", or stopped to say nice things about their beautiful cart; and rabbits, sitting at their front doors in the hedgerows, held up their forepaws, and said, "O my! O my! O my!"

Late in the evening, tired and happy and miles from home, they drew up on a remote common far from habitations, turned the horse loose to graze, and ate their simple supper sitting on the grass by the side of the cart. Toad talked big about all he was going to do in the days to come, while stars grew fuller and larger all around them, and a yellow moon, appearing suddenly and silently from nowhere in particular, came to keep them company and listen to their talk. At last they turned into their little bunks in the cart; and Toad, kicking out his legs, sleepily said, "Well, good night, you fellows! This is the real life for a gentleman! Talk about your old river!"

"I *don't* talk about my river," replied the patient Rat. "You know I don't, Toad. But I *think* about it," he added pathetically, in a lower tone: "I think about it—all the time!"

The Mole reached out from under his blanket, felt for the Rat's paw in the darkness, and gave it a squeeze. "I'll do whatever you like, Ratty," he whispered. "Shall we run away to-morrow morning, quite early—*very* early—and go back to our dear old hole on the river?"

"No, no, we'll see it out," whispered back the Rat. "Thanks awfully, but I ought to stick by Toad till this trip is ended. It wouldn't be safe for him to be left to himself It won't take very long. His fads never do. Good night!"

The end was indeed nearer than even the Rat suspected.

After so much open air and excitement the Toad slept very soundly, and no amount of shaking could rouse him out of bed next morning. So the Mole and Rat turned to, quietly and manfully, and while the Rat saw to the horse, and lit a fire, and cleaned last night's cups and platters, and got things ready for breakfast, the Mole trudged off to the nearest village, a long way off, for milk and eggs and various necessaries the Toad had, of course, forgotten to provide. The hard work had all been done, and the two animals were resting, thoroughly exhausted, by the time Toad appeared on the scene, fresh and gay, remarking what a pleasant easy life it was they were all leading now, after the cares and worries and fatigues of housekeeping at home.

They had a pleasant ramble that day over grassy downs and along narrow by-lanes, and camped, as before, on a common, only this time the two guests took care that Toad should do his fair share of work. In consequence, when the time came for starting next morning, Toad was by no means so rapturous about the simplicity of the primitive life, and indeed attempted to resume his place in his bunk, whence he was hauled by force. Their way lay, as before, across country by narrow lanes, and it was not till the afternoon that they came out on the high road their first high road; and there disaster, fleet and unforeseen, sprang out on them—disaster momentous indeed to their expedition, but simply overwhelming in its effect on the after-career of Toad.

They were strolling along the high road easily, the Mole by the horse's head, talking to him, since the horse had complained that he was being frightfully left out of it, and nobody considered him in the least; the Toad and the Water Rat walking behind the cart talking together—at least Toad was talking, and Rat was saying at intervals, "Yes, precisely; and what did *you* say to *him*?"—and thinking all the time of something very different, when far behind them they heard a faint warning hum, like the drone of a distant bee. Glancing back, they saw a small cloud of dust, with a dark centre of energy advancing on them at incredible speed, while from out of the dust a faint "Poop-poop!" wailed like an uneasy animal in pain. Hardly regarding it, they turned to resume their conversation, when in an instant (as it seemed) the peaceful scene was changed, and with a blast of wind and a whirl of sound that made them jump for the nearest ditch, it was on them! The "poop-poop" rang with a brazen shout in their ears, they had a moment's glimpse of an interior of glittering plate-glass and rich morocco, and the magnificent motor-car, immense, breath-snatching, passionate, with its pilot tense and hugging his wheel, possessed all earth and air for the fraction of a second, flung an enveloping cloud of dust that blinded and enwrapped them utterly, and then dwindled to a speck in the far distance, changed back into a droning bee once more.

The old grey horse, dreaming, as he plodded along, of his quiet paddock, in a new raw situation such as this simply abandoned himself to his natural emotions. Rearing, plunging, backing steadily, in spite of all the Mole's efforts at his head, and all the Mole's lively language directed at his better feelings, he drove the cart backwards towards the deep ditch at the side of the road. It wavered an instant—then there was a heartrending crash—and the canary-coloured cart, their pride and their joy, lay on its side in the ditch, an irredeemable wreck.

The Rat danced up and down in the road, simply transported with passion. "You villains!" he shouted, shaking both fists, "You scoundrels, you highwaymen, you—you—road-hogs!—I'll have the law on you! I'll report you! I'll take you through all the Courts!" His home-sickness had quite slipped away from him, and for the moment he was the skipper of the canary-coloured vessel driven on a shoal by the reckless jockeying of rival mariners, and he was trying to recollect all the fine and biting things he used to say to masters of steam-launches when their wash, as they drove too near the bank, used to flood his parlour carpet at home.

Toad sat straight down in the middle of the dusty road, his legs stretched out before him, and stared fixedly in the direction of the disappearing motor-car. He breathed short, his face wore a placid, satisfied expression, and at intervals he faintly murmured "Poop-poop!"

The Mole was busy trying to quiet the horse, which he succeeded in doing after a time. Then he went to look at the cart, on its side in the ditch. It was indeed a sorry sight. Panels and windows smashed, axles hopelessly bent, one wheel off, sardine-tins scattered over the wide world, and the bird in the bird-cage sobbing pitifully and calling to be let out.

The Rat came to help him, but their united efforts were not sufficient to right the cart. "Hi! Toad!" they cried. "Come and bear a hand, can't you!"

The Toad never answered a word, or budged from his seat in the road; so they went to see what was the matter with him. They found him in a sort of trance, a happy smile on his face, his eyes still fixed on the dusty wake of their destroyer. At intervals he was still heard to murmur "Poop-poop!"

The Rat shook him by the shoulder. "Are you coming to help us, Toad?" he demanded sternly.

"Glorious, stirring sight!" murmured Toad, never offering to move. "The poetry of motion! The *real* way to travel! The *only* way to travel! Here to-day—in next week to-morrow! Villages skipped, towns and cities jumped—always somebody else's horizon! O bliss! O poop-poop! O my! O my!"

"O *stop* being an ass, Toad!" cried the Mole despairingly.

"And to think I never *knew*!" went on the Toad in a dreamy monotone. "All those wasted years that lie behind me. I never knew, never even *dreamt*! But now—but *now* that I know, now that I fully realize! O what a flowery track lies spread before me, hence-forth! What dust-clouds shall spring up behind me as I speed on my reckless way! What carts I shall fling carelessly into the ditch in the wake of my magnificent onset! Horrid little carts—common carts—canary-coloured carts!"

"What are we to do with him?" asked the Mole of the Water Rat.

"Nothing at all," replied the Rat firmly. "Because there is really nothing to be done. You see, I know him from of old. He is now possessed. He has got a new craze, and it always takes him that way, in its first stage. He'll continue like that for days now, like an animal walking in a happy dream, quite useless for all practical purposes. Never mind him. Let's go and see what there is to be done about the cart."

A careful inspection showed them that, even if they succeeded in righting it by themselves, the cart would travel no longer. The axles were in a hopeless state, and the missing wheel was shattered into pieces.

The Rat knotted the horse's reins over his back and took him by the head, carrying the bird-cage and its hysterical occupant in the other hand. "Come on!" he said grimly to the Mole. "It's five or six miles to the nearest town, and we shall just have to walk it. The sooner we make a start the better."

"But what about Toad?" asked the Mole anxiously, as they set off together. "We can't leave him here, sitting in the middle of the road by himself, in the distracted state he's in! It's not safe. Supposing another Thing were to come along?"

"O, *bother* Toad," said the Rat savagely; "I've done with him." They had not proceeded very far on their way, however, when there was a pattering of feet behind them, and Toad caught them up and thrust a paw inside the elbow of each of them; still breathing short and staring into vacancy.

"Now, look here, Toad!" said the Rat sharply: "as soon as we get to the town, you'll have to go straight to the police-station, and see if they know anything about that motor-car and who it belongs to, and lodge a complaint against it. And then you'll have to go to a blacksmith's or a wheelwright's and arrange for the cart to be fetched and mended and put to rights. It'll take time, but it's not quite a hopeless smash. Meanwhile, the Mole and I will go to an inn and find comfortable rooms where we can stay till the cart's ready, and till your nerves have recovered their shock."

"Police-station! Complaint!" murmured Toad dreamily. "Me *complain* of that beautiful, that heavenly vision that has been vouchsafed me! *Mend* the *cart*! I've done with carts for ever. I never want to see the cart, or to hear of it again. O Ratty! You can't think how obliged I am to you for consenting to come on this trip! I wouldn't have gone without you, and then I might never have seen that—that swan, that sunbeam, that thunderbolt! I might never have heard that entrancing sound, or smelt that bewitching smell! I owe it all to you, my best of friends!"

The Rat turned from him in despair. "You see what it is?" he said to the Mole, addressing him across Toad's head: "He's quite hopeless. I give it up—when we get to the town we'll go to the railway station, and with luck we may pick up a train there that'll get us back to River Bank to-night. And if ever you catch me going a-pleasuring with this provoking animal again—" He snorted, and during the rest of that weary trudge addressed his remarks exclusively to Mole.

On reaching the town they went straight to the station and deposited Toad in the second-class waiting-room, giving a porter twopence to keep a strict eye on him. They then left the horse at an inn stable, and gave what directions they could about the cart and its contents. Eventually, a slow train having landed them at a station not very far from Toad Hall, they escorted the spellbound, sleep-walking Toad to his door, put him inside it, and instructed his housekeeper to feed him, undress him, and put him to bed. Then they got out their boat from the boat-house, sculled down the river home, and at a very late hour sat down to supper in their own cosy riverside parlour, to the Rat's great joy and contentment.

The following evening the Mole, who had risen late and taken things very easy all day, was sitting on the bank fishing, when the Rat, who had been looking up his friends and gossiping, cane strolling along to find him. "Heard the news?" he said. "There's nothing else being talked about, all along the river bank. Toad went up to Town by an early train this morning. And he has ordered a large and very expensive motor-car."

CHAPTER 3

The Wild Wood

The Mole had long wanted to make the acquaintance of the Badger. He seemed, by all accounts, to be such an important personage and, though rarely visible, to make his unseen influence felt by everybody about the place. But whenever the Mole mentioned his wish to the Water Rat he always found himself put off. "It's all right," the Rat would say. "Badger'll turn up some day or other—he's always turning up—and then I'll introduce you. The best of fellows! But you must not only take him as you find him, but *when* you find him."

"Couldn't you ask him here—dinner or something?" said the Mole.

"He wouldn't come," replied the Rat simply. "Badger hates Society, and invitations, and dinner, and all that sort of thing."

"Well, then, supposing we go and call on *him*?" suggested the Mole.

"O, I'm sure he wouldn't like that at *all*," said the Rat, quite alarmed. "He's so very shy, he'd be sure to be offended. I've never even ventured to call on him at his own home myself, though I know him so well. Besides, we can't. It's quite out of the question, because he lives in the very middle of the Wild Wood."

"Well, supposing he does," said the Mole. "You told me the Wild Wood was all right, you know."

"Oh, I know, I know, so it is," replied the Rat evasively. "But I think we won't go there just now. Not *just* yet. It's a long way, and he wouldn't be at home at this time of year anyhow, and he'll be coming along some day, if you'll wait quietly."

The Mole had to be content with this. But the Badger never came along, and every day brought its amusements, and it was not till summer was long over, and cold and frost and miry ways kept them much indoors, and the swollen river raced past outside their windows with a speed that mocked at boating of any sort or kind, that he found his thoughts dwelling again with much persistence on the solitary grey Badger, who lived

his own life by himself, in his hole in the middle of
the Wild Wood.

In the winter time the Rat slept a great deal, retir-
ing early and rising late. During his short day he
sometimes scribbled poetry or did other small
domestic jobs about the house; and, of course,
there were always animals dropping in for a chat,
and consequently there was a good deal of story-
telling and comparing notes on the past summer
and all its doings.

Such a rich chapter it had been, when one came
to look back on it all! With illustrations so numerous and so very highly coloured! The pageant of the
river bank had marched steadily along, unfolding
itself in scene-pictures that succeeded each other in
stately procession. Purple loosestrife arrived early,
shaking luxuriant tangled locks along the edge of
the mirror whence its own face laughed back at it.
Willow-herb, tender and wistful, like a pink sunset
cloud was not slow to follow. Comfrey, the purple
hand-in-hand with the white, crept forth to take its
place in the line; and at last one morning the diffi-
dent and delaying dog-rose stepped delicately on
the stage, and one knew, as if string music had
announced it in stately chords that strayed into a

gavotte, that June at last was here. One member of
the company was still awaited; the shepherd-boy for
the nymphs to woo, the knight for whom the ladies
waited at the window, the prince that was to kiss the
sleeping summer back to life and love. But when
meadow-sweet, debonair and odorous in amber
jerkin, moved graciously to his place in the group,
then the play was ready to begin.

And what a play it had been! Drowsy animals,
snug in their holes while wind and rain were batter-
ing at their doors, recalled still keen mornings an
hour before sunrise, when the white mist, as yet
undispersed, clung closely along the surface of the
water; then the shock of the early plunge, the scam-
per along the bank, and the radiant transformation
of earth, air, and water, when suddenly the sun was
with them again, and grey was gold and colour was
born and sprang out of the earth once more. They
recalled the languorous siesta of hot midday, deep in
green undergrowth, the sun striking through in tiny
golden shafts and spots; the boating and bathing of
the afternoon, the rambles along dusty lanes and
through yellow cornfields; and the long cool evening
at last, when so many threads were gathered up, so
many friendships rounded, and so many adventures

planned for the morrow. There was plenty to talk
about on those short winter days when the animals
found themselves round the fire; still, the Mole had
a good deal of spare time on his hands, and so one
afternoon, when the Rat in his arm-chair before the
blaze was alternately dozing and trying over rhymes
that wouldn't fit, he formed the resolution to go out
by himself and explore the Wild Wood, and perhaps
strike up an acquaintance with Mr Badger.

It was a cold still afternoon with a hard steely sky
overhead, when he slipped out of the warm parlour
into the open air. The country lay bare and entirely
leafless around him, and he thought that he had
never seen so far and so intimately into the insides
of things as on that winter day when Nature was
deep in her annual slumber and seemed to have
kicked the clothes off. Copses, dells, quarries and
all hidden places, which had been mysterious mines
for exploration in leafy summer, now exposed
themselves and their secrets pathetically, and
seemed to ask him to overlook their shabby poverty
for a while, till they could riot in rich masquerade as
before, and trick and entice him with the old decep-
tions. It was pitiful in a way, and yet cheering—even
exhilarating. He was glad that he liked the country

undecorated, hard, and stripped of its finery. He had got down to the bare bones of it, and they were fine and strong and simple. He did not want the warm clover and the play of seeding grasses; the screens of quickset, the billowy drapery of beech and elm seemed best away; and with great cheerfulness of spirit he pushed on towards the Wild Wood, which lay before him low and threatening, like a black reef in some still southern sea.

There was nothing to alarm him at first entry. Twigs crackled under his feet, logs tripped him, funguses on stumps resembled caricatures, and startled him for the moment by their likeness to something familiar and far away; but that was all fun, and exciting. It led him on, and he penetrated to where the light was less, and trees crouched nearer and nearer, and holes made ugly mouths at him on either side.

Everything was very still now. The dusk advanced on him steadily, rapidly, gathering in behind and before; and the light seemed to be draining away like flood-water.

Then the faces began.

It was over his shoulder, and indistinctly, that he first thought he saw a face: a little evil wedge-shaped face, looking out at him from a hole. When he turned and confronted it, the thing had vanished. He quickened his pace, telling himself cheerfully not to begin imagining things, or there would be simply no end to it. He passed another hole, and another, and another; and then—yes!—no!—yes! certainly a little narrow face, with hard eyes, had flashed up for an instant from a hole, and was gone. He hesitated— braced himself up for an effort and strode on. Then suddenly, and as if it had been so all the time, every hole, far and near, and there were hundreds of them, seemed to possess its face, coming and going rapidly, all fixing on him glances of malice and hatred: all hard-eyed and evil and sharp.

If he could only get away from the holes in the banks, he thought, there would be no more faces. He swung off the path and plunged into the untrodden places of the wood.

Then the whistling began.

Very faint and shrill it was, and far behind him, when first he heard it; but somehow it made him hurry forward. Then, still very faint and shrill, it sounded far ahead of him, and made him hesitate and want to go back. As he halted in indecision it broke out on either side, and seemed to be caught up and passed on throughout the whole length of the wood to its furthest limit. They were up and alert and ready, evidently, whoever they were! And he—he was alone, and unarmed, and far from any help; and the night was closing in.

Then the pattering began.

He thought it was only falling leaves at first, so slight and delicate was the sound of it. Then as it grew it took a regular rhythm, and he knew it for nothing else but the pat-pat-pat of little feet, still a very long way off. Was it in front or behind? It seemed to be first one, then the other, then both. It grew and it multiplied, till from every quarter as he listened anxiously, leaning this way and that, it seemed to be closing in on him. As he stood still to hearken, a rabbit came running hard towards him through the trees. He waited, expecting it to slacken pace, or to swerve from him into a different course. Instead, the animal almost brushed him as it dashed past, his face set and hard, his eyes staring. "Get out of this, you fool, get out," the Mole heard him mutter as he swung round a stump and disappeared down a friendly burrow.

The pattering increased till it sounded like sudden hail on the dry-leaf carpet spread around him. The whole wood seemed running now, running hard, hunting, chasing, closing in round something or—somebody? In panic, he began to run too, aimlessly, he knew not whither. He ran up against things, he fell over things and into things, he darted under things and dodged round things. At last he took refuge in the dark deep hollow of an old beech tree, which offered shelter, concealment— perhaps even safety, but who could tell? Anyhow, he was too tired to run any further, and could only snuggle down into the dry leaves which had drifted into the hollow and hope he was safe for the time. and as he lay there panting and trembling, and listened to the whistlings and the patterings outside, he knew it at last, in all its fullness, that dread thing which other little dwellers in field and hedgerow had encountered here, and known as their darkest moment—that thing which the Rat had vainly tried to shield him from—the Terror of the Wild Wood!

Meantime the Rat, warm and comfortable, dozed by his fireside. His paper of half-finished verses slipped from his knee, his head fell back, his mouth opened, and he wandered by the verdant banks of dream-rivers. Then a coal slipped, the fire crackled and sent up a spurt of flame, and he woke with a start. Remembering what he had been engaged upon, he reached down to the floor for his verses, pored over them for a minute, and then looked round for the Mole to ask him if he knew a good rhyme for something or other.

But the Mole was not there.

He listened for a time. The house seemed very quiet.

Then he called "Moly!" several times, and, receiving no answer, got up and went out into the hall.

The Mole's cap was missing from its accustomed peg. His goloshes, which always lay by the umbrella-stand, were also gone.

The Rat left the house and carefully examined the muddy surface of the ground outside, hoping to find the Mole's tracks. There they were, sure enough. The goloshes were new, just bought for the winter, and the pimples on their soles were fresh and sharp. He could see the imprints of them in the mud, running along straight and purposeful, leading direct to the Wild Wood.

The Rat looked very grave, and stood in deep thought for a minute or two. Then he re-entered the house, strapped a belt round his waist, shoved a brace of pistols into it, took up a stout cudgel that stood in a corner of the hall, and set off for the Wild Wood at a smart pace.

It was already getting towards dusk when he reached the first fringe of trees and plunged without hesitation into the wood, looking anxiously on either side for any sign of his friend. Here and there wicked little faces popped out of holes, but vanished immediately at sight of the valorous animal, his pistols, and the great ugly cudgel in his grasp; and the whistling and pattering, which he had heard quite plainly on his first entry, died away and ceased, and all was very still. He made his way manfully through the length of the wood, to its furthest edge; then, forsaking all paths, he set himself to traverse it, laboriously working over the whole ground, and all the time calling out cheerfully, "Moly, Moly, Moly! Where are you? It's me—it's old Rat!"

He had patiently hunted through the wood for an hour or more, when at last to his joy he heard a little answering cry. Guiding himself by the sound, he made his way through the gathering darkness to the foot of an old beech tree, with a hole in it, and from out of the hole came a feeble voice, saying, "Ratty! Is that really you?"

The Rat crept into the hollow, and there he found the Mole, exhausted and still trembling. "O, Rat!" he cried, "I've been so frightened, you can't think!"

"Oh, I quite understand," said the Rat soothingly. "You shouldn't really have gone and done it, Mole. I did my best to keep you from it. We river-bankers, we hardly ever come here by ourselves. If we have to come, we come in couples, at least; then we're generally all right. Besides, there are a hundred things one has to know, which we understand all about and you don't, as yet. I mean passwords, and signs, and sayings which have power and effect, and plants you carry in your pocket, and verses you repeat, and dodges and tricks you practise; all simple enough when you know them, but they've got to be known if you're small, or you'll find yourself in trouble. Of course if you were Badger or Otter, it would be quite another matter."

"Surely the brave Mr Toad wouldn't mind coming here by himself, would he?" inquired the Mole.

"Old Toad?" said the Rat, laughing heartily. "He wouldn't show his face here alone, not for a whole hatful of golden guineas, Toad wouldn't."

The Mole was greatly cheered by the sound of the Rat's careless laughter, as well as by the sight of his stick and his gleaming pistols, and he stopped shivering and began to feel bolder and more himself again.

"Now then," said the Rat presently, "we really must pull ourselves together and make a start for home while there's still a little light left. It will never do to spend the night here, you understand. Too cold, for one thing."

"Dear Ratty," said the poor Mole, "I'm dreadfully sorry, but I'm simply dead beat and that's a solid fact. You *must* let me rest here a while longer, and get my strength back, if I'm to get home at all."

"O, all right," said the good-natured Rat, "rest away. It's pretty nearly pitch dark now, anyhow; and there ought to be a bit of a moon later."

So the Mole got well into the dry leaves and stretched himself out, and presently dropped off into sleep, though of a broken and troubled sort; while the Rat covered himself up, too, as best he might, for warmth, and lay patiently waiting, with a pistol in his paw.

When at last the Mole woke up, much refreshed and in his usual spirits, the Rat said, "Now then! I'll just take a look outside and see if everything's quiet, and then we really must be off."

He went to the entrance of their retreat and put his head out. Then the Mole heard him saying quietly to himself, "Hullo! hullo! here—*is*—a—go!"

"What's up, Ratty?" asked the Mole.

"*Snow* is up," replied the Rat briefly; "or rather, *down*. It's snowing hard."

The Mole came and crouched beside him, and, looking out, saw the wood that had been so dreadful to him in quite a changed aspect. Holes, hollows, pools, pitfalls, and other black menaces to the wayfarer were vanishing fast, and a gleaming carpet of faery was springing up everywhere, that looked too delicate to be trodden upon by rough feet. A fine powder filled the air and caressed the cheek with a tingle in its touch, and the black boles of the trees showed up in a light that seemed to come from below.

"Well, well, it can't be helped," said the Rat after pondering. "We must make a start, and take our chance, I suppose. The worst of it is, I don't exactly know where we are. And now this snow makes everything look so very different."

It did indeed. The Mole would not have known that it was the same wood. However, they set out bravely, and took the line that seemed most promising, holding on to each other and pretending with invincible cheerfulness that they recognized an old friend in every fresh tree that grimly and silently greeted them, or saw openings, gaps, or paths with a familiar turn in them, in the monotony of white space and black tree-trunks that refused to vary.

An hour or two later—they had lost all count of time—they pulled up, dispirited, weary, and hopelessly at sea, and sat down on a fallen tree-trunk to recover their breath and consider what was to be done. They were aching with fatigue and bruised with tumbles; they had fallen into several holes and got wet through; the snow was getting so deep that they could hardly drag their little legs through it, and the trees were thicker and more like each other than ever. There seemed to be no end to this wood, and no beginning, and no difference in it, and, worst of all, no way out.

"We can't sit here very long," said the Rat. "We shall have to make another push for it, and do something or other. The cold is too awful for anything, and the snow will soon be too deep for us to wade through." He peered about him and considered. "Look here," he went on, "this is what occurs to me; There's a sort of dell down there in front of us, where the ground seems all hilly and humpy and hummocky. We'll make our way down into that, and try and find some sort of shelter, a cave or hole with a dry floor to it, out of the snow and the wind, and there we'll have a good rest before we try again, for we're both of us pretty dead beat. Besides, the snow may leave off, or something may turn up."

So once more they got on their feet, and struggled down into the dell, where they hunted about for a cave or some corner that was dry and a protection from the keen wind and the whirling snow. They were investigating one of the hummocky bits the Rat had spoken of, when suddenly the Mole tripped up and fell forward on his face with a squeal.

"O, my leg!" he cried. "O, my poor shin!" and he sat upon the snow and nursed his leg in both his front paws.

"Poor old Mole!" said the Rat kindly. "You don't seem to be having much luck to-day, do you? Let's have a look at the leg. Yes," he went on, going down on his knees to look, "you've cut your shin, sure enough. Wait till I get at my handkerchief, and I'll tie it up for you."

"I must have tripped over a hidden branch or a stump," said the Mole miserably. "O my! O my!"

"It's a very clean cut," said the Rat, examining it again attentively. "That was never done by a branch or a stump. Looks as if it was made by a sharp edge of something in metal. Funny!" He pondered a while, and examined the humps and slopes that surrounded them.

"Well, never mind what done it," said the Mole, forgetting his grammar in his pain. "It hurts just the same, whatever done it."

But the Rat, after carefully tying up the leg with his handkerchief, had left him and was busy scraping in the snow. He scratched and shovelled and explored, all four legs working busily, while the Mole waited impatiently, remarking at intervals, "O, *come* on, Rat!"

Suddenly the Rat cried "Hooray" and then "Hooray-oo-ray-oo-ray-oo-ray!" and fell to executing a feeble jig in the snow.

"What *have* you found, Ratty?" asked the Mole, still nursing his leg.

"Come and see!" said the delighted Rat, as he jigged on.

The Mole hobbled up to the spot and had a good look.

"Well," he said at last, slowly, "I *see* it right enough. Seen the same sort of thing before, lots of times. Familiar object, I call it. A door-scraper! Well, what of it? Why dance jigs round a door-scraper?"

"But don't you see what it *means*, you—you dull-witted animal?" cried the Rat impatiently.

"Of course I see what it means," replied the Mole. "It simply means that some *very* careless and forgetful person has left his door-scraper lying about in the middle of the Wild Wood, *just* where it's *sure* to trip *everybody* up. Very thoughtless of him, I call it. When I get home I shall go and complain about it to—to somebody or other, see if I don't!"

"O dear! O dear!" cried the Rat, in despair at his obtuseness.

"Here, stop arguing and come and scrape!" And he set to work again and made the snow fly in all directions around him.

After some further toil his efforts were rewarded, and a very shabby door-mat lay exposed to view.

"There, what did I tell you?" exclaimed the Rat in great triumph.

"Absolutely nothing whatever," replied the Mole, with perfect truthfulness. "Well now," he went on, "you seem to have found another piece of domestic litter, done for and thrown away, and I suppose you're perfectly happy. Better go ahead and dance your jig round that if you've got to, and get it over, and then perhaps we can go on and not waste any more time over rubbish-heaps. Can we *eat* a door-mat? Or sleep under a door-mat? Or sit on a door-mat and sledge home over the snow on it, you exasperating rodent?"

"Do—you—mean—to—say," cried the excited Rat, "that this door-mat doesn't *tell* you anything?"

"Really, Rat," said the Mole quite pettishly, "I think we've had enough of this folly. Who ever heard of a door-mat telling any one anything? They simply don't do it. They are not that sort at all. Door-mats know their place."

"Now look here, you—you thick-headed beast," replied the Rat, really angry, "this must stop. Not another word, but scrape—scrape and scratch and dig and hunt round, especially on the sides of the hummocks, if you want to sleep dry and warm tonight, for it's our last chance!"

The Rat attacked a snow-bank beside them with ardour, probing with his cudgel everywhere and then digging with fury; and the Mole scraped busily too, more to oblige the Rat than for any other reason, for his opinion was that his friend was getting light-headed.

Some ten minutes' hard work, and the point of the Rat's cudgel struck something that sounded hollow. He worked till he could get a paw through and feel; then called the Mole to come and help him. Hard at it went the two animals, till at last the result of their labours stood full in view of the astonished and hitherto incredulous Mole.

In the side of what had seemed to be a snow-bank stood a solid-looking little door, painted a dark green. An iron bell-pull hung by the side, and below it, on a small brass plate, neatly engraved in square capital letters, they could read by the aid of moonlight:

MR BADGER

The Mole fell backwards on the snow from sheer surprise and delight. "Rat!" he cried in penitence, "you're a wonder! A real wonder, that's what you are. I see it all now! You argued it out, step by step, in that wise head of yours, from the very moment that I fell and cut my shin, and you looked at the cut, and at once your majestic mind said to itself, 'Door-scraper!' And then you turned to and found the very door-scraper that done it! Did you stop there? No. Some people would have been quite satisfied; but not you. Your intellect went on working. 'Let me

only just find a door-mat,' says you to yourself, 'and my theory is proved!' And of course you found your door-mat. You're so clever, I believe you could find anything you liked. 'Now,' says you, 'that door exists, as plain as if I saw it. There's nothing else remains to be done but to find it!' Well, I've read about that sort of thing in books, but I've never come across it before in real life. You ought to go where you'll be properly appreciated. You're simply wasted here, among us fellows. If I only had your head, Ratty—"

"But as you haven't," interrupted the Rat rather unkindly, "I suppose you're going to sit on the snow all night and talk? Get up at once and hang on to that bell-pull you see there, and ring hard, as hard as you can, while I hammer!"

While the Rat attacked the door with his stick, the Mole sprang up at the bell-pull, clutched it and swung there, both feet well off the ground, and from quite a long way off they could faintly hear a deep-toned bell respond.

CHAPTER 4

Mr Badger

They waited patiently for what seemed a very long time, stamping in the snow to keep their feet warm. At last they heard the sound of slow shuffling footsteps approaching the door from the inside. It seemed, as the Mole remarked to the Rat, like some one walking in carpet slippers that were too large for him and down at heel; which was intelligent of Mole, because that was exactly what it was.

There was the noise of a bolt shot back, and the door opened a few inches, enough to show a long snout and a pair of sleepy blinking eyes.

"Now, the *very* next time this happens," said a gruff and suspicious voice, "I shall be exceedingly angry. Who is it *this* time, disturbing people on such a night? Speak up!"

"O, Badger," cried the Rat, "let us in, please. It's me, Rat, and my friend Mole, and we've lost our way in the snow."

"What, Ratty, my dear little man!" exclaimed the Badger, in quite a different voice. "Come along in, both of you, at once. Why, you must be perished. Well I never! Lost in the snow! And in the Wild Wood too, and at this time of night! But come in with you."

The two animals tumbled over each other in their eagerness to get inside, and heard the door shut behind them with great joy and relief.

The Badger, who wore a long dressing-gown, and whose slippers were indeed very down-at-heel, carried a flat candlestick in his paw and had probably been on his way to bed when their summons sounded. He looked kindly down on them and patted both their heads. "This is not the sort of night for small animals to be out," he said paternally. "I'm afraid you've been up to some of your pranks again, Ratty. But come along; come into the kitchen. There's a first-rate fire there, and supper and everything."

He shuffled on in front of them, carrying the light, and they followed him, nudging each other in an anticipating sort of way, down a long, gloomy, and to tell the truth, decidedly shabby passage, into a sort of a central hall, out of which they could dimly see other long tunnel-like passages branching, passages mysterious and without apparent end. But there were doors in the hall as well—stout oaken comfortable-looking doors. One of these the Badger flung open, and at once they found themselves in all the glow and warmth of a large fire-lit kitchen.

The floor was well-worn red brick, and on the wide hearth burnt a fire of logs, between two attractive chimney-corners tucked away in the wall, well out of any suspicion of draught. A couple of high-backed settles, facing each other on either side of the fire, gave further sitting accommodation for the sociably disposed. In the middle of the room stood a long table of plain boards placed on trestles, with benches down each side. At one end of it, where an arm-chair stood pushed back, were spread the remains of the Badger's plain but ample supper. Rows of spotless plates winked from the shelves of the dresser at the far end of the room, and from the rafters overhead hung hams, bundles of dried herbs, nets of onions, and baskets of eggs. It seemed a place where heroes could fitly feast after victory, where weary harvesters could line up in scores along the table and keep their Harvest Home with

mirth and song, or where two or three friends of
simple tastes could sit about as they pleased and eat
and smoke and talk in comfort and contentment.
The ruddy brick floor smiled up at the smoky ceil-
ing; the oaken settles, shiny with long wear,
exchanged cheerful glances with each other; plates
on the dresser grinned at pots on the shelf, and the
merry firelight flickered and played over everything
without distinction.

The kindly Badger thrust them down on a settle to
toast themselves at the fire, and bade them remove
their wet coats and boots. Then he fetched them
dressing-gowns and slippers, and himself bathed the
Mole's shin with warm water and mended the cut
with sticking-plaster till the whole thing was just as
good as new, if not better. In the embracing light and
warmth, warm and dry at last, with weary legs
propped up in front of them, and a suggestive clink of
plates being arranged on the table behind, it seemed
to the storm-driven animals, now in safe anchorage,
that the cold and trackless Wild Wood just left
outside was miles and miles away, and all that they
had suffered in it a half-forgotten dream.

When at last they were thoroughly toasted, the
Badger summoned them to the table, where he had

been busy laying a repast. They had felt pretty hungry before, but when they actually saw at last the supper that was spread for them, really it seemed only a question of what they should attack first where all was so attractive, and whether the other things would obligingly wait for them till they had time to give them attention. Conversation was impossible for a long time; and when it was slowly resumed, it was that regrettable sort of conversation that results from talking with your mouth full. The Badger did not mind that sort of thing at all, nor did he take any notice of elbows on the table, or everybody speaking at once. As he did not go into Society himself, he had got an idea that these things belonged to the things that didn't really matter. (We know of course that he was wrong, and took too narrow a view; because they do matter very much, though it would take too long to explain why.) He sat in his arm-chair at the head of the table, and nodded gravely at intervals as the animals told their story; and he did not seem surprised or shocked at anything, and he never said, "I told you so," or, "Just what I always said," or remarked that they ought to have done so-and-so, or ought not to have done something else. The Mole began to feel very friendly towards him.

When supper was really finished at last, and each animal felt that his skin was now as tight as was decently safe, and that by this time he didn't care a hang for anybody or anything, they gathered round the glowing embers of the great wood fire, and thought how jolly it was to be sitting up so late, and so independent, and so full; and after they had chatted for a time about things in general, the Badger said heartily, "Now then! tell us the news from your part of the world. How's old Toad going on?"

"O, from bad to worse," said the Rat gravely, while the Mole, cocked up on a settle and basking in the firelight, his heels higher than his head, tried to look properly mournful. "Another smash-up only last week, and a bad one. You see, he will insist on driving himself, and he's hopelessly incapable. If he'd only employ a decent, steady, well-trained animal, pay him good wages, and leave everything to him, he'd get on all right. But no; he's convinced he's a heaven-born driver, and nobody can teach him anything; and all the rest follows."

"How many has he had?" inquired the Badger gloomily.

"Smashes, or machines?" asked the Rat. "O, well, after all, it's the same thing—with Toad. This is the seventh. As for the others—you know that coach-house of his? Well, it's piled up—literally piled up to the roof—with fragments of motor-cars, none of them bigger than your hat! That accounts for the other six—so far as they can be accounted for."

"He's been in hospital three times," put in the Mole; "and as for the fines he's had to pay, it's simply awful to think of."

"Yes, and that's part of the trouble," continued the Rat. "Toad's rich, we all know; but he's not a millionaire. And he's a hopelessly bad driver, and quite regardless of law and order. Killed or ruined—it's got to be one of the two things, sooner or later. Badger! we're his friends—oughtn't we to do something?"

The Badger went through a bit of hard thinking. "Now look here!" he said at last, rather severely; "of course you know I can't do anything *now*?"

His two friends assented, quite understanding his point. No animal, according to the rules of animal-etiquette, is ever expected to do anything strenu-ous, or heroic, or even moderately active during the off-season of winter. All are sleepy—some actually asleep. All are weather-bound, more or less; and all are resting from arduous days and nights, during which every muscle in them has been severely tested, and every energy kept at full stretch.

"Very well then!" continued the Badger. "*But*, when once the year has really turned, and the nights are shorter, and half-way through them one rouses and feels fidgety and wanting to be up and doing by sunrise, if not before—*you* know—!"

Both animals nodded gravely. *They* knew!

"Well, *then*," went on the Badger, "we—that is, you and me and our friend the Mole here—we'll take Toad seriously in hand. We'll stand no nonsense whatever. We'll bring him back to reason, by force if need be. We'll *make* him be a sensible Toad. We'll—you're asleep, Rat!"

"Not me!" said the Rat, waking up with a jerk.

"He's been asleep two or three times since supper," said the Mole laughing. He himself was feeling quite wakeful and even lively, though he didn't know why. The reason was, of course, that he being naturally an underground animal by birth and breeding, the situation of Badger's house exactly suited him and made him feel at home; while the Rat, who slept every night in a bedroom the windows of which opened on a breezy river, naturally felt the atmosphere still and oppressive.

"Well, it's time we were all in bed," said the Badger, getting up and fetching flat candlesticks. "Come along, you two, and I'll show you your quarters. And take your time to-morrow morning— breakfast at any hour you please!"

He conducted the two animals to a long room that seemed half bedchamber and half loft. The Badger's winter stores, which indeed were visible everywhere, took up half the room—piles of apples, turnips, and potatoes, baskets full of nuts, and jars of honey; but the two little white beds on the remainder of the floor looked soft and inviting, and the linen on them, though coarse, was clean and smelt beautifully of lavender; and the Mole and the Water Rat, shaking off their garments in some thirty seconds, tumbled in between the sheets in great joy and contentment.

In accordance with the kindly Badger's injunctions, the two tired animals came down to breakfast very late next morning, and found a bright fire burning in the kitchen, and two young hedgehogs sitting on a bench at the table, eating oatmeal porridge out of wooden bowls. The hedgehogs dropped their spoons, rose to their feet, and ducked their heads respectfully as the two entered.

"There, sit down, sit down," said the Rat pleasantly, "and go on with your porridge. Where have you youngsters come from? Lost your way in the snow, I suppose?"

"Yes, please, sir," said the elder of the two hedgehogs respectfully. "Me and little Billy here, we was trying to find our way to school—mother *would* have us go, was the weather ever so—and of course we lost ourselves, sir, and Billy he got frightened and took and cried, being young and faint-hearted. And at last we happened up against Mr Badger's back door, and made so bold as to knock, sir, for Mr Badger he's a kind-hearted gentleman, as everyone knows—"

"I understand," said the Rat, cutting himself some rashers from a side of bacon, while the Mole dropped some eggs into a saucepan. "And what's the weather like outside? You needn't 'sir' me quite so much," he added.

"O, terrible bad, sir, terrible deep the snow is," said the hedgehog. "No getting out for the likes of you gentlemen to-day."

"Where's Mr Badger?" inquired the Mole, as he warmed the coffee-pot before the fire.

"The master's gone into his study, sir," replied the hedgehog, "and he said as how he was going to be particular busy this morning, and on no account was he to be disturbed."

This explanation, of course, was thoroughly understood by everyone present. The fact is, as already set forth, when you live a life of intense activity for six months in the year, and of comparative or actual somnolence for the other six, during the latter period you cannot be continually pleading sleepiness when there are people about or things to be done. The excuse gets monotonous. The animals well knew that Badger, having eaten a hearty breakfast, had retired to his study and settled himself in an arm-chair with his legs up on another and a red cotton handkerchief over his face, and was being "busy" in the usual way at this time of the year.

The front-door bell clanged loudly, and the Rat, who was very greasy with buttered toast, sent Billy, the smaller hedgehog, to see who it might be. There was a sound of much stamping in the hall, and presently Billy returned in front of the Otter, who threw himself on the Rat with an embrace and a shout of affectionate greeting.

"Get off!" spluttered the Rat, with his mouth full.

"Thought I should find you here all right," said the Otter cheerfully. "They were all in a great state of alarm along River Bank when I arrived this morning. Rat never been home all night—nor Mole either— something dreadful must have happened, they said; and the snow had covered up all your tracks, of course. But I knew that when people were in any fix they mostly went to Badger, or else Badger got to know of it somehow, so I came straight off here, through the Wild Wood and the snow! My! it was fine, coming through the snow as the red sun was rising and showing against the black tree-trunks! As you went along in the stillness, every now and then masses of snow slid off the branches suddenly with a flop! making you jump and run for cover. Snow-castles and snow-caverns had sprung up out of nowhere in the night—and snow bridges, terraces, ramparts—I could have stayed and played with them for hours. Here and there great branches had been torn away by the sheer weight of the snow, and robins perched and hopped on them in their perky conceited way, just as if they had done it themselves. A ragged string of wild geese passed overhead, high on the grey sky, and a few rooks whirled over the trees, inspected, and flapped off homewards with a disgusted expression; but I met no sensible being to ask the news of. About half-way across I came on a rabbit sitting on a stump, cleaning his silly face with his paws. He was a pretty scared animal when I crept up behind him and placed a heavy forepaw on his shoulder. I had to cuff his head once or twice to get any sense out of it at all. At last I managed to extract from him that Mole had been seen in the Wild Wood last night by one of them. It was the talk of the burrows, he said, how Mole, Mr Rat's particular friend, was in a bad fix; how he had lost his way, and 'They' were up and out hunting, and were chivvying him round and round. 'Then why didn't any of you *do* something?' I asked. 'You mayn't be blest with brains, but there are hundreds and hundreds of you, big, stout fellows, as fat as butter, and your burrows running in all directions, and you could have taken him in and made him safe and comfortable, or tried to, at all events.' 'What, *us*?' he merely said: '*do* something? us rabbits?' So I cuffed him again and left him. There was nothing else to be done. At any rate, I had learnt something; and if I had had the luck to meet any of 'Them' I'd have learnt something more—or *they* would."

"Weren't you at all—er—nervous?" asked the Mole, some of yesterday's terror coming back to him at the mention of the Wild Wood.

"Nervous?" The Otter showed a gleaming set of strong white teeth as he laughed. "I'd give 'em nerves if any of them tried anything on with me. Here, Mole, fry me some slices of ham, like the good little chap you are. I'm frightfully hungry, and I've got any amount to say to Ratty here. Haven't seen him for an age."

So the good-natured Mole, having cut some slices of ham, set the hedgehogs to fry it, and returned to his own breakfast, while the Otter and the Rat, their heads together, eagerly talked river-shop, which is long shop and talk that is endless, running on like the babbling river itself.

A plate of fried ham had just been cleared and sent back for more, when the Badger entered, yawning and rubbing his eyes, and greeted them all in his quiet, simple way, with kind inquiries for every one. "It must be getting on for luncheon time," he remarked to the Otter. "Better stop and have it with us. You must be hungry, this cold morning."

"Rather!" replied the Otter, winking at the Mole. "The sight of these greedy young hedgehogs stuffing themselves with fried ham makes me feel positively famished."

The hedgehogs, who were just beginning to feel hungry again after their porridge, and after working so hard at their frying, looked timidly up at Mr Badger, but were too shy to say anything.

"Here, you two youngsters be off home to your mother," said the Badger kindly. "I'll send some one with you to show you the way. You won't want any dinner to-day, I'll be bound."

He gave them sixpence apiece and a pat on the head, and they went off with much respectful swinging of caps and touching of forelocks.

Presently they all sat down to luncheon together. The Mole found himself placed next to Mr Badger, and, as the other two were still deep in river-gossip from which nothing could divert them, he took the opportunity to tell Badger how comfortable and homelike it all felt to him. "Once well under-ground," he said, "you know exactly where you are. Nothing can happen to you, and nothing can get at you. You're entirely your own master, and you don't have to consult anybody or mind what they say. Things go on all the same overhead, and you let 'em, and don't bother about 'em. When you want to, up you go, and there the things are, wait-ing for you."

The Badger simply beamed on him. "That's exactly what I say," he replied. "There's no security, or peace and tranquillity, except underground. And then, if your ideas get larger and you want to expand—why, a dig and a scrape, and there you are! If you feel your house is a bit too big, you stop up a hole or two, and there you are again! No builders, no tradesmen, no remarks passed on you by fellows looking over your wall, and, above all, no weather. Look at Rat, now. A couple of feet of flood-water, and he's got to move into hired lodgings; uncomfortable, inconveniently situated, and horribly expensive. Take Toad. I say nothing against Toad Hall; quite the best house in these parts, *as* a house. But supposing a fire breaks out— where's Toad? Supposing tiles are blown off, or walls sink or crack, or windows get broken— where's Toad? Supposing the rooms are draughty—I *hate* a draught myself—where's Toad? No, up and out of doors is good enough to roam about and get one's living in; but underground to come back to at last—that's my idea of *home*!"

The Mole assented heartily; and the Badger in consequence got very friendly with him. "When lunch is over," he said, "I'll take you all round this little place of mine. I can see you'll appreciate it. You understand what domestic architecture ought to be, you do."

After luncheon, accordingly, when the other two had settled themselves into the chimney-corner and had started a heated argument on the subject of *eels*, the Badger lighted a lantern and bade the Mole follow him. Crossing the hall, they passed down one of the principal tunnels, and the wavering light of the lantern gave glimpses on either side of rooms both large and small, some mere cupboards, others nearly as broad and imposing as Toad's dining-hall. A narrow passage at right angles led them into another corridor, and here the same thing was repeated. The Mole was staggered at the size, the extent, the ramifications of it all; at the length of the dim passages, the solid vaultings of the crammed store-chambers, the masonry everywhere, the pillars, the arches, the pavements. "How on earth, Badger," he said at last, "did you ever find time and strength to do all this? It's astonishing!"

"It *would* be astonishing indeed," said the Badger simply, "if I had done it. But as a matter of fact I did none of it—only cleaned out the passages and chambers, as far as I had need of them. There's lots more of it, all round about. I see you don't understand, and I must explain it to you. Well, very long ago, on the spot where the Wild Wood waves now, before ever it had planted itself and grown up to what it now is, there was a city—a city of people, you know. Here, where we are standing, they lived, and walked, and talked, and slept, and carried on their business. Here they stabled their horses and feasted, from here they rode out to fight or drove out to trade. They were a powerful people, and rich, and great builders. They built to last, for they thought their city would last for ever."

"But what has become of them all?" asked the Mole.

"Who can tell?" said the Badger. "People come— they stay for a while, they flourish, they build—and they go. It is their way. But we remain. There were badgers here, I've been told, long before that same city ever came to be. And now there are badgers here again. We are an enduring lot, and we may move out for a time, but we wait, and are patient, and back we come. And so it will ever be."

"Well, and when they went at last, those people?" said the Mole.

"When they went," continued the Badger, "the strong winds and persistent rains took the matter in hand, patiently, ceaselessly, year after year. Perhaps we badgers too, in our small way, helped a little—who knows? It was all down, down, down, gradually—ruin and levelling and disappearance. Then it was all up, up, up, gradually, as seeds grew to saplings, and saplings to forest trees, and bramble and fern came creeping in to help. Leaf-mould rose and obliterated, streams in their winter freshets brought sand and soil to clog and to cover, and in course of time our home was ready for us again, and we moved in. Up above us, on the surface, the same thing happened. Animals arrived, liked the look of the place, took up their quarters, settled down, spread, and flourished. They didn't bother themselves about the past—they never do; they're too busy. The place was a bit humpy and hillocky, naturally, and full of holes; but that was rather an advantage. And they don't bother about the future, either—the future when perhaps the people will move in again—for a time—as may very well be. The Wild Wood is pretty well populated by now; with all the usual lot, good, bad, and indifferent—I name no names. It takes all sorts to make a world. But I fancy you know something about them yourself by this time."

"I do indeed," said the Mole, with a slight shiver.

"Well, well," said the Badger, patting him on the shoulder, it was your first experience of them, you see. They're not so bad really; and we must all live and let live. But I'll pass the word round to-morrow, and I think you'll have no further trouble. Any friend of *mine* walks where he likes in this country, or I'll know the reason why!"

When they got back to the kitchen again, they found the Rat walking up and down, very restless. The underground atmosphere was oppressing him and getting on his nerves, and he seemed really to be afraid that the river would run away if he wasn't there to look after it. So he had his overcoat on, and his pistols thrust into his belt again. "Come along, Mole," he said anxiously, as soon as he caught sight of them. "We must get off while it's daylight. Don't want to spend another night in the Wild Wood again."

"It'll be all right, my fine fellow," said the Otter. "I'm coming along with you, and I know every path blindfold; and if there's a head that needs to be punched, you can confidently rely upon me to punch it."

"You really needn't fret, Ratty," added the Badger placidly. "My passages run further than you think, and I've bolt-holes to the edge of the wood in several directions, though I don't care for everybody to know about them. When you really have to go, you shall leave by one of my short cuts. Meantime, make yourself easy, and sit down again."

The Rat was nevertheless still anxious to be off and attend to his river, so the Badger, taking up his lantern again, led the way along a damp and airless tunnel that wound and dipped, part vaulted, part hewn through solid rock, for a weary distance that seemed to be miles. At last daylight began to show itself confusedly through tangled growth overhanging the mouth of the passage; and the Badger, bidding them a hasty good-bye, pushed them hurriedly through the opening, made everything look as natural as possible again, with creepers, brushwood, and dead leaves, and retreated.

They found themselves standing on the very edge of the Wild Wood. Rocks and brambles and tree-roots behind them, confusedly heaped and tangled; in front, a great space of quiet fields, hemmed by lines of hedges black on the snow, and, far ahead, a glint of the familiar old river, while the wintry sun hung red and low on the horizon. The Otter, as knowing all the paths, took charge of the party, and they trailed out on a bee-line for a distant stile. Pausing there a moment and looking back, they saw the whole mass of the Wild Wood, dense, menacing, compact, grimly set in vast white surroundings; simultaneously they turned and made swiftly for home, for firelight and the familiar things it played on, for the voice, sounding cheerily outside their window, of the river that they knew and trusted in all its moods, that never made them afraid with any amazement.

As he hurried along, eagerly anticipating the moment when he would be at home again among the things he knew and liked, the Mole saw clearly that he was an animal of tilled field and hedgerow, linked to the ploughed furrow, the frequented pasture, the lane of evening lingerings, the cultivated garden-plot. For others the asperities, the stubborn endurance, or the clash of actual conflict, that went with Nature in the rough; he must be wise, must keep to the pleasant places in which his lines were laid and which held adventure enough, in their way, to last for a lifetime.

CHAPTER 5

Dulce Domum

The sheep ran huddling together against the hurdles, blowing out thin nostrils and stamping with delicate fore-feet, their heads thrown back and a light steam rising from the crowded sheep-pen into the frosty air, as the two animals hastened by in high spirits, with much chatter and laughter. They were returning across country after a long day's outing with Otter, hunting and exploring on the wide uplands where certain streams tributary to their own river had their first small beginnings; and the shades of the short winter day were closing in on them, and they had still some distance to go. Plodding at random across the plough, they had heard the sheep and had made for them; and now, leading from the sheep-pen, they found a beaten

track that made walking a lighter business, and responded, moreover, to that small inquiring something which all animals carry inside them, saying unmistakably, "Yes, quite right; *this* leads home!"

"It looks as if we were coming to a village," said the Mole somewhat dubiously, slackening his pace, as the track, that had in time become a path and then had developed into a lane, now handed them over to the charge of a well-metalled road. The animals did not hold with villages, and their own highways, thickly frequented as they were, took an independent course, regardless of church, post office, or public-house.

"Oh, never mind!" said the Rat. "At this season of the year they're all safe indoors by this time, sitting round the fire; men, women, and children, dogs and cats and all. We shall slip through all right, without any bother or unpleasantness, and we can have a look at them through their windows if you like, and see what they're doing."

The rapid nightfall of mid-December had quite beset the little village as they approached it on soft feet over a first thin fall of powdery snow. Little was visible but squares of a dusky orange-red on either side of the street, where the firelight or lamplight of each cottage overflowed through the casements into the dark world without. Most of the low latticed windows were innocent of blinds, and to the lookers-in from outside, the inmates, gathered round the tea-table, absorbed in handiwork, or talking with laughter and gesture, had each that happy grace which is the last thing the skilled actor shall capture—the natural grace which goes with perfect unconsciousness of observation. Moving at will from one theatre to another, the two spectators, so far from home themselves, had something of wistfulness in their eyes as they watched a cat being stroked, a sleepy child picked up and huddled off to bed, or a tired man stretch and knock out his pipe on the end of a smouldering log.

But it was from one little window, with its blind drawn down, a mere blank transparency on the night, that the sense of home and the little curtained world within walls—the larger stressful world of outside Nature shut out and forgotten—most pulsated. Close against the white blind hung a bird-cage, clearly silhouetted, every wire, perch, and appurtenance distinct and recognisable, even to yesterday's dull-edged lump of sugar. On the middle perch the fluffy occupant, head tucked well into feathers, seemed so near to them as to be easily stroked, had they tried; even the delicate tips of his plumped-out plumage pencilled plainly on the illuminated screen. As they looked, the sleepy little fellow stirred uneasily, woke, shook himself and raised his head. They could see the gape of his tiny beak as he yawned in a bored sort of way, looked round, and then settled his head into his back again, while the ruffled feathers gradually subsided into perfect stillness. Then a gust of bitter wind took them in the back of the neck, a small sting of frozen sleet on the skin woke them as from a dream, and they knew their toes to be cold and their legs tired and their own home distant a weary way.

Once beyond the village, where the cottages ceased abruptly, on either side of the road they could smell through the darkness the friendly fields again; and they braced themselves for the last long stretch, the home stretch, the stretch that we know is bound to end, some time, in the rattle of the door-latch, the sudden firelight, and the sight of familiar things greeting us as long-absent travellers from far oversea. They plodded along steadily and silently, each of them thinking his own thoughts. The Mole's ran a good deal on supper, as it was pitch dark, and it was all a strange country to him as far as he knew, and he was following obediently in the wake of the Rat, leaving the guidance entirely to him. As for the Rat, he was walking a little way ahead, as his habit was, his shoulders humped, his eyes fixed on the straight grey road in front of him; so he did not notice poor Mole when suddenly the summons reached him, and took him like an electric shock.

We others, who have long lost the more subtle of the physical senses, have not even proper terms to express an animal's intercommunications with his surroundings, living or otherwise; and have only the word "smell", for instance, to include the whole range of delicate thrills which murmur in the nose of the animal night and day, summoning, warning, inciting, repelling. It was one of these mysterious fairy calls from out the void that suddenly reached Mole in the darkness, making him tingle through and through with its very familiar appeal, even while as yet he could not clearly remember what it was. He stopped dead in his tracks, his nose searching hither and thither in its efforts to recapture the fine filament, the telegraphic current, that had so strongly moved him. A moment, and he had caught it again; and with it this time came recollection in fullest flood.

Home! That was what they meant, those caressing appeals, those soft touches wafted through the air, those invisible little hands pulling and tugging, all one way! Why, it must be quite close by him at that moment, his old home that he had hurriedly forsaken and never sought again, that day when he first found the river! And now it was sending out its scouts and its messengers to capture him and ring him in. Since his escape on that bright morning he had hardly given it a thought, so absorbed had he been in his new life, in all its pleasures, its surprises, its fresh and captivating experiences. Now, with a rush of old memories, how clearly it stood up before him, in the darkness! Shabby indeed, and small and poorly furnished, and yet his, the home he had made for himself, the home he had been so happy to get back to after his day's work. And the home had been happy with him, too, evidently, and was missing him, and wanted him back, and was telling him so, through his nose, sorrowfully, reproachfully, but with no bitterness or anger; only with plaintive reminder that it was there, and wanted him.

The call was clear, the summons was plain. He must obey it instantly, and go. "Ratty!" he called, full of joyful excitement, "hold on! Come back! I want you, quick!"

"O, *come* along, Mole, do!" replied the Rat cheerfully, still plodding along.

"*Please* stop, Ratty!" pleaded the poor Mole, in anguish of heart. "You don't understand! It's my home, my old home! I've just come across the smell of it, and it's close by here, really quite close. And I *must* go to it, I must, I must! O, come back, Ratty! Please, please come back!"

The Rat was by this time very far ahead, too far to hear clearly what the Mole was calling, too far to catch the sharp note of painful appeal in his voice. And he was much taken up with the weather, for he too could smell something—something suspiciously like approaching snow.

"Mole, we mustn't stop now, really!" he called back. "We'll come for it tomorrow, whatever it is you've found. But I daren't stop now—it's late, and the snow's coming on again, and I'm not sure of the way! And I want your nose, Mole, so come on quick, there's a good fellow!" And the Rat pressed forward on his way without waiting for an answer.

Poor Mole stood alone in the road, his heart torn asunder, and a big sob gathering, gathering, somewhere low down inside him, to leap up to the surface presently, he knew, in passionate escape. But even under such a test as this his loyalty to his friend stood firm. Never for a moment did he dream of abandoning him. Meanwhile, the wafts from his old home pleaded, whispered, conjured, and finally claimed him imperiously. He dared not tarry longer within their magic circle. With a wrench that tore his very heartstrings he set his face down the road and followed submissively in the track of the Rat, while faint, thin little smells, still dogging his retreating nose, reproached him for his new friendship and his callous forgetfullness.

With an effort he caught up the unsuspecting Rat, who began chattering cheerily about what they would do when they got back, and how jolly a fire of logs in the parlour would be, and what a supper he meant to eat; never noticing his companion's silence and distressful state of mind At last, however, when they had gone some considerable way further, and were passing some tree-stumps at the edge of a copse that bordered the road, he stopped and said kindly, "Look here, Mole, old chap, you seem dead tired. No talk left in you, and your feet dragging like lead. We'll sit down here for a minute and rest. The snow has held off so far, and the best part of our journey is over."

The Mole subsided forlornly on a tree-stump and tried to control himself, for he felt it surely coming. The sob he had fought with so long refused to be beaten. Up and up, it forced its way to the air, and then another, and another, and others thick and fast; till poor Mole at last gave up the struggle, and cried freely and helplessly and openly, now that he knew it was all over and he had lost what he could hardly be said to have found.

The Rat, astonished and dismayed at the violence of Mole's paroxysm of grief, did not dare to speak for a while. At last he said, very quietly and sympathetically, "What is it, old fellow? Whatever can be the matter? Tell us your trouble, and let me see what I can do."

Poor Mole found it difficult to get any words out between the upheavals of his chest that followed one upon another so quickly and held back speech and choked it as it came. "I know it's a—shabby, dingy little place," he sobbed forth at last, brokenly: "not like—your cosy quarters—or Toad's beautiful hall—or Badger's great house—but it was my own little home—and I was fond of it—and I went away and forgot all about it—and then I smelt it suddenly—on the road, when I called and you wouldn't listen, Rat—and everything came back to me with a rush—and I *wanted* it!—O dear, O dear—and when you *wouldn't* turn back, Ratty—and I had to leave it, though I was smelling it all the time—I thought my heart would break.—We might have just gone and had one look at it, Ratty—only one look—it was close by—but you wouldn't turn back, Ratty, you wouldn't turn back! O dear, O dear!"

Recollection brought fresh waves of sorrow, and sobs again took full charge of him, preventing further speech.

The Rat stared straight in front of him, saying nothing, only patting Mole gently on the shoulder. After a time he muttered gloomily, "I see it all now! What a *pig* I have been! A pig—that's me! Just a pig—a plain pig."

He waited till Mole's sobs became gradually less stormy and more rhythmical; he waited till at last sniffs were frequent and sobs only intermittent. Then he rose from his seat, and, remarking carelessly, "Well, now we'd really better be getting on, old chap!" set off up the road again, over the toilsome way they had come.

"Wherever are you (hic) going to (hic), Ratty?" cried the tearful Mole, looking up in alarm.

"We're going to find that home of yours, old fellow," replied the Rat pleasantly; "so you had better come along, for it will take some finding, and we shall want your nose."

"O, come back, Ratty, do!" cried the Mole, getting up and hurrying after him. "It's no good, I tell you! It's too late, and too dark, and the place is to far off, and the snow's coming! And—and I never meant to let you know I was feeling that way about it—it was all an accident and a mistake! And think of River Bank, and your supper!"

"Hang River Bank, and supper too!" said the Rat heartily. "I tell you, I'm going to find this place now, if I stay out all night. So cheer up, old chap, and take my arm, and we'll very soon be back there again."

Still snuffling, pleading, and reluctant, Mole suffered himself to be dragged back along the road by his imperious companion, who by a flow of cheerful talk and anecdote endeavoured to beguile his spirits back and make the weary way seem shorter. When at last it seemed to the Rat that they must be nearing that part of the road where the Mole had been "held up", he said, "Now, no more talking. Business! Use your nose, and give your mind to it."

They moved on in silence for some little way, when suddenly the Rat was conscious, through his arm that was linked in Mole's, of a faint sort of electric thrill that was passing down that animal's body. Instantly he disengaged himself, fell back a pace, and waited, all attention.

The signals were coming through!

Mole stood a moment rigid, while his uplifted nose, quivering slightly, felt the air.

Then a short, quick run forward—a fault—a check—a try back; and then a slow, steady, confident advance.

The Rat, much excited, kept close to his heels as the Mole, with something of the air of a sleep-walker, crossed a dry ditch, scrambled through a hedge, and nosed his way over a field open and trackless and bare in the faint starlight.

Suddenly, without giving warning, he dived; but the Rat was on the alert, and promptly followed him down the tunnel to which his unerring nose had faithfully led him.

It was close and airless, and the earthy smell was strong, and it seemed a long time to Rat ere the passage ended and he could stand erect and stretch and shake himself. The Mole struck a match, and by its light the Rat saw that they were standing in an open space, neatly swept and sanded underfoot, and directly facing them was Mole's little front door, with "Mole End" painted, in Gothic lettering, over the bell-pull at the side.

Mole reached down a lantern from a nail on the wall and lit it, and the Rat, looking round him, saw that they were in a sort of fore-court. A garden-seat stood on one side of the door, and on the other, a roller; for the Mole, who was a tidy animal when at home, could not stand having his ground kicked up by other animals into little runs that ended in earth-heaps. On the walls hung wire baskets with ferns in them, alternating with brackets carrying plaster statuary—Garibaldi, and the infant Samuel, and Queen Victoria, and other heroes of modern Italy. Down one side of the fore-court ran a skittle-alley, with benches along it and little wooden tables marked with rings that hinted at beer-mugs. In the middle was a small round pond containing goldfish and surrounded by a cockleshell border. Out of the centre of the pond rose a fanciful erection clothed in more cockle-shells and topped by a large silvered glass ball that reflected everything all wrong and had a very pleasing effect.

Mole's face beamed at the sight of all these objects so dear to him, and he hurried Rat through the door, lit a lamp in the hall, and took one glance round his old home. He saw the dust lying thick on everything, saw the cheerless, deserted look of the long-neglected house, and its narrow, meagre dimensions, its worn and shabby contents—and collapsed again on a hall-chair, his nose in his paws. "O, Ratty!" he cried dismally, "why ever did I do it? Why did I bring you to this poor, cold little place, on a night like this, when you might have been at River Bank by this time, toasting your toes before a blazing fire, with all your own nice things about you!"

The Rat paid no heed to his doleful self-reproaches. He was running here and there, opening doors, inspecting rooms and cupboards, and lighting lamps and candles and sticking them up everywhere. "What a capital little house this is!" he called out cheerily. "So compact! So well planned! Everything here and everything in its place! We'll make a jolly night of it. The first thing we want is a good fire; I'll see to that—I always know where to find things. So this is the parlour? Splendid! Your own idea, those little sleeping-bunks in the wall? Capital! Now, I'll fetch the wood and the coals, and you get a duster, Mole—you'll find one in the drawer of the kitchen table—and try and smarten things up a bit. Bustle about, old chap!"

Encouraged by his inspiriting companion, the Mole roused himself and dusted and polished with energy and heartiness, while the Rat, running to and fro with armfuls of fuel, soon had a cheerful blaze roaring up the chimney. He hailed the Mole to come and warm himself; but Mole promptly had another fit of the blues, dropping down on a couch in dark despair and burying his face in his duster.

"Rat," he moaned, "how about your supper, you poor, cold, hungry, weary animal? I've nothing to give you—nothing—not a crumb!"

"What a fellow you are for giving in!" said the Rat reproachfully.

"Why, only just now I saw a sardine-opener on the kitchen dresser, quite distinctly; and everybody knows that means there are sardines about somewhere in the neighbourhood. Rouse yourself! pull yourself together, and come with me and forage."

They went and foraged accordingly, hunting through every cupboard and turned out every drawer. The result was not so very depressing after all, though of course it might have been better; a tin of sardines—a box of captain's biscuits, nearly full—and a German sausage encased in silver paper.

"There's a banquet for you!" observed the Rat, as he arranged the table. "I know some animals who would give their ears to be sitting down to supper with us to-night!"

"No bread!" groaned the Mole dolorously; "no butter, no—"

"No *pâté de foie gras*, no champagne!" continued the Rat, grinning. "And that reminds me—what's that little door at the end of the passage? Your

cellar, of course! Every luxury in this house! Just you wait a minute."

He made for the cellar door, and presently reappeared, somewhat dusty, with a bottle of beer in each paw and another under each arm. "Self-indulgent beggar you seem to be, Mole," he observed. "Deny yourself nothing. This is really the jolliest little place I ever was in. Now, wherever did you pick up those prints? Make the place look so home-like, they do. No wonder you're so fond of it, Mole. Tell us all about it, and how you came to make it what it is."

Then, while the Rat busied himself fetching plates, and knives and forks, and mustard which he mixed in an egg-cup, the Mole, his bosom still heaving with the stress of his recent emotion, related—somewhat shyly at first, but with more freedom as he warmed to his subject—how this was planned, and how that was thought out, and how this was got through a windfall from an aunt, and that was a wonderful find and a bargain, and this other thing was bought out of laborious savings and a certain amount of "going without". His spirits finally quite restored, he must needs go and caress his possessions, and take a lamp and show off their points to his visitor, and expatiate on them, quite forgetful of the supper they both so much needed; Rat, who was desperately hungry but strove to conceal it, nodding seriously, examining with a puckered brow, and saying, "Wonderful", and "Most remarkable", at intervals, when the chance for an observation was given him.

At last the Rat succeeded in decoying him to the table, and had just got seriously to work with the sardine-opener when sounds were heard from the forecourt without—sounds like the scuffing of small feet in the gravel and a confused murmur of tiny voices, while broken sentences reached them— "Now, all in a line—hold the lantern up a bit,

Tommy—clear your throats first—no coughing after I say one, two, three.—Where's young Bill?— Here, come on, do, we're all a-waiting—"

"What's up?" inquired the Rat, pausing in his labours.

"I think it must be the field-mice," replied the Mole, with a touch of pride in his manner. "They go round carol-singing regularly at this time of the year. They're quite an institution in these parts. And they never pass me over—they come to Mole End last of all; and I used to give them hot drinks, and supper too sometimes, when I could afford it. It will be like old times to hear them again."

"Let's have a look at them!" cried the Rat, jumping up and running to the door.

It was a pretty sight, and a seasonable one, that met their eyes when they flung the door open. In the fore-court, lit by the dim rays of a horn lantern, some eight or ten little field-mice stood in a semi-circle, red worsted comforters round their throats, their forepaws thrust deep into their pockets, their feet jigging for warmth. With bright beady eyes they glanced shyly at each other, sniggering a little, sniffing and applying coat-sleeves a good deal. As the door opened, one of the elder ones that carried the

lantern was just saying, "Now then, one, two, three!" and forthwith their shrill little voices uprose on the air, singing one of the old-time carols that their forefathers composed in fields that were fallow and held by frost, or when snow-bound in chimney corners, and handed down to be sung in the miry street to lamp-lit windows at Yule-time.

CAROL

Villagers all this frosty tide,
Let your doors swing open wide,
Though wind may follow, and snow beside,
Yet draw us in by your fire to bide;
Joy shall be yours in the morning!

Here we stand in the cold and the sleet,
Blowing fingers and stamping feet,
Come from far away you to greet—
You by the fire and we in the street—
* Bidding you joy in the morning!*

For here one half of the night was gone,
Sudden a star has led us on,
Raining bliss and benison—
Bliss to-morrow and more anon
* Joy for every morning!*

Good man Joseph toiled through the snow—
Saw the star o'er a stable low;
Mary she might not further go—
Welcome thatch, and litter below!
* Joy was hers in the morning!*

And then they heard the angels tell
"Who were the first to cry Nowell?
Animals all as it befell,
In the stable where they did dwell!
* Joy shall be theirs in the morning."*

The voices ceased, the singers, bashful but smiling, exchanged sidelong glances, and silence succeeded—

but for a moment only. Then, from up above and far away, down the tunnel they had so lately travelled was borne to their ears in a faint musical hum the sound of distant bells ringing a joyful and clangorous peal.

"Very well sung, boys!" cried the Rat heartily. "And now come along in, all of you, and warm yourselves by the fire, and have something hot!"

"Yes, come along, field-mice," cried the Mole eagerly. "This is quite like old times! Shut the door after you. Pull up that settle to the fire. Now, you just wait a minute, while we—O, Ratty!" he cried in despair, plumping down on a seat, with tears impending. "Whatever are we doing? We've nothing to give them!"

"You leave all that to me," said the masterful Rat. "Here, you with the lantern! Come over this way. I want to talk to you. Now, tell me, are there any shops open at this hour of the night?"

"Why, certainly, sir," replied the field-mouse respectfully. "At this time of the year our shops keep open to all sorts of hours."

"Then look here!" said the Rat. "You go off at once, you and your lantern, and you get me—"

Here much muttered conversation ensued, and the Mole only heard bits of it, such as—"Fresh, mind!—no, a pound of that will do—see you get Buggins's, for I won't have any other—no, only the best—if you can't get it there, try somewhere else—yes, of course, home-made, no tinned stuff—well then, do the best you can!" Finally, there was a chink of coin passing from paw to paw, the field-mouse was provided with an ample basket for his purchases, and off he hurried, he and his lantern.

The rest of the field-mice, perched in a row on the settle, their small legs swinging, gave themselves up to enjoyment of the fire, and toasted their chilblains till they tingled; while the Mole, failing to draw them into easy conversation, plunged into family history and made each of them recite the names of his numerous brothers, who were too young, it appeared, to be allowed to go out a-carolling this year, but looked forward very shortly to winning the parental consent

The Rat, meanwhile, was busy examining the label on one of the beer-bottles. "I perceive this to be Old Burton," he remarked approvingly. "*Sensible* Mole! The very thing! Now we shall be able to mull some ale! Get the things ready, Mole, while I draw the corks."

It did not take long to prepare the brew and thrust the tin heater well into the red heart of the fire; and soon every field-mouse was sipping and coughing and choking (for a little mulled ale goes a long way) and wiping his eyes and laughing and forgetting he had ever been cold in all his life.

"They act plays too, these fellows," the Mole explained to the Rat. "Make them up all by themselves, and act them afterwards. And very well they do it, too! They gave us a capital one last year, about a field-mouse who was captured at sea by a Barbary corsair, and made to row in a galley; and when he escaped and got home again, his lady-love had gone into a convent. Here, you! You were in it, I remember. Get up and recite a bit."

The field-mouse addressed got up on his legs, giggled shyly, looked round the room, and remained absolutely tongue-tied. His comrades cheered him on, Mole coaxed and encouraged him, and the Rat went so far as to take him by the shoulders and shake him; but nothing could overcome his stage-fright. They were all busily engaged on him like watermen applying the Royal Humane Society's regulations to a case of long submersion, when the latch clicked, the door opened, and the field-mouse with the lantern reappeared, staggering under the weight of his basket.

There was no more talk of play-acting once the very real and solid contents of the basket had been tumbled out on the table. Under the generalship of Rat, everybody was set to do something or to fetch something. In a very few minutes supper was ready, and Mole, as he took the head of the table in a sort of dream, saw a lately barren board set thick with savoury comforts; saw his little friends' faces brighten and beam as they fell to without delay; and then let himself loose—for he was famished indeed—on the provender so magically provided, thinking what a happy home-coming this had turned out, after all. As they ate, they talked of old times, and the field-mice gave him the local gossip up to date, and answered as well as they could the hundred questions he had to ask them. The Rat said little or nothing, only taking care that each guest had what he wanted, and plenty of it, and that Mole had no trouble or anxiety about anything.

They clattered off at last, very grateful and showering wishes of the season, with their jacket pockets stuffed with remembrances for the small brothers and sisters at home. When the door had closed on the last of them and the chink of the lanterns had died away, Mole and Rat kicked the fire up, drew their chairs in, brewed themselves a last nightcap of mulled ale, and discussed the events of the long day. At last the Rat, with a tremendous yawn, said, "Mole, old chap, I'm ready to drop. Sleepy is simply not the word. That your own bunk over on that side? Very well, then, I'll take this. What a ripping little house this is! Everything so handy!"

He clambered into his bunk and rolled himself well up in the blankets, and slumber gathered him forthwith, as a swath of barley is folded into the arms of the reaping-machine.

The weary Mole also was glad to turn in without delay, and soon had his head on his pillow, in great joy and contentment. But ere he closed his eyes he let them wander round his old room, mellow in the glow of the firelight that played or rested on familiar and friendly things which had long been unconsciously a part of him, and now smilingly received him back, without rancour. He was now in just the frame of mind that the tactful Rat had quietly worked to bring about in him. He saw clearly how plain and simple—how narrow, even—it all was; but clearly, too, how much it all meant to him, and the special value of some such anchorage in one's existence. He did not at all want to abandon the new life and its splendid spaces, to turn his back on sun and air and all they offered him and creep home and stay there; the upper world was all too strong, it called to him still, even down there, and he knew he must return to the larger stage. But it was good to think he had this to come back to, this place which was all his own, these things which were so glad to see him again and could always be counted upon for the same simple welcome.

CHAPTER 6

Mr Toad

It was a bright morning in the early part of summer; the river had resumed its wonted banks and its accustomed pace, and a hot sun seemed to be pulling everything green and bushy and spiky up out of the earth towards him, as if by strings. The Mole and the Water Rat had been up since dawn, very busy on matters connected with boats and the opening of the boating season; painting and varnishing, mending paddles, repairing cushions, hunting for missing boat-hooks, and so on; and were finishing breakfast in their little parlour and eagerly discussing their plans for the day, when a heavy knock sounded at the door.

"Bother!" said the Rat, all over egg. "See who it is, Mole, like a good chap, since you've finished."

The Mole went to attend the summons, and the Rat heard him utter a cry of surprise. Then he flung the parlour door open, and announced with much importance, "Mr Badger!"

This was a wonderful thing, indeed, that the Badger should pay a formal call on them, or indeed on anybody. He generally had to be caught, if you wanted him badly, as he slipped quietly along a hedgerow of an early morning or a late evening, or else hunted up in his own house in the middle of the wood, which was a serious undertaking.

The Badger strode heavily into the room, and stood looking at the two animals with an expression full of seriousness. The Rat let his egg-spoon fall on the table-cloth, and sat open-mouthed.

"The hour has come!" said the Badger at last with great solemnity.

"What hour?" asked the Rat uneasily, glancing at the clock on the mantelpiece.

"*Whose* hour, you should rather say," replied the Badger. "Why, Toad's hour! The hour of Toad! I said I would take him in hand as soon as the winter was well over, and I'm going to take him in hand to-day!"

"Toad's hour, of course!" cried the Mole delightedly. "Hooray! I remember now! *We'll* teach him to be a sensible Toad!"

"This very morning," continued the Badger, taking an arm-chair, "as I learnt last night from a trustworthy source, another new and exceptionally powerful motor-car will arrive at Toad Hall on approval or return. At this very moment, perhaps, Toad is busily arranging himself in those singularly hideous habiliments so dear to him, which transform him from a (comparatively) good-looking Toad into an Object which throws any decent-minded animal that comes across it into a violent fit. We must be up and doing, ere it is too late. You two animals will accompany me instantly to Toad Hall, and the work of rescue shall be accomplished."

"Right you are!" cried the Rat, starting up. "We'll rescue the poor unhappy animal! We'll convert him! He'll be the most converted Toad that ever was before we've done with him!"

They set off up the road on their mission of mercy, Badger leading the way. Animals when in company walk in a proper and sensible manner, in single file, instead of sprawling all across the road and being of no use or support to each other in case of sudden trouble or danger.

They reached the carriage-drive of Toad Hall to find, as the Badger had anticipated, a shiny new motor-car, of great size, painted a bright red (Toad's favourite colour), standing in front of the house. As they neared the door it was flung open, and Mr Toad, arrayed in goggles, cap, gaiters, and enormous overcoat, came swaggering down the steps, drawing on his gauntleted gloves.

"Hullo! come on, you fellows!" he cried cheerfully on catching sight of them. "You're just in time to come with me for a jolly—to come for a jolly—for a—er jolly—"

His hearty accents faltered and fell away as he noticed the stern unbending look on the countenances of his silent friends, and his invitation remained unfinished.

The Badger strode up the steps. "Take him inside," he said sternly to his companions. Then, as Toad was hustled through the door, struggling and protesting, he turned to the chauffeur in charge of the new motor-car.

"I'm afraid you won't be wanted to-day," he said. "Mr Toad has changed his mind. He will not

require the car. Please understand that this is final
You needn't wait." Then he followed the others
inside and shut the door.

"Now, then!" he said to the Toad, when the four
of them stood together in the hall, "first of all, take
those ridiculous things off!"

"Shan't!" replied Toad, with great spirit. "What
is the meaning of this gross outrage? I demand an
instant explanation."

"Take them off him, then, you two," ordered the
Badger briefly.

They had to lay Toad out on the floor, kicking and
calling all sorts of names, before they could get to work
properly. Then the Rat sat on him, and the Mole got
his motor-clothes off him bit by bit, and they stood
him up on his legs again. A good deal of his blustering
spirit seemed to have evaporated with the removal of
his fine panoply. Now that he was merely Toad, and
no longer the Terror of the Highway, he giggled feebly
and looked from one to the other appealingly, seeming
quite to understand the situation.

"You knew it must come to this, sooner or later,
Toad," the Badger explained severely. "You've disre-
garded all the warnings we've given you, you've
gone on squandering the money your father left you,

and you're getting us animals a bad name in the district by your furious driving and your smashes and your rows with the police. Independence is all very well, but we animals never allow our friends to make fools of themselves beyond a certain limit; and that limit you've reached. Now, you're a good fellow in many respects, and I don't want to be too hard on you. I'll make one more effort to bring you to reason. You will come with me into the smoking-room, and there you will hear some facts about yourself; and we'll see whether you come out of that room the same Toad that you went in."

He took Toad firmly by the arm, led him into the smoking-room, and closed the door behind them.

"That's no good!" said the Rat contemptuously. "*Talking* to Toad'll never cure him. He'll *say* anything."

They made themselves comfortable in arm-chairs and waited patiently. Through the closed door they could just hear the long continuous drone of the Badger's voice, rising and falling in waves of oratory; and presently they noticed that the sermon began to be punctuated at intervals by long-drawn sobs, evidently proceeding from the bosom of Toad, who was a soft-hearted and affectionate fellow, very easily converted—for the time being—to any point of view.

After some three-quarters of an hour the door opened, and the Badger reappeared, solemnly leading by the paw a very limp and dejected Toad. His skin hung baggily about him, his legs wobbled, and his cheeks were furrowed by the tears so plentifully called forth by the Badger's moving discourse.

"Sit down there Toad," said the Badger kindly, pointing to a chair. "My friends," he went on, "I am pleased to inform you that Toad has at last seen the error of his ways. He is truly sorry for his misguided conduct in the past, and he has undertaken to give up motor-cars entirely and for ever. I have his solemn promise to that effect."

"That is very good news," said the Mole gravely.

"Very good news indeed," observed the Rat dubiously, "if only—*if* only—"

He was looking very hard at Toad as he said this, and could not help thinking he perceived something vaguely resembling a twinkle in that animal's still sorrowful eye.

"There's only one thing more to be done," continued the gratified Badger. "Toad, I want you solemnly to repeat, before your friends here, what you fully admitted to me in the smoking-room just now. First, you are sorry for what you've done, and you see the folly of it all?"

There was a long, long pause. Toad looked desperately this way and that, while the other animals waited in grave silence. At last he spoke.

"No!" he said a little sullenly, but stoutly; "I'm *not* sorry. And it wasn't folly at all! It was simply glorious!"

"What?" cried the Badger, greatly scandalized. "You backsliding animal, didn't you tell me just now, in there—"

"O, yes, yes, in *there*," said Toad impatiently. "I'd have said anything in there. You're so eloquent, dear Badger, and so moving, and so convincing, and put all your points so frightfully well—you can do what you like with me in *there*, and you know it. But I've been searching my mind since, and going over things in it, and I find that I'm not a bit sorry or repentant really, so it's no earthly good saying I am; now, is it?"

"Then you don't promise," said the Badger, "never to touch a motor-car again?"

"Certainly not!" replied Toad emphatically. "On the contrary, I faithfully promise that the very first motor-car I see, poop-poop! off I go in it!"

"Told you so, didn't I?" observed the Rat to the Mole.

"Very well, then," said the Badger firmly, rising to his feet. "Since you won't yield to persuasion, we'll try what force can do. I feared it would come to this all along. You've often asked us three to come and stay with you, Toad, in this handsome house of yours; well, now we're going to. When we've converted you to a proper point of view we may quit, but not before. Take him upstairs, you two, and lock him up in his bedroom, while we arrange matters between ourselves."

"It's for your own good, Toady, you know," said the Rat kindly, as Toad, kicking and struggling, was hauled up the stairs by his two faithful friends. "Think what fun we shall all have together, just as we used to, when you've quite got over this—this painful attack of yours!"

"We'll take great care of everything for you till you're well, Toad," said the Mole; "and we'll see your money isn't wasted, as it has been."

"No more of those regrettable incidents with the police, Toad," said the Rat, as they thrust him into his bedroom.

"And no more weeks in hospital, being ordered about by female nurses, Toad," added the Mole, turning the key on him.

They descended the stair, Toad shouting abuse at them through the keyhole; and the three friends then met in conference on the situation.

"It's going to be a tedious business," said the Badger, sighing. "I've never seen Toad so determined. However, we will see it out. He must never be left an instant unguarded. We shall have to take it in turns to be with him, till the poison has worked itself out of his system."

They arranged watches accordingly. Each animal took it in turns to sleep in Toad's room at night, and they divided the day up between them. At first Toad was undoubtedly very trying to his careful guardians. When his violent paroxysms possessed him he would arrange bedroom chairs in rude resemblance of a motor-car and would crouch on the foremost of them, bent forward and staring fixedly ahead, making uncouth and ghastly noises, till the climax was reached, when, turning a complete somersault, he would lie prostrate amidst the ruins of the chairs, apparently completely satisfied for the moment. As time passed, however, these painful seizures grew gradually less frequent, and his friends strove to divert his mind into fresh channels. But his interest in other matters did not seem to revive, and he grew apparently languid and depressed.

One fine morning the Rat, whose turn it was to go on duty, went upstairs to relieve Badger, whom he found fidgeting to be off and stretch his legs in a long ramble round his wood and down his earths and burrows. "Toad's still in bed," he told the Rat, outside the door. "Can't get much out of him, except, 'O, leave him alone, he wants nothing, perhaps he'll be better presently, it may pass off in time, don't be unduly anxious,' and so on. Now, you look out, Rat! When Toad's quiet and submissive, and playing at being the hero of a Sunday-School prize, then he's at his artfullest. There's sure to be something up. I know him. Well, now I must be off."

"How are you to-day, old chap?" inquired the Rat cheerfully, as he approached Toad's bedside.

He had to wait some minutes for an answer. At last a feeble voice replied, "Thank you so much, dear Ratty! So good of you to inquire! But first tell me how you are yourself, and the excellent Mole?"

"O, *we're* all right," replied the Rat. "Mole," he added incautiously, "is going out for a run round with Badger. They'll be out till luncheon-time, so you and I will spend a pleasant morning together, and I'll do my best to amuse you. Now jump up, there's a good fellow, and don't lie moping there on a fine morning like this!"

"Dear, kind Rat," murmured Toad, "how little you realize my condition, and how very far I am from 'jumping up' now—if ever! But do not trouble about me. I hate being a burden to my friends, and I do not expect to be one much longer. Indeed, I almost hope not."

"Well, I hope not, too," said the Rat heartily. "You've been a fine bother to us all this time, and I'm glad to hear it's going to stop. And in weather like this, and the boating season just beginning! It's too bad of you, Toad! It isn't the trouble we mind, but you're making us miss such an awful lot."

"I'm afraid it *is* the trouble you mind, though," replied the Toad languidly. "I can quite understand it. It's natural enough. You're tired of bothering about me. I mustn't ask you to do anything further. I'm a nuisance, I know."

"You are, indeed," said the Rat "But I tell you, I'd take any trouble on earth for you, if only you'd be a sensible animal."

"If I thought that, Ratty," murmured Toad, more feebly than ever, "then I would beg you—for the last time, probably—to step round to the village as quickly as possible—even now it may be too late—and fetch the doctor. But don't you bother. It's only a trouble, and perhaps we may as well let things take their course."

"Why, what do you want a doctor for?" inquired the Rat, coming closer and examining him. He certainly lay very still and flat, and his voice was weaker and his manner much changed.

"Surely you have noticed of late—" murmured Toad. "But no—why should you? Noticing things is only a trouble. To-morrow, indeed, you may be saying to yourself, 'O, if only I had noticed sooner! If only I had done something!' But no; it's a trouble. Never mind—forget that I asked."

"Look here, old man," said the Rat, beginning to get rather alarmed, "of course I'll fetch a doctor to you, if you really think you want him. But you can hardly be bad enough for that yet. Let's talk about something else."

"I fear, dear friend," said Toad, with a sad smile, "that 'talk' can do little in a case like this—or doctors either, for that matter; still, one must grasp at the slightest straw. And, by the way—while you are about it—I *hate* to give you additional trouble, but I happen to remember that you will pass the door—would you mind at the same time asking the lawyer to step up? It would be a convenience to me, and there are moments—perhaps I should say there is a moment—when one must face disagreeable tasks, at whatever cost to exhausted nature!"

"A lawyer! O, he must be really bad!" the affrighted Rat said to himself, as he hurried from the room, not forgetting, however, to lock the door carefully behind him.

Outside, he stopped to consider. The other two were far away, and he had no one to consult.

"It's best to be on the safe side," he said, on reflection. "I've known Toad fancy himself frightfully bad before, without the slightest reason; but I've never heard him ask for a lawyer! If there's nothing really the matter, the doctor will tell him he's an old ass, and cheer him up; and that will be something gained. I'd better humour him and go; it won't take very long." So he ran off to the village on his errand of mercy.

The Toad, who had hopped lightly out of bed as soon as he heard the key turned in the lock,

watched him eagerly from the window till he disappeared down the carriage-drive. Then, laughing
heartily, he dressed as quickly as possible in the
smartest suit he could lay hands on at the moment,
filled his pockets with cash which he took from a
small drawer in the dressing-table, and next, knot-
ting the sheets from his bed together and tying one
end of the improvised rope round the central
mullion of the handsome Tudor window which
formed such a feature of his bedroom, he scrambled
out, slid lightly to the ground, and, taking the opposite direction to the Rat, marched off light-heart-
edly, whistling a merry tune.

It was a gloomy luncheon for Rat when the
Badger and the Mole at length returned, and he had
to face them at table with his pitiful and unconvinc-
ing story. The Badger's caustic, not to say brutal,
remarks may be imagined, and therefore passed
over; but it was painful to the Rat that even the
Mole, though he took his friend's side as far as possible, could not help saying, "You've been a bit of a
duffer this time, Ratty! Toad, too, of all animals!"

"He did it awfully well," said the crestfallen Rat.

"He did *you* awfully well!" rejoined the Badger
hotly. "However, talking won't mend matters. He's

got clear away for the time, that's certain; and the worst of it is, he'll be so conceited with what he'll think is his cleverness that he may commit any folly. One comfort is, we're free now, and needn't waste any more of our precious time doing sentry-go. But we'd better continue to sleep at Toad Hall for a while longer. Toad may be brought back at any moment— on a stretcher, or between two policemen."

So spoke the Badger, not knowing what the future held in store, or how much water, and of how turbid a character, was to run under bridges before Toad should sit at ease again in his ancestral Hall.

Meanwhile, Toad, gay and irresponsible, was walking briskly along the high road, some miles from home. At first he had taken by-paths, and crossed many fields, and changed his course several times, in case of pursuit; but now, feeling by this time safe from recapture, and the sun smiling brightly on him, and all nature joining in a chorus of approval to the song of self-praise that his own heart was singing to him, he almost danced along the road in his satisfaction and conceit.

"Smart piece of work that!" he remarked to himself, chuckling. "Brain against brute force—and

brain came out on the top—as it's bound to do.
Poor old Ratty! My! won't he catch it when the
Badger gets back! A worthy fellow, Ratty, with
many good qualities, but very little intelligence and
absolutely no education. I must take him in hand
some day, and see if I can make something of him."

Filled full of conceited thoughts such as these he
strode along, his head in the air, till he reached a
little town, where the sign of "The Red Lion",
swinging across the road half-way down the main
street, reminded him that he had not breakfasted
that day, and that he was exceedingly hungry after
his long walk. He marched into the inn, ordered the
best luncheon that could be provided at so short a
notice, and sat down to eat it in the coffee-room.

He was about half-way through his meal when an
only too familiar sound, approaching down the
street, made him start and fall a-trembling all over.
The poop-poop! drew nearer and nearer, the car
could be heard to turn into the inn-yard and come
to a stop, and Toad had to hold on to the leg of the
table to conceal his over-mastering emotion.
Presently the party entered the coffee-room,
hungry, talkative and gay, voluble on their experiences of the morning and the merits of the chariot

that had brought them along so well. Toad listened eagerly, all ears, for a time; at last he could stand it no longer. He slipped out of the room quietly, paid his bill at the bar, and as soon as he got outside sauntered round quietly to the inn-yard. "There cannot be any harm," he said to himself, "in my only just *looking* at it!"

The car stood in the middle of the yard, quite unattended, the stable-helps and other hangers-on being all at their dinner. Toad walked slowly round it, inspecting, criticizing, musing deeply.

"I wonder," he said to himself presently, "I wonder if this sort of car *starts* easily?"

Next moment, hardly knowing how it came about, he found he had hold of the handle and was turning it As the familiar sound broke forth, the old passion seized on Toad and completely mastered him, body and soul. As if in a dream he found himself, somehow, seated in the driver's seat; as if in a dream, he pulled the lever and swung the car round the yard and out through the archway; and, as if in a dream, all sense of right and wrong, all fear of obvious consequences, seemed temporarily suspended. He increased his pace, and as the car devoured the street and leapt forth on the high road through the open country, he was only conscious that he was Toad once more, Toad at his best and highest, Toad the terror, the traffic-queller, the Lord of the lone trail, before whom all must give way or be smitten into nothingness and everlasting night. He chanted as he flew, and the car responded with sonorous drone; the miles were eaten up under him as he sped he knew not whither, fulfilling his instincts, living his hour, reckless of what might come to him.

"To my mind," observed the Chairman of the Bench of Magistrates cheerfully, "the *only* difficulty that presents itself in this otherwise very clear case is, how we can possibly make it sufficiently hot for the incorrigible rogue and hardened ruffian whom we see cowering in the dock before us. Let me see: he has been found guilty, on the clearest evidence, first, of stealing a valuable motor-car; secondly, of driving to the public danger; and, thirdly, of gross impertinence to the rural police. Mr Clerk, will you tell us, please, what is the very stiffest penalty we can impose for each of these offences? Without, of course, giving the prisoner the benefit of any doubt, because there isn't any."

The Clerk scratched his nose with his pen.

"Some people would consider," he observed, "that stealing the motor-car was the worst offence; and so it is.

"But cheeking the police undoubtedly carries the severest penalty, and so it ought. Supposing you were to say twelve months for the theft, which is mild; and three years for the furious driving, which is lenient; and fifteen years for the cheek, which was pretty bad sort of cheek, judging by what we've heard from the witness-box, even if you only believe one-tenth part of what you heard, and I never believe more myself—those figures, if added together correctly, tot up to nineteen years—"

"First rate!" said the Chairman.

"—So you had better make it a round twenty years and be on the safe side," concluded the Clerk.

"An excellent suggestion!" said the Chairman approvingly. "Prisoner! Pull yourself together and try and stand up straight. It's going to be twenty years for you this time. And mind, if you appear before us again, upon any charge whatever, we shall have to deal with you very seriously!"

Then the brutal minions of the law fell upon the hapless Toad; loaded him with chains, and dragged him from the Court House, shrieking, praying, protesting; across the market-place, where the play-ful populace, always as severe upon detected crime as they are sympathetic and helpful when one is merely "wanted", assailed him with jeers, carrots, and popular catch-words; past hooting school children, their innocent faces lit up with the pleasure they ever derive from the sight of a gentleman in difficulties; across the hollow-sounding drawbridge, below the spiky portcullis, under the frowning arch-way of the grim old castle, whose ancient towers soared high overhead; past guardrooms full of grin-ning soldiery off duty, past sentries who coughed in a horrid sarcastic way, because that is as much as a sentry on his post dare do to show his contempt and abhorrence of crime; up time-worn winding stairs, past men-at-arms in casquet and corselet of steel, darting threatening looks through their vizards; across courtyards, where mastiffs strained at their leash and pawed the air to get at him; past ancient warders, their halberds leant against the wall, dozing over a pasty and a flagon of brown ale; on and on, past the rack-chamber and the thumb-screw-room, past the turning that led to the private scaffold, till they reached the door of the grimmest dungeon that lay in the heart of the innermost keep.

There at last they paused, where an ancient gaoler sat fingering a bunch of mighty keys.

"Oddsbodikin," said the sergeant of police, taking off his helmet and wiping his forehead. "Rouse thee, old loon, and take over from us this vile Toad, a criminal of deepest guilt and matchless artfulness and resource. Watch and ward him with all thy skill; and mark thee well, grey-beard, should aught untoward befall, thy old head shall answer for his—and a murrain on both of them!"

The gaoler nodded grimly, laying his withered hand on the shoulder of the miserable Toad. The rusty key creaked in the lock, the great door clanged behind them; and Toad was a helpless prisoner in the remotest dungeon of the best-guarded keep of the stoutest castle in all the length and breadth of Merry England.

CHAPTER 7

The Piper at the Gates of Dawn

The Willow-Wren was twittering his thin little song, hidden himself in the dark selvedge of the river bank. Though it was past ten o'clock at night, the sky still clung to and retained some lingering skirts of light from the departed day; and the sullen heats of the torrid afternoon broke up and rolled away at the dispersing touch of the cool fingers of the short midsummer night. Mole lay stretched on the bank, still panting from the stress of the fierce day that had been cloudless from dawn to late sunset, and waited for his friend to return. He had been on the river with some companions, leaving the Water Rat free to keep an engagement of long standing with Otter; and he had come back to find the house dark and deserted, and no sign of Rat, who was doubtless keeping it up late with his old comrade. It was still too hot to think of staying indoors, so he lay on some cool dock-leaves, and thought over the past day and its doings, and how very good they all had been.

The Rat's light footfall was presently heard approaching over the parched grass. "O, the blessed coolness!" he said, and sat down, gazing thought-fully into the river, silent and preoccupied.

"You stayed to supper, of course?" said the Mole presently.

"Simply had to," said the Rat. "They wouldn't hear of my going before. You know how kind they always are. And they made things as jolly for me as ever they could, right up to the moment I left. But I felt a brute all the time, as it was clear to me they were very unhappy, though they tried to hide it. Mole, I'm afraid they're in trouble. Little Portly is missing again; and you know what a lot his father thinks of him, though he never says much about it."

"What, that child?" said the Mole lightly. "Well, suppose he is; why worry about it? He's always straying off and getting lost, and turning up again; he's so adventurous. But no harm ever happens to him. Everybody hereabouts knows him and likes him, just as they do old Otter, and you may be sure some animal or other will come across him and bring him back again all right. Why, we've found him ourselves, miles from home, and quite self-possessed and cheerful!"

"Yes; but this time it's more serious," said the Rat gravely. "He's been missing for some days now, and the Otters have hunted everywhere, high and low, without finding the slightest trace. And they've asked every animal, too, for miles around, and no one knows anything about him. Otter's evidently more anxious than he'll admit. I got out of him that young Portly hasn't learnt to swim very well yet, and I can see he's thinking of the weir. There's a lot of water coming down still, considering the time of year, and the place always had a fascination for the child. And then there are—well, traps and things—*you* know. Otter's not the fellow to be nervous about any son of his before it's time. And now he *is* nervous. When I left, he came out with me—said he wanted some air, and talked about stretching his legs. But I could see it wasn't that, so I drew him out and pumped him, and got it all from him at last. He was going to spend the night watching by the ford. You know the place where the old ford used to be, in bygone days before they built the bridge?"

"I know it well," said the Mole. "But why should Otter choose to watch there?"

"Well, it seems that it was there he gave Portly his first swimming lesson," continued the Rat. "From that shallow, gravelly spit near the bank. And it was there he used to teach him fishing, and there young Portly caught his first fish, of which he was so very proud. The child loved the spot, and Otter thinks that if he came wandering back from wherever he is—if he *is* anywhere by this time, poor little chap—he might make for the ford he was so fond of; or if he came across it he'd remember it well, and stop there and play, perhaps. So Otter goes there every night and watches—on the chance, you know, just on the chance!"

They were silent for a time, both thinking of the same thing—the lonely, heart-sore animal, crouched by the ford, watching and waiting, the long night through—on the chance.

"Well, well," said the Rat presently, "I suppose we ought to be thinking about turning in." But he never offered to move.

"Rat," said the Mole, "I simply can't go and turn in, and go to sleep, and *do* nothing, even though there doesn't seem to be anything to be done. We'll get the boat out, and paddle upstream. The moon will be up in an hour or so, and then we will search as well as we can—anyhow, it will be better than going to bed and doing *nothing*."

"Just what I was thinking myself," said the Rat. "It's not the sort of night for bed anyhow; and daybreak is not so very far off, and then we may pick up some news of him from early risers as we go along."

They got the boat out, and the Rat took the sculls, paddling with caution. Out in midstream there was a clear, narrow track that faintly reflected the sky; but wherever shadows fell on the water from bank, bush, or tree, they were as solid to all appearance as the banks themselves, and the Mole had to steer with judgment accordingly. Dark and deserted as it was, the night was full of small noises, song and chatter and rustling, telling of the busy little population who were up and about, plying their trades and vocations through the night till sunshine should fall on them at last and send them off to their well-earned repose. The water's own noises, too, were more apparent than by day, its gurglings and "cloops" more unexpected and near at hand; and constantly they started at what seemed a sudden clear call from an actual articulate voice.

The line of the horizon was clear and hard against the sky, and in one particular quarter it showed black against a silvery climbing phosphorescence that grew and grew. At last, over the rim of the waiting earth the moon lifted with slow majesty till it swung clear of the horizon and rode off, free of moorings; and once more they began to see surfaces—meadows widespread, and quiet gardens, and the river itself from bank to bank, all softly disclosed, all washed clean of mystery and terror, all radiant again as by day, but with a difference that was tremendous. Their old haunts greeted them again in other raiment, as if they had slipped away and put on this pure new apparel and come quietly back, smiling as they shyly waved to see if they would be recognized again under it.

Fastening their boat to a willow, the friends landed in this silent, silver kingdom, and patiently explored the hedges, the hollow trees, the runnels and their little culverts, the ditches and dry waterways. Embarking again and crossing over, they worked their way up the stream in this manner, while the moon, serene and detached in a cloudless sky, did what she could, though so far off, to help them in their quest; till her hour came and she sank;

earthwards reluctantly, and left them, and mystery once more held field and river.

Then a change began slowly to declare itself The horizon became clearer, field and tree came more into sight, and somehow with a different look; the mystery began to drop away from them. A bird piped suddenly, and was still; and a light breeze sprang up and set the reeds and bulrushes rustling. Rat, who was in the stern of the boat while Mole sculled, sat up suddenly and listened with a passionate intentness. Mole, who with gentle strokes was just keeping the boat moving while he scanned the banks with care, looked at him with curiosity.

"It's gone!" sighed the Rat, sinking back in his seat again. "So beautiful and strange and new! Since it was to end so soon, I almost wish I had never heard it. For it has roused a longing in me that is pain, and nothing seems worth while but just to hear that sound once more and go on listening to it for ever. No! There it is again!" he cried, alert once more. Entranced, he was silent for a long space, spellbound.

"Now it passes on and I begin to lose it," he said presently. "O, Mole! the beauty of it! The merry bubble and joy, the thin, clear happy call of the distant piping! Such music I never dreamed of, and the call in it is stronger even than the music is sweet! Row on, Mole, row! For the music and the call must be for us."

The Mole, greatly wondering, obeyed. "I hear nothing myself," he said, "but the wind playing in the reeds and rushes and osiers."

The Rat never answered, if indeed he heard. Rapt, transported, trembling, he was possessed in all his senses by this new divine thing that caught up his helpless soul and swung and dandled it, a powerless but happy infant in a strong sustaining grasp.

In silence Mole rowed steadily, and soon they came to a point where the river divided, a long backwater branching off to one side. With a slight movement of his head Rat, who had long dropped the rudder-lines, directed the rower to take the backwater. The creeping tide of light gained and gained, and now they could see the colour of the flowers that gemmed the water's edge.

"Clearer and nearer still," cried the Rat joyously. "Now you must surely hear it! Ah—at last—I see you do!"

Breathless and transfixed the Mole stopped rowing as the liquid run of that glad piping broke on him like a wave, caught him up, and possessed him utterly. He saw the tears on his comrade's cheeks, and bowed his head and understood. For a space they hung there, brushed by the purple loosestrife that fringed the bank; then the clear imperious summons that marched hand-in-hand with the intoxicating melody imposed its will on Mole, and mechanically he bent to his oars again. And the light grew steadily stronger, but no birds sang as they were wont to do at the approach of dawn; and but for the heavenly music all was marvellously still.

On either side of them, as they glided onwards, the rich meadow-grass seemed that morning of a freshness and a greenness unsurpassable. Never had they noticed the roses so vivid, the willow-herb so riotous, the meadow-sweet so odorous and pervading. Then the murmur of the approaching weir began to hold the air, and they felt a consciousness that they were nearing the end, whatever it might be, that surely awaited their expedition.

A wide half-circle of foam and glinting lights and shining shoulders of green water, the great weir closed the backwater from bank to bank, troubled all the quiet surface with twirling eddies and floating foam-streaks, and deadened all other sounds with its solemn and soothing rumble. In midmost of the stream, embraced in the weir's shimmering arm-spread, a small island lay anchored, fringed close with willow and silver birch and alder. Reserved, shy, but full of significance, it hid whatever it might hold behind a veil, keeping it till the hour should come, and, with the hour, those who were called and chosen.

Slowly, but with no doubt or hesitation whatever, and in something of a solemn expectancy, the two animals passed through the broken, tumultuous water and moored their boat at the flowery margin of the island. In silence they landed, and pushed through the blossom and scented herbage and undergrowth that led up to the level ground, till they stood on a little lawn of a marvellous green, set round with Nature's own orchard-trees—crab-apple, wild cherry, and sloe.

"This is the place of my song-dream, the place the music played to me," whispered the Rat, as if in a trance. "Here, in this holy place, here if anywhere, surely we shall find Him!"

Then suddenly the Mole felt a great Awe fall upon him, an awe that turned his muscles to water, bowed his head, and rooted his feet to the ground. It was no panic terror—indeed he felt wonderfully at peace and happy—but it was an awe that smote and held him and, without seeing, he knew it could only mean that some august Presence was very, very near. With difficulty he turned to look for his friend, and saw him at his side cowed, stricken, and trembling violently. And still there was utter silence in the populous bird-haunted branches around them; and still the light grew and grew.

Perhaps he would never have dared to raise his eyes, but that, though the piping was now hushed, the call and the summons seemed still dominant and imperious. He might not refuse, were Death himself waiting to strike him instantly, once he had looked with mortal eye on things rightly kept hidden. Trembling he obeyed, and raised his humble head; and then, in that utter clearness of the imminent dawn, while Nature, flushed with fullness of incredible colour, seemed to hold her breath for the event, he looked in the very eyes of the Friend and Helper; saw the backward sweep of the curved horns, gleaming in the growing daylight; saw the stern, hooked nose between the kindly eyes that were looking down on them humorously, while the bearded mouth broke into a half-smile at the corners; saw the rippling muscles on the arm that lay across the broad chest, the long supple hand still holding the pan-pipes only just fallen away from the parted lips; saw the splendid curves of the shaggy limbs disposed in majestic ease on the sward; saw, last of all, nestling between his very hooves, sleeping soundly in entire peace and contentment, the little, round, podgy, childish form of the baby otter. All this he saw, for one moment breathless and intense, vivid on the morning sky; and still, as he looked, he lived; and still, as he lived, he wondered.

"Rat!" he found breath to whisper, shaking. "Are you afraid?"

"Afraid?" murmured the Rat, his eyes shining with unutterable love. "Afraid! Of *Him*? O, never, never! And yet—and yet—O, Mole, I am afraid!" Then the two animals, crouching to the earth, bowed their heads and did worship.

Sudden and magnificent, the sun's broad golden disc showed itself over the horizon facing them; and the first rays, shooting across the level water-meadows, took the animals full in the eyes and dazzled them. When they were able to look once more, the Vision had vanished, and the air was full of the carol of birds that hailed the dawn.

As they stared blankly, in dumb misery deepening as they slowly realized all they had seen and all they had lost, a capricious little breeze, dancing up from the surface of the water, tossed the aspens, shook the dewy roses, and blew lightly and caressingly in their faces, and with its soft touch came instant oblivion. For this is the last best gift that the kindly demi-god is careful to bestow on those to whom he has revealed himself in their helping: the gift of forgetfulness. Lest the awful remembrance should remain and grow, and overshadow mirth and pleasure, and the great haunting memory should spoil all the after-lives of little animals

helped out of difficulties, in order that they should
be happy and light-hearted as before.

Mole rubbed his eyes and stared at Rat, who was
looking about him in a puzzled sort of way. "I beg
your pardon; what did you say, Rat?" he asked.

"I think I was only remarking," said Rat slowly,
"that this was the right sort of place, and that here,
if anywhere, we should find him. And look! Why,
there he is, the little fellow!" And with a cry of
delight he ran towards the slumbering Portly.

But Mole stood still a moment, held in thought. As
one wakened suddenly from a beautiful dream, who
struggles to recall it, and can recapture nothing but a
dim sense of the beauty of it, the beauty! Till that, too,
fades away in its turn, and the dreamer bitterly
accepts the hard, cold waking and all its penalties; so
Mole, after struggling with his memory for a brief
space, shook his head sadly and followed the Rat.

Portly woke up with a joyous squeak, and wriggled with pleasure at the sight of his father's friends,
who had played with him so often in past days. In a
moment, however, his face grew blank, and he fell
to hunting round in a circle with pleading whine. As
a child that has fallen happily asleep in its nurse's
arms, and wakes to find itself alone and laid in a

strange place, and searches corners and cupboards, and runs from room to room, despair growing silently in its heart, even so Portly searched the island and searched, dogged and unwearying, till at last the black moment came for giving it up, and sitting down and crying bitterly.

The Mole ran quickly to comfort the little animal; but Rat, lingering, looked long and doubtfully at certain hoof-marks deep in the sward.

"Some—great—animal—has been here," he murmured slowly and thoughtfully; and stood musing, musing; his mind strangely stirred.

"Come along, Rat!" called the Mole. "Think of poor Otter, waiting up there by the ford!"

Portly had soon been comforted by the promise of a treat—a jaunt on the river in Mr Rat's real boat; and the two animals conducted him to the water's side, placed him securely between them in the bottom of the boat, and paddled off down the backwater. The sun was fully up by now, and hot on them, birds sang lustily and without restraint, and flowers smiled and nodded from either bank, but somehow—so thought the animals—with less of richness and blaze of colour than they seemed to remember seeing quite recently somewhere—they wondered where.

The main river reached again, they turned the boat's head up stream, towards the point where they knew their friend was keeping his lonely vigil. As they drew near the familiar ford, the Mole took the boat in to the bank, and they lifted Portly out and set him on his legs on the tow-path, gave him his marching orders and a friendly farewell pat on the back, and shoved out into mid-stream. They watched the little animal as he waddled along the path contentedly and with importance; watched him till they saw his muzzle suddenly lift and his waddle break into a clumsy amble as he quickened his pace with shrill whines and wriggles of recognition. Looking up the river, they could see Otter start up, tense and rigid, from out of the shallows where he crouched in dumb patience, and could hear his amazed and joyous bark as he bounded up through the osiers on to the path. Then the Mole, with a strong pull on one oar, swung the boat round and let the full stream bear them down again whither it would, their quest now happily ended.

"I feel strangely tired, Rat," said the Mole, leaning wearily over his oars as the boat drifted. "It's being up all night, you'll say, perhaps; but thats nothing. We do as much half the nights of the week, at this time of the year. No; I feel as if I had been through something very exciting and rather terrible, and it was just over; and yet nothing particular has happened."

"Or something very surprising and splendid and beautiful," murmured the Rat, leaning back and closing his eyes. "I feel just as you do, Mole; simply dead tired, though not body-tired. It's lucky we've got the stream with us, to take us home. Isn't it jolly to feel the sun again, soaking into one's bones! And hark to the wind playing in the reeds!"

"It's like music—far-away music," said the Mole, nodding drowsily.

"So I was thinking," murmured the Rat, dreamful and languid. "Dance-music—the lilting sort that runs on without a stop—but with words in it, too—it passes into words and out of them again—I catch them at intervals then it is dance-music once more, and then nothing but the reeds' soft thin whispering."

"You hear better than I," said the Mole sadly. "I cannot catch the words."

"Let me try and give you them," said the Rat softly, his eyes still close. "Now it is turning into words again—faint but clear—*Lest the awe should dwell—And turn your frolic to fret—You shall look on my power at the helping hour—But then you shall forget!* Now the reeds take it up—*forget, forget,* they sigh, and it dies away in a rustle and a whisper. Then the voice returns—

"*Lest limbs be reddened and rent—I spring the trap that is set—As I loose the snare you may glimpse me there—For surely you shall forget!* Row nearer, Mole, nearer to the reeds! It is hard to catch, and grows each minute fainter.

"*Helper and healer, I cheer—Small waifs in the woodland wet— Strays I find in it, wounds I bind in it— Bidding them all forget!* Nearer, Mole, nearer! No, it is no good; the song has died away into reed-talk."

"But what do the words mean?" asked the wondering Mole.

"That I do not know," said the Rat simply. "I passed them on to you as they reached me. Ah! now they return again, and this time full and clear! This time, at last, it is the real, the unmistakable thing, simple—passionate—perfect—"

"Well, let's have it, then," said the Mole, after he had waited patiently for a few minutes, half dozing in the hot sun.

But no answer came. He looked, and understood the silence. With a smile of much happiness on his face, and something of a listening look still lingering there, the weary Rat was fast asleep.

CHAPTER 8

Toad's Adventures

When Toad found himself immured in a dank and noisome dungeon, and knew that all the grim darkness of a medieval fortress lay between him and the outer world of sunshine and well-metalled high roads where he had lately been so happy, disporting himself as if he had bought up every road in England, he flung himself at full length on the floor, and shed bitter tears, and abandoned himself to dark despair. "This is the end of everything" (he said), "at least it is the end of the career of Toad, which is the same thing; the popular and handsome Toad, the rich and hospitable Toad, the Toad so free and careless and debonair! How can I hope to be ever set at large again" (he said), "who have been imprisoned so justly for stealing so handsome a motor-car in such an audacious manner, and for such lurid and imaginative cheek, bestowed upon such a number of fat, red-faced policemen!" (Here his sobs choked him.) "Stupid animal that I was" (he said), "now I must languish in this dungeon, till people who were proud to say they knew me, have forgotten the very name of Toad! O wise old Badger!" (he said), "O clever, intelligent Rat and sensible Mole! What sound judgments, what a knowledge of men and matters you possess! O unhappy and forsaken Toad!" With lamentations such as these he passed his days and nights for several weeks, refusing his meals or intermediate light refreshments, though the grim and ancient gaoler, knowing that Toad's pockets were well lined, frequently pointed out that many comforts, and indeed luxuries, could by arrangement be sent in—at a price—from outside.

Now the gaoler had a daughter, a pleasant wench and good-hearted, who assisted her father in the lighter duties of his post. She was particularly fond of animals, and, besides her canary, whose cage hung on a nail in the massive wall of the keep by day, to the great annoyance of prisoners who relished an after-dinner nap, and was shrouded in an antimacassar on the parlour table at night, she kept several piebald mice and a restless revolving squirrel. This kind-hearted girl, pitying the misery of Toad, said to her father one day, "Father! I can't bear to see that poor beast so unhappy, and getting so thin! You let me have the managing of him. You know how fond of animals I am. I'll make him eat from my hand, and sit up, and do all sorts of things."

Her father replied that she could do what she liked with him. He was tired of Toad, and his sulks and his airs and his meanness. So that day she went on her errand of mercy, and knocked at the door of Toad's cell.

"Now, cheer up, Toad," she said coaxingly, on entering, "and sit up and dry your eyes and be a sensible animal. And do try and eat a bit of dinner. See, I've brought you some of mine, hot from the oven!"

It was bubble-and-squeak, between two plates, and its fragrance filled the narrow cell. The penetrating smell of cabbage reached the nose of Toad as he lay prostrate in his misery on the floor, and gave him the idea for a moment that perhaps life was not such a blank and desperate thing as he had imagined. But still he wailed, and kicked with his legs, and refused to be comforted. So the wise girl retired for the time, but, of course, a good deal of the smell of hot cabbage remained behind, as it will do, and Toad, between his sobs, sniffed and reflected, and gradually began to think new and inspiring thoughts: of chivalry, and poetry, and deeds still to be done; of broad meadows, and cattle browsing in them, raked by sun and wind; of kitchen-gardens, and straight herb-borders, and warm snap-dragon beset by bees; and of the comforting clink of dishes set down on the table at Toad Hall, and the scrape of chair-legs on the floor as every one pulled himself close up to his work. The air of the narrow cell took on a rosy tinge; he began to think of his friends, and how they would surely be able to do something; of lawyers, and how they would have enjoyed his case, and what an ass he had been not to get in a few; and lastly, he thought of his own great cleverness and resource, and all that he was capable of if he only gave his great mind to it; and the cure was almost complete.

When the girl returned, some hours later, she carried a tray, with a cup of fragrant tea steaming on it; and a plate piled up with very hot buttered toast, cut thick, very brown on both sides, with the butter running through the holes in it in great golden drops, like honey from the honey-comb.

The smell of that buttered toast simply talked to Toad, and with no uncertain voice; talked of warm kitchens, of breakfasts on bright frosty mornings, of cosy parlour firesides on winter evenings, when one's ramble was over and slippered feet were propped on the fender; of the purring of contented cats, and the twitter of sleepy canaries. Toad sat up on end once-more, dried his eyes, sipped his tea and munched his toast, and soon began talking freely about himself, and the house he lived in, and his doings there, and how important he was, and what a lot his friends thought of him.

The gaoler's daughter saw that the topic was doing him as much good as the tea, as indeed it was, and encouraged him to go on.

"Tell me about Toad Hall," said she. "It sounds beautiful."

"Toad Hall," said the Toad proudly, "is an eligible self-contained gentleman's residence, very unique; dating in part from the fourteenth century, but replete with every modern convenience. Up-to-date sanitation. Five minutes from church, post office, and golf-links. Suitable for—"

"Bless the animal," said the girl, laughing, "I don't want to *take* it. Tell me something *real* about it. But first wait till I fetch you some more tea and toast."

She tripped away, and presently returned with a fresh trayful; and Toad, pitching into the toast with avidity, his spirits quite restored to their usual level, told her about the boat-house, and the fish-pond, and the old walled kitchen-garden; and about the pig-styes, and the stables, and the pigeon-house, and the hen-house; and about the dairy, and the wash-house, and the china-cupboards, and the linen-presses (she liked that bit especially); and about the banqueting-hall, and the fun they had there when the other animals were gathered round the table and Toad was at his best, singing songs, telling stories, carrying on generally. Then she wanted to know about his animal-friends, and was very interested in all he had to tell her about them and how they lived, and what they did to pass their time. Of course, she did not say she was fond of animals as *pets*, because she had the sense to see that Toad would be extremely offended. When she said good night, having filled his water jug and shaken up his straw for him, Toad was very much the same sanguine, self-satisfied animal that he had been of old. He sang a little song or two, of the sort he used to sing at his dinner-parties, curled himself up in the straw, and had an excellent night's rest and the pleasantest of dreams.

They had many interesting talks together, after that, as the dreary days went on; and the gaoler's daughter grew very sorry for Toad, and thought it a great shame that a poor little animal should be locked up in prison for what seemed to her a very trivial offence. Toad, of course, in his vanity, thought that her interest in him proceeded from a growing tenderness; and he could not help half regretting that the social gulf between them was so very wide, for she was a comely lass, and evidently admired him very much.

One morning the girl was very thoughtful, and answered at random, and did not seem to Toad to be paying proper attention to his witty sayings and sparkling comments.

"Toad," she said presently, "just listen, please. I have an aunt who is a washerwoman."

"There, there," said Toad graciously and affably, "never mind; think no more about it. *I* have several aunts who *ought* to be washerwomen."

"Do be quiet a minute, Toad," said the girl. "You talk too much, that's your chief fault, and I'm trying to think, and you hurt my head. As I said, I have an aunt who is a washerwoman; she does the washing for all the prisoners in this castle—we try to keep any paying business of that sort in the family, you understand. She takes out the washing on Monday morning, and brings it in on Friday evening. This is a Thursday. Now, this is what occurs to me: you're very rich—at least you're always telling me so—and she's very poor. A few pounds wouldn't make any difference to you, and it would mean a lot to her. Now, I think if she were properly approached—squared, I believe, is the word you animals use—you could come to some arrangement by which she would let you have her dress and bonnet and so on, and you could escape from the castle as the official washerwoman. You're very alike in many respects—particularly about the figure."

"We're *not*," said the Toad in a huff. "I have a very elegant figure—for what I am."

"So has my aunt," replied the girl, "for what *she* is. But have it your own way. You horrid, proud, ungrateful animal, when I'm sorry for you, and trying to help you!"

"Yes, yes, that's all right; thank you very much indeed," said the Toad hurriedly. "But look here! you wouldn't surely have Mr Toad, of Toad Hall, going about the country disguised as a washerwoman!"

"Then you can stop here as a Toad," replied the girl with much spirit. "I suppose you want to go off in a coach-and-four!"

Honest Toad was always ready to admit himself in the wrong. "You are a good, kind, clever girl," he said, "and I am indeed a proud and a stupid toad. Introduce me to your worthy aunt, if you will be so kind, and I have no doubt that the excellent lady and I will be able to arrange terms satisfactory to both parties."

Next evening the girl ushered her aunt into Toad's cell, bearing his week's washing pinned up in a towel. The old lady had been prepared before-hand for the interview, and the sight of certain golden sovereigns that Toad had thoughtfully placed on the table in full view practically completed the matter and left little further to discuss. In return for his cash, Toad received a cotton print gown, an apron, a shawl, and a rusty black bonnet; the only stipulation the old lady made being that she should be gagged and bound and dumped down in a corner. By this not very convinc-ing artifice, she explained, aided by picturesque fiction which she could supply herself, she hoped to retain her situation, in spite of the suspicious appearance of things.

Toad was delighted with the suggestion. It would enable him to leave the prison in some style, and with his reputation for being a desperate and dangerous fellow untarnished; and he readily helped the gaoler's daughter to make her aunt appear as much as possible the victim of circumstances over which she had no control.

"Now it's your turn, Toad," said the girl. "Take off that coat and waistcoat of yours; you're fat enough as it is."

Shaking with laughter, she proceeded to "hook-and-eye" him into the cotton print gown, arranged the shawl with a professional fold, and tied the strings of the rusty bonnet under his chin.

"You're the very image of her," she giggled, "only I'm sure you never looked half so respectable in all your life before. Now, goodbye, Toad, and good luck. Go straight down the way you came up; and if any one says anything to you, as they probably will, being but men, you can chaff back a bit, of course, but remember you're a widow woman, quite alone in the world, with a character to lose."

With a quaking heart, but as firm a footstep as he could command, Toad set forth cautiously on what seemed to be a most hare-brained and hazardous undertaking; but he was soon agreeably surprised to find how easy everything was made for him, and a little humbled at the thought that both his popularity, and the sex that seemed to inspire it, were really another's. The washerwoman's squat figure in its familiar cotton print seemed a passport for every barred door and grim gateway; even when he hesitated, uncertain as to the right turning to take, he found himself helped out of his difficulty by the warder at the next gate, anxious to be off to his tea, summoning him to come along sharp and not keep him waiting there all night. The chaff and the humorous sallies to which he was subjected, and to which, of course, he had to provide prompt and effective reply, formed, indeed, his chief danger; for Toad was an animal with a strong sense of his own dignity, and the chaff was mostly (he thought) poor and clumsy, and the humour of the sallies entirely lacking. However, he kept his temper, though with great difficulty, suited his retorts to his company and his supposed character, and did his best not to overstep the limits of good taste.

It seemed hours before he crossed the last court-
yard, rejected the pressing invitations from the last
guardroom, and dodged the outspread arms of the
last warder, pleading with simulated passion for just
one farewell embrace. But at last he heard the
wicket-gate in the great outer door click behind
him, felt the fresh air of the outer world upon his
anxious brow, and knew that he was free!

Dizzy with the easy success of his daring exploit,
he walked quickly towards the lights of the town,
not knowing in the least what he should do next,
only quite certain of one thing, that he must remove
himself as quickly as possible from a neighbourhood where the lady he was forced to represent was
so well-known and so popular a character.

As he walked along, considering, his attention
was caught by some red and green lights a little
way off, to one side of the town, and the sound of
the puffing and snorting of engines and the banging of shunted trucks fell on his ear. "Aha!" he
thought, "this is a piece of luck! A railway-station is
the thing I want most in the whole world at this
moment; and what's more, I needn't go through
the town to get to it, and shan't have to support
this humiliating character by repartees which,

though thoroughly effective, do not assist one's sense of self-respect."

He made his way to the station accordingly, consulted a time-table, and found that a train, bound more or less in the direction of his home, was due to start in half an hour. "More luck!" said Toad, his spirits rising rapidly, and went off to the booking-office to buy his ticket.

He gave the name of the station that he knew to be nearest to the village of which Toad Hall was the principal feature, and mechanically put his fingers, in search of the necessary money, where his waistcoat pocket should have been. But here the cotton gown, which had nobly stood by him so far, and which he had basely forgotten, intervened, and frustrated his efforts. In a sort of nightmare he struggled with the strange uncanny thing that seemed to hold his hands, turn all muscular strivings to water, and laugh at him all the time; while other travellers, forming up in a line behind, waited with impatience, making suggestions of more or less value and comments of more or less stringency and point. At last—somehow—he never rightly understood how—he burst the barriers, attained the goal, arrived at where all waistcoat pockets are eternally situated, and found—not only no money, but no pocket to hold it, and no waistcoat to hold the pocket!

To his horror he recollected that he had left both coat and waistcoat behind him in his cell, and with them his pocket-book, money, keys, watch, matches, pencil-case—all that makes life worth living, all that distinguishes the many-pocketed animal, the lord of creation, from the inferior one-pocketed or no-pocketed productions that hop or trip about permissively, unequipped for the real contest.

In his misery he made one desperate effort to carry the thing off, and, with a return to his fine old manner—a blend of the Squire and the College Don—he said, "Look here! I find I've left my purse behind. Just give me that ticket, will you, and I'll send the money on to-morrow. I'm well-known in these parts."

The clerk stared at him and the rusty black bonnet a moment, and then laughed. "I should think you were pretty well-known in these parts," he said, "if you've tried this game on often. Here, stand away from the window, please, madam; you're obstructing the other passengers!"

An old gentleman who had been prodding him in the back for some moments here thrust him away, and, what was worse, addressed him as his good woman, which angered Toad more than anything that had occurred that evening.

Baffled and full of despair, he wandered blindly down the platform where the train was standing, and tears trickled down each side of his nose. It was hard, he thought, to be within sight of safety and almost of home, and to be baulked by the want of a few wretched shillings and by the pettifogging mistrustfulness of paid officials. Very soon his escape would be discovered, the hunt would be up, he would be caught, reviled, loaded with chains, dragged back again to prison and bread-and-water and straw; his guards and penalties would be doubled; and O, what sarcastic remarks the girl would make! What was to be done? He was not swift of foot; his figure was unfortunately recognizable. Could he not squeeze under the seat of a carriage? He had seen this method adopted by schoolboys, when the journey-money provided by thoughtful parents had been diverted to other and better ends. As he pondered, he found himself opposite the engine, which was being oiled, wiped, and generally caressed by its affectionate driver, a burly man with an oil-can in one hand and a lump of cotton-waste in the other.

"Hullo, mother!" said the engine-driver, "what's the trouble? You don't look particularly cheerful."

"O, sir!" said Toad, crying afresh, "I am a poor unhappy washerwoman, and I've lost all my money, and can't pay for a ticket, and I must get home tonight somehow, and whatever I am to do I don't know. O dear, O dear!"

"That's a bad business, indeed," said the engine-driver reflectively. "Lost your money—and can't get home—and got some kids, too, waiting for you, I dare say?"

"Any amount of 'em," sobbed Toad. "and they'll be hungry—and playing with matches—and upsetting lamps, the little innocents!—and quarrelling, and going on generally. O dear, O dear!"

"Well, I'll tell you what I'll do," said the good engine-driver. "You're a washerwoman to your trade, says you. Very well, that's that. And I'm an engine-driver, as you well may see, and there's no denying it's terribly dirty work. Uses up a power of shirts, it does, till my missus is fair tired of washing of 'em. If you'll wash a few shirts for me when you get home, and send 'em along, I'll give you a ride on my engine. It's against the Company's regulations, but we're not so very particular in these out-of-the-way parts."

The Toad's misery turned into rapture as he eagerly scrambled up into the cab of the engine. Of course, he had never washed a shirt in his life, and couldn't if he tried and, anyhow, he wasn't going to begin; but he thought: "When I get safely home to Toad Hall, and have money again, and pockets to put it in, I will send the engine-driver enough to pay for quite a quantity of washing, and that will be the same thing, or better."

The guard waved his welcome flag, the engine-driver whistled in cheerful response, and the train moved out of the station. As the speed increased, and the Toad could see on either side of him real fields, and trees, and hedges, and cows, and horses, all a-flying past him, and as he thought how every minute was bringing him nearer to Toad Hall and sympathetic friends, and money to chink in his pocket, and a soft bed to sleep in, and good things to eat, and praise and admiration at the recital of his adventures and his surpassing cleverness, he began to skip up and down and shout and sing snatches of song, to the great astonishment of the engine-driver, who had come across washerwomen before, at long intervals, but never one at all like this.

They had covered many and many a mile, and Toad was already considering what he would have for supper as soon as he got home, when he noticed that the engine-driver, with a puzzled expression on his face, was leaning over the side of the engine and listening hard. Then he saw him climb on to the coals and gaze out over the top of the train; then he returned and said to Toad: "It's very strange; we're the last train running in this direction to-night, yet I could be sworn that I heard another following us!"

Toad ceased his frivolous antics at once. He became grave and depressed, and a dull pain in the lower part of his spine, communicating itself to his legs, made him want to sit down and try desperately not to think of all the possibilities.

By this time the moon was shining brightly, and the engine-driver, steadying himself on the coal, could command a view of the line behind them for a long distance.

Presently he called out, "I can see it clearly now! It is an engine, on our rails, coming along at a great pace! It looks as if we were being pursued!"

The miserable Toad, crouching in the coal-dust, tried hard to think of something to do, with dismal want of success.

"They are gaining on us fast!" cried the engine-driver. "And the engine is crowded with the queerest lot of people! Men like ancient warders, waving halberds; policemen in their helmets, waving truncheons; and shabbily dressed men in pot-hats, obvious and unmistakable plain-clothes detectives even at this distance, waving revolvers and walking-sticks; all waving, and all shouting the same thing—'Stop, stop, stop!'"

Then Toad fell on his knees among the coals and, raising his clasped paws in supplication, cried, "Save me, only save me, dear kind Mr Engine-driver, and I will confess everything! I am not the simple washerwoman I seem to be! I have no children waiting for me, innocent or otherwise! I am a toad—the well-known and popular Mr Toad, a landed proprietor; I have just escaped, by my great daring and cleverness, from a loathsome dungeon into which my enemies had flung me; and if those fellows on that engine recapture me, it will be chains and bread-and-water and straw and misery once more for poor, unhappy, innocent Toad!"

The engine-driver looked down upon him very sternly, and said, "Now tell the truth; what were you put in prison for?"

"It was nothing very much," said poor Toad, colouring deeply. "I only borrowed a motor-car while the owners were at lunch; they had no need of it at the time. I didn't mean to steal it, really; but people—especially magistrates—take such harsh views of thoughtless and high-spirited actions."

The engine-driver looked very grave and said, "I fear that you have been indeed a wicked toad, and by rights I ought to give you up to offended justice. But you are evidently in sore trouble and distress, so I will not desert you. I don't hold with motor-cars, for one thing; and I don't hold with being ordered about by policemen when I'm on my own engine, for another. And the sight of an animal in tears always makes me feel queer and soft-hearted. So cheer up, Toad! I'll do my best, and we may beat them yet!"

They piled on more coals, shovelling furiously; the furnace roared, the sparks flew, the engine leapt and swung, but still their pursuers slowly gained. The engine-driver, with a sigh, wiped his brow with a handful of cotton-waste, and said, "I'm afraid it's no good, Toad. You see, they are running light, and they have the better engine. There's just one thing left for us to do, and it's your only chance, so attend very carefully to what I tell you. A short way ahead of us is a long tunnel, and on the other side of that the line passes through a thick wood. Now, I will put on all the speed I can while we are running through the tunnel but the other fellows will slow down a bit, naturally, for fear of an accident. When we are through, I will shut off steam and put on brakes as hard as I can, and the moment it's safe to do so you must jump and hide in the wood, before they get through the tunnel and see you. Then I will go full speed ahead again, and they can chase me if they like, for as long as they like, and as far as they like. Now mind and be ready to jump when I tell you!"

They piled on more coals, and the train shot into the tunnel, and the engine rushed and roared and rattled, till at last they shot out at the other end into fresh air and the peaceful moonlight, and saw the wood lying dark and helpful upon either side of the line. The driver shut off steam and put on brakes, the Toad got down on the step, and as the train slowed down to almost a walking pace he heard the driver call out, "Now, jump!"

Toad jumped, rolled down a short embankment, picked himself up unhurt, scrambled into the wood and hid.

Peeping out, he saw his train get up speed again and disappear at a great pace. Then out of the tunnel burst the pursuing engine, roaring and whistling, her motley crew waving their various weapons and shouting, "Stop! stop! stop!" When they were past, the Toad had a hearty laugh—for the first time since he was thrown into prison.

But he soon stopped laughing when he came to consider that it was now very late and dark and cold, and he was in an unknown wood, with no money and no chance of supper, and still far from friends and home; and the dead silence of everything, after the roar and rattle of the train, was something of a shock. He dared not leave the shelter of the trees, so he struck into the wood, with the idea of leaving the railway as far as possible behind him.

After so many weeks within walls, he found the wood strange and unfriendly and inclined, he thought, to make fun of him. Nightjars, sounding their mechanical rattle, made him think that the wood was full of searching warders, closing in on him. An owl, swooping noiselessly towards him, brushed his shoulder with its wing, making him jump with the horrid certainty that it was a hand; then flitted off, moth-like, laughing its low ho! ho! ho! which Toad thought in very poor taste. Once he met a fox, who stopped, looked him up and down in a sarcastic sort of way, and said, "Hullo, washerwoman! Half a pair of socks and a pillow-case short this week! Mind it doesn't occur again!" and swaggered off, sniggering. Toad looked about for a stone to throw at him, but could not succeed in finding one, which vexed him more than anything. At last, cold, hungry, and tired out, he sought the shelter of a hollow tree, where with branches and dead leaves he made himself as comfortable a bed as he could, and slept soundly till the morning.

CHAPTER 9

Wayfarers All

The Water Rat was restless, and he did not exactly know why. To all appearances the summer's pomp was still at fullest height, and although in the tilled acres green had given way to gold, though rowans were reddening, and the woods were dashed here and there with a tawny fierceness, yet light and warmth and colour were still present in undiminished measure, clean of any chilly premonitions of the passing year. But the constant chorus of the orchards and hedges had shrunk to a casual evensong from a few yet unwearied performers; the robin was beginning to assert himself once more; and there was a feeling in the air of change and departure. The cuckoo, of course, had long been silent; but many another feathered friend, for months a part of the familiar landscape and its small society, was missing too, and it seemed that the ranks thinned steadily day by day. Rat, ever observant of all winged movement, saw that it was taking daily a southing tendency; and even as he lay in bed at night he thought he could make out, passing in the darkness overhead, the beat and quiver of impatient pinions, obedient to the peremptory call.

Nature's Grand Hotel has its Season, like the others. As the guests one by one pack, pay, and depart, and the seats at the *table d'hôte* shrink pitifully at each succeeding meal; as suites of rooms are closed, carpets taken up, and waiters sent away; those boarders who are staying on, *en pension*, until the next year's full reopening, cannot help being somewhat affected by all these flittings and farewells, this eager discussion of plans, routes, and fresh quarters, this daily shrinkage in the stream of comradeship. One gets unsettled, depressed, and inclined to be querulous. Why this craving for change? Why not stay on quietly here, like us, and be jolly? You don't know this hotel out of the season, and what fun we have among ourselves, we fellows who remain and see the whole interesting year out. All very true, no doubt, the others always reply; we quite envy you—and some other year perhaps—but just now we have engagements—and there's the bus at the door—our time is up! So they depart, with a smile and a nod, and we miss them, and feel resentful. The Rat was a self-sufficing sort of animal, rooted to the land, and, whoever went, he stayed; still, he could not help noticing what was in the air, and feeling some of its influence in his bones.

It was difficult to settle down to anything seriously, with all this flitting going on. Leaving the water-side, where rushes stood thick and tall in a stream that was becoming sluggish and low, he wandered country-wards, crossed a field or two of pasturage already looking dusty and parched, and thrust into the great realm of wheat, yellow, wavy, and murmurous, full of quiet motion and small whisperings. Here he often loved to wander, through the forest of stiff strong stalks that carried their own golden sky away over his head—a sky that was always dancing, shimmering, softly talking; or swaying strongly to the passing wind and recovering itself with a toss and a merry laugh. Here, too, he had many small friends, a society complete in itself, leading full and busy lives, but always with a spare moment to gossip and exchange news with a visitor.

To-day, however, though they were civil enough, the field-mice and harvest-mice seemed preoccupied. Many were digging and tunnelling busily; others, gathered together in small groups, examined plans and drawings of small flats, stated to be desirable and compact, and situated conveniently near the Stores. Some were hauling out dusty trunks and dress-baskets, others were already elbow-deep packing their belongings; while everywhere piles and bundles of wheat, oats, barley, beech-mast and nuts, lay about ready for transport.

"Here's old Ratty!" they cried as soon as they saw him. "Come and bear a hand, Rat, and don't stand about idle!"

"What sort of games are you up to?" said the Water Rat severely. "You know it isn't time to be thinking of winter quarters yet, by a long way!"

"O yes, we know that," explained a field-mouse rather shamefacedly; "but it's always as well to be in good time, isn't it? We really *must* get all the furniture and baggage and stores moved out of this before those horrid machines begin clicking round the fields; and then, you know, the best flats get picked up so quickly nowadays, and if you're late you have to put up with *anything*, and they want such a lot of doing up, too, before they're fit to move into. Of course, we're early, we know that; but we're only just making a start."

"O, bother *starts*," said the Rat. 'It's a splendid day. Come for a row, or a stroll along the hedges, or a picnic in the woods, or something."

"Well, I *think* not *to-day*, thank you," replied the field- mouse hurriedly. "Perhaps some *other* day— when we've more *time*"—

The Rat, with a snort of contempt, swung round to go, tripped over a hat-box, and fell, with undignified remarks.

"If people would be more careful," said a field-mouse rather stiffly, "and look where they're going, people wouldn't hurt themselves and forget themselves. Mind that hold-all, Rat! You'd better sit down somewhere. In an hour or two we may be more free to attend to you."

"You won't be 'free,' as you call it, much this side of Christmas, I can see that," retorted the Rat grumpily, as he picked his way out of the field.

He returned somewhat despondently to his river again—his faithful, steady-going old river, which never packed up, flitted, or went into winter quarters.

In the osiers which fringed the bank he spied a swallow sitting. Presently it was joined by another, and then by a third; and the birds, fidgeting restlessly on their bough, talked together earnestly and low.

"What, *already*?" said the Rat, strolling up to them. "What's the hurry? I call it simply ridiculous."

"O, we're not off yet, if that's what you mean," replied the first swallow. "We're only making plans and arranging things. Talking it over, you know— what route we're taking this year, and where we'll stop, and so on. That's half the fun!"

"Fun?" said the Rat; "now that's just what I don't understand. If you've *got* to leave this pleasant place, and your friends who will miss you, and your snug homes that you've just settled into, why, when the hour strikes I've no doubt you'll go bravely, and face all the trouble and discomfort and change and newness, and make believe that you're not very unhappy. But to want to talk about it, or even think about it, till you really need—"

"No, you don't understand, naturally," said the second swallow. "First, we feel it stirring within us, a sweet unrest; then back come the recollections one by one, like homing pigeons. They flutter through our dreams at night, they fly with us in our wheelings and circlings by day. We hunger to inquire of each other, to compare notes and assure ourselves that it was all really true, as one by one the scents and sounds and names of long-forgotten places come gradually back and beckon to us."

"Couldn't you stop on for just this year," suggested the Water Rat wistfully. "We'll all do our best to make you feel at home. You've no idea what good times we have here, while you are far away."

"I tried 'stopping on' one year," said the third swallow. "I had grown so fond of the place that when the time came I hung back and let the others go on without me. For a few weeks it was all well enough, but afterwards, O the weary length of the nights! The shivering, sunless days! The air so clammy and chill, and not an insect in an acre of it! No, it was no good; my courage broke down, and one cold, stormy night I took wing, flying well inland on account of the strong easterly gales. It was snowing hard as I beat through the passes of the great mountains, and I had a stiff fight to win through; but never shall I forget the blissful feeling of the hot sun again on my back as I sped down to the lakes that lay so blue and placid below me, and the taste of my first fat insect! The past was like a bad dream; the future was all happy holiday as I moved Southwards week by week, easily, lazily, lingering as long as I dared, but always heeding the call! No, I had had my warning; never again did I think of disobedience."

"Ah, yes, the call of the South, of the South!" twittered the other two dreamily. "Its songs, its hues, its radiant air! O, do you remember—" and, forgetting the Rat, they slid into passionate reminiscence, while he listened fascinated, and his heart burned within him. In himself, too, he knew that it was vibrating at last, that chord hitherto dormant and unsuspected. The mere chatter of these southern-bound birds, their pale and second-hand reports, had yet power to awaken this wild new sensation and thrill him through and through with it; what would one moment of the real thing work in him—one passionate touch of the real southern sun, one waft of the authentic odour? With closed eyes he dared to dream a moment in full abandonment, and when he looked again the river seemed steely and chill, the green fields grey and lightless. Then his loyal heart seemed to cry out on his weaker self for its treachery.

"Why do you ever come back, then, at all?" he demanded of the swallows jealously. "What do you find to attract you in this poor drab little country?"

"And do you think," said the first swallow, "that the other call is not for us too, in its due season? The call of lush meadow-grass, wet orchards, warm, insect-haunted ponds, of browsing cattle, of haymaking, and all the farm-buildings clustering round the House of the perfect Eaves?"

"Do you suppose," asked the second one, "that you are the only living thing that craves with a hungry longing to hear the cuckoo's note again?"

"In due time," said the third, "we shall be home-sick once more for quiet water-lilies swaying on the surface of an English stream. But to-day all that seems pale and thin and very far away. Just now our blood dances to other music."

They fell a-twittering among themselves once more, and this time their intoxicating babble was of violet seas, tawny sands, and lizard-haunted walls.

Restlessly the Rat wandered off once more, climbed the slope that rose gently from the north bank of the river, and lay looking out towards the great ring of Downs that barred his vision further southwards—his simple horizon hitherto, his Mountains of the Moon, his limit behind which lay nothing he had cared to see or to know. To-day, to him gazing south with a new-born need stirring in his heart, the clear sky over their long low outline seemed to pulsate with promise; to-day, the unseen was everything, the unknown the only real fact of life. On this side of the hills was now the real blank, on the other lay the crowded and coloured panorama that his inner eye was seeing so clearly. What seas lay beyond, green, leaping, and crested! What sun-bathed coasts, along which the white villas glittered against the olive woods! What quiet harbours, thronged with gallant shipping bound for purple islands of wine and spice, islands set low in languorous waters!

He rose and descended river-wards once more; then changed his mind and sought the side of the dusty lane. There, lying half-buried in the thick, cool under-hedge tangle that bordered it, he could muse on the metalled road and all the wondrous world that it led to; on all the wayfarers, too, that might have trodden it, and the fortunes and adventures they had gone to seek or found unseeking—out there, beyond—beyond!

Footsteps fell on his ear, and the figure of one that walked somewhat wearily came into view; and he saw that it was a Rat, and a very dusty one. The wayfarer, as he reached him, saluted with a gesture of courtesy that had something foreign about it—hesitated a moment—then with a pleasant smile turned from the track and sat down by his side in the cool herbage. He seemed tired, and the Rat let him rest unquestioned, understanding something of what was in his thoughts; knowing, too, the value all animals attach at times to mere silent companionship, when the weary muscles slacken and the mind marks time.

The wayfarer was lean and keen-featured, and somewhat bowed at the shoulders; his paws were thin and long, his eyes much wrinkled at the corners, and he wore small gold earrings in his neatly-set, well-shaped ears. His knitted jersey was of a faded blue, his breeches, patched and stained, were based on a blue foundation, and his small belongings that he carried were tied up in a blue cotton handkerchief.

When he had rested awhile the stranger sighed, snuffed the air, and looked about him.

"That was clover, that warm whiff on the breeze!" he remarked; "and those are cows we hear cropping the grass behind us and blowing softly between mouthfuls. There is a sound of distant reapers, and yonder rises a blue line of cottage smoke against the woodland. The river runs somewhere close by, for I hear the call of a moorhen, and I see by your build that you're a freshwater mariner. Everything seems asleep, and yet going on all the time. It is a goodly life that you lead, friend; no doubt the best in the world, if only you are strong enough to lead it!"

"Yes, it's *the* life, the only life, to live," responded the Water Rat dreamily, and without his usual whole-hearted conviction.

"I did not say exactly that," replied the stranger cautiously; "but no doubt it's the best. I've tried it, and I know. And because I've just tried it—six months of it—and know it's the best, here am I, foot-sore and hungry, tramping away from it, tramping southward, following the old call, back to the old life, *the* life which is mine and which will not let me go."

"Is this, then, yet another of them?" mused the Rat. "And where have you just come from?" he asked. He hardly dared to ask where he was bound for; he seemed to know the answer only too well.

"Nice little farm," replied the wayfarer briefly. "Up along in that direction"—he nodded north-wards. "Never mind about it. I had everything I could want—everything I had any right to expect of life, and more; and here I am! Glad to be here all the same, though, glad to be here! So many miles further on the road, so many hours nearer to my heart's desire!"

His shining eyes held fast to the horizon, and he seemed to be listening for some sound that was wanting from that inland acreage, vocal as it was with the cheerful music of pasturage and farmyard.

"You are not one of *us*," said the Water Rat, "nor yet a farmer; nor even, I should judge, of this country."

"Right," replied the stranger. "I'm a seafaring rat, I am, and the port I originally hail from is

Constantinople, though I'm a sort of a foreigner there too, in a manner of speaking. You will have heard of Constantinople, friend? A fair city, and an ancient and glorious one. And you may have heard, too, of Sigurd, King of Norway, and how he sailed thither with sixty ships, and how he and his men rode up through streets all canopied in their honour with purple and gold; and how the Emperor and Empress came down and banqueted with him on board his ship. When Sigurd returned home, many of his Northmen remained behind and entered the Emperor's body-guard, and my ancestor, a Norwegian born, stayed behind too, with the ships that Sigurd gave the Emperor. Seafarers we have ever been, and no wonder; as for me, the city of my birth is no more my home than any pleasant port between there and the London River. I know them all, and they know me. Set me down on any of their quays or foreshores, and I am home again."

"I suppose you go on great voyages," said the Water Rat with growing interest. "Months and months out of sight of land, and provisions running short, and allowanced as to water, and your mind communing with the mighty ocean, and all that sort of thing?"

"By no means," said the Sea Rat frankly. "Such life as you describe would not suit me at all. I'm in the coasting trade, and rarely out of sight of land. It's the jolly times on shore that appeal to me, as much as any seafaring. O, those southern seaports! The smell of them, the riding-lights at night, the glamour!"

"Well, perhaps you have chosen the better way," said the Water Rat, but rather doubtfully. "Tell me something of your coasting, then, if you have a mind to, and what sort of harvest an animal of spirit might hope to bring home from it to warm his latter days with gallant memories by the fireside; for my life, I confess to you, feels to me to-day somewhat narrow and circumscribed."

"My last voyage," began the Sea Rat, "that landed me eventually in this country, bound with high hopes for my inland farm, will serve as a good example of any of them, and, indeed, as an epitome of my highly-coloured life. Family troubles, as usual, began it. The domestic storm-cone was hoisted, and I shipped myself on board a small trading vessel bound from Constantinople, by classic seas whose every wave throbs with a deathless memory, to the Grecian Islands and the Levant. Those were golden days and balmy nights! In and out of harbour all the time—old friends everywhere—sleeping in some cool temple or ruined cistern during the heat of the day—feasting and song after sundown, under great stars set in a velvet sky! Thence we turned and coasted up the Adriatic, its shores swimming in an atmosphere of amber, rose, and aquamarine; we lay in wide land-locked harbours, we roamed through ancient and noble cities, until at last one morning, as the sun rose royally behind us, we rode into Venice down a path of gold. O, Venice is a fine city, wherein a rat can wander at his ease and take his pleasure! Or, when weary of wandering, can sit at the edge of the Grand Canal at night, feasting with his friends, when the air is full of music and the sky fill of stars, and the lights flash and shimmer on the polished steel prows of the swaying gondolas, parked so that you could walk across the canal on them from side to side! And then the food—do you like shell-fish? Well, well, we won't linger over that now."

He was silent for a time; and the Water Rat, silent too and enthralled, floated on dream-canals and heard a phantom song pealing high between vaporous grey wave-lapped walls.

"Southwards we sailed again at last," continued the Sea Rat, "coasting down the Italian shore, till finally we made Palermo, and there I quitted for a long, happy spell on shore. I never stick too long to one ship; one gets narrow-minded and prejudiced. Besides, Sicily is one of my happy hunting-grounds. I know everybody there, and their ways just suit me. I spent many jolly weeks in the island, staying with friends up country. When I grew restless again I took advantage of a ship that was trading to Sardinia and Corsica; and very glad I was to feel the fresh breeze and the sea-spray in my face once more."

"But isn't it very hot and stuffy, down in the— hold, I think you call it?" asked the Water Rat.

The seafarer looked at him with the suspicion of a wink. "I'm an old hand," he remarked with much simplicity. "The captain's cabin's good enough for me."

"It's a hard life, by all accounts," murmured the Rat, sunk deep in thought.

"For the crew it is," replied the seafarer gravely, again with the ghost of a wink.

"From Corsica," he went on, "I made use of a ship that was taking wine to the mainland. We made Alassio in the evening, lay to, hauled up our wine-casks, and hove them overboard, tied one to the other by a long line. Then the crew took to the boats and rowed shorewards, singing as they went, and drawing after them the long bobbing procession of casks, like a mile of porpoises. On the sands they had horses waiting, which dragged the casks up the steep street of the little town with a fine rush and clatter and scramble. When the last cask was in, we went and refreshed and rested, and sat late into the night, drinking with our friends; and next morning I was off to the great olive-woods for a spell and a rest. For now I had done with islands for the time, and ports and shipping were plentiful; so I led a lazy life among the peasants, lying and watching them work, or stretched high on the hillside with the blue Mediterranean far below me. And so at length, by easy stages, and partly on foot, partly by sea, to Marseilles, and the meeting of old shipmates, and the visiting of great ocean-bound vessels, and feasting once more. Talk of shell-fish! Why, sometimes I dream of the shell-fish of Marseilles, and wake up crying!"

"That reminds me," said the polite Water Rat; "you happened to mention that you were hungry, and I ought to have spoken earlier. Of course you will stop and take your midday meal with me? My hole is close by; it is some time past noon, and you are very welcome to whatever there is."

"Now I call that kind and brotherly of you," said the Sea Rat. "I was indeed hungry when I sat down, and ever since I inadvertently happened to mention shell-fish, my pangs have been extreme. But couldn't you fetch it along out here? I am none too fond of going under hatches, unless I'm obliged to; and then, while we eat, I could tell you more concerning my voyages and the pleasant life I lead—at least, it is very pleasant to me, and by your attention I judge it commends itself to you; whereas if we go indoors it is a hundred to one that I shall presently fall asleep."

"That is indeed an excellent suggestion," said the Water Rat, and hurried off home. There he got out the luncheon-basket and packed a simple meal, in which, remembering the stranger's origin and preferences, he took care to include a yard of long French bread, a sausage out of which the garlic sang, some cheese which lay down and cried, and a long-necked straw-covered flask containing bottled sunshine shed and garnered on far Southern slopes. Thus laden, he returned with all speed, and blushed for pleasure at the old seaman's commendations of his taste and judgment, as together they unpacked the basket and laid out the contents on the grass by the roadside.

The Sea Rat, as soon as his hunger was somewhat assuaged, continued the history of his latest
voyage, conducting his simple hearer from port to
port of Spain, landing him at Lisbon, Oporto, and
Bordeaux, introducing him to the pleasant
harbours of Cornwall and Devon, and so up the
Channel to that final quayside, where, landing after
winds long contrary, storm-driven and weather-
beaten, he had caught the first magical hints and
heraldings of another Spring, and, fired by these,
had sped on a long tramp inland, hungry for the
experiment of life on some quiet farmstead, very far
from the weary beating of any sea.

Spellbound and quivering with excitement, the
Water Rat followed the Adventurer league by
league, over stormy bays, through crowded road-
steads, across harbour bars on a racing tide, up
winding rivers that hid their busy little towns round
a sudden turn, and left him with a regretful sigh
planted at his dull inland farm, about which he
desired to hear nothing.

By this time their meal was over, and the
Seafarer, refreshed and strengthened, his voice
more vibrant, his eye lit with a brightness that
seemed caught from some far-away sea-beacon,

filled his glass with the red and glowing vintage of the South, and, leaning towards the Water Rat, compelled his gaze and held him, body and soul, while he talked. Those eyes were of the changing foam-streaked grey-green of leaping Northern seas; in the glass shone a hot ruby that seemed the very heart of the South, beating for him who had courage to respond to its pulsation. The twin lights, the shifting grey and the steadfast red, mastered the Water Rat and held him bound, fascinated, powerless. The quiet world outside their rays receded far away and ceased to be. And the talk, the wonderful talk flowed on—or was it speech entirely, or did it pass at times into song—shanty of the sailors weighing the dripping anchor, sonorous hum of the shrouds in a tearing North-Easter, ballad of the fisherman hauling his nets at sundown against an apricot sky, chords of guitar and mandoline from gondola or caique? Did it change into the cry of the wind, plaintive at first, angrily shrill as it freshened, rising to a tearing whistle, sinking to a musical trickle of air from the leech of the bellying sail? All these sounds the spellbound listener seemed to hear, and with them the hungry complaint of the gulls and the sea-mews, the soft thunder of the breaking wave, the cry of the protesting shingle. Back into speech again it passed, and with beating heart he was following the adventures of a dozen seaports, the fights, the escapes, the rallies, the comradeships, the gallant undertakings; or he searched islands for treasure, fished in still lagoons and dozed day-long on warm white sand. Of deep-sea fishings he heard tell, and mighty silver gatherings of the mile-long net; of sudden perils, noise of breakers on a moonless night, or the tall bows of the great liner taking shape overhead through the fog; of the merry home-coming, the headland rounded, the harbour lights opened out: the groups seen dimly on the quay, the cheery hail, the splash of the hawser; the trudge up the steep little street towards the comforting glow of red-curtained windows.

Lastly, in his waking dream it seemed to him that the Adventurer had risen to his feet, but was still speaking, still holding him fast with his sea-grey eyes.

"And now," he was softly saying, "I take to the road again, holding on south-westwards for many a long and dusty day; till at last I reach the little grey sea town I know so well, that clings along one steep side of the harbour. There through dark doorways you look down flights of stone steps, overhung by great pink tufts of valerian and ending in a patch of sparkling blue water. The little boats that lie tethered to the rings and stanchions of the old sea-wall are gaily painted as those I clambered in and out of in my own childhood; the salmon leap on the flood tide, schools of mackerel flash and play past quay-sides and foreshores, and by the windows the great vessels glide, night and day, up to their moorings or forth to the open sea. There, sooner or later, the ships of all seafaring nations arrive; and there, at its destined hour, the ship of my choice will let go its anchor. I shall take my time, I shall tarry and bide, till at last the right one lies waiting for me, warped out into midstream, loaded low, her bowsprit pointing down harbour. I shall slip on board, by boat or along hawser; and then one morning I shall wake to the song and tramp of the sailors, the clink of the capstan, and the rattle of the anchor-chain coming merrily in. We shall break out the jib and the fore-sail, the white houses on the harbour side will glide slowly past us as she gathers steering-way, and the voyage will have begun! As she forges towards the headland she will clothe herself with canvas; and then, once outside, the sounding slap of great green seas as she heels to the wind, pointing South!

"And you, you will come too, young brother; for the days pass, and never return, and the South still waits for you. Take the Adventure, heed the call, now ere the irrevocable moment passes! 'Tis but a banging of the door behind you, a blithesome step forward, and you are out of the old life and into the new! Then some day, some day long hence, jog home here if you will, when the cup has been drained and the play has been played, and sit down by your quiet river with a store of goodly memories for company. You can easily over-take me on the road, for you are young, and I am ageing and go softly. I will linger, and look back; and at last I will surely see you coming, eager and light-hearted, with all the South in your face!"

The voice died away and ceased, as an insect's tiny trumpet dwindles swiftly into silence; and the Water Rat, paralysed and staring, saw at last but a distant speck on the white surface of the road.

Mechanically he rose and proceeded to repack the luncheon-basket, carefully and without haste. Mechanically he returned home, gathered together a few small necessaries and special treasures he was fond of, and put them in a satchel; acting with slow deliberation, moving about the room like a sleep-walker; listening ever with parted lips. He swung the satchel over his shoulder, carefully selected a stout stick for his wayfaring, and with no haste, but with no hesitation at all, he stepped across the threshold just as the Mole appeared at the door.

"Why, where are you off to, Ratty?" asked the Mole in great surprise, grasping him by the arm.

"Going South, with the rest of them," murmured the Rat in a dreamy monotone, never looking at him. "Seawards first and then on shipboard, and so to the shores that are calling me!"

He pressed resolutely forward, still without haste, but with dogged fixity of purpose; but the Mole, now thoroughly alarmed, placed himself in front of him, and looking into his eyes saw that they were glazed and set and turned a streaked and shifting grey— not his friend's eyes, but the eyes of some other animal! Grappling with him strongly he dragged him inside, threw him down, and held him.

The Rat struggled desperately for a few moments, and then his strength seemed suddenly to leave him, and he lay still and exhausted, with closed eyes, trembling. Presently the Mole assisted him to rise and placed him in a chair, where he sat collapsed and shrunken into himself, his body shaken by a violent shivering, passing in time into an hysterical fit of dry sobbing. Mole made the door fast, threw the satchel into a drawer and locked it, and sat down quietly on the table by his friend, waiting for the strange seizure to pass. Gradually the Rat sank into a troubled doze, broken by starts and confused murmurings of things strange and wild and foreign to the unenlightened Mole; and from that he passed into a deep slumber.

Very anxious in mind, the Mole left him for a time and busied himself with household matters; and it was getting dark when he returned to the parlour and found the Rat where he had left him, wide awake indeed, but listless, silent, and dejected. He took one hasty glance at his eyes; found them, to his great gratification, clear and dark and brown again as before; and then sat down and tried to cheer him up and help him to relate what had happened to him.

Poor Ratty did his best, by degrees, to explain things; but how could he put into cold words what had mostly been suggestion? How recall, for another's benefit, the haunting sea voices that had sung to him, how reproduce at second-hand the magic of the Seafarer's hundred reminiscences? Even to himself, now the spell was broken and the glamour gone, he found it difficult to account for what had seemed, some hours ago, the inevitable and only thing. It is not surprising, then, that he failed to convey to the Mole any clear idea of what he had been through that day.

To the Mole this much was plain: the fit, or attack, had passed away, and had left him sane again, though shaken and cast down by the reaction. But he seemed to have lost all interest for the time in the things that went to make up his daily life, as well as in all pleasant forecastings of the altered days and doings that the changing season was surely bringing.

Casually, then, and with seeming indifference, the Mole turned his talk to the harvest that was being gathered in, the towering wagons and their straining teams, the growing ricks, and the large moon rising over bare acres dotted with sheaves. He talked of the reddening apples around, of the browning nuts, of jams and preserves and the distilling of cordials; till by easy stages such as these he reached mid-winter, its hearty joys and its snug home life, and then he became simply lyrical.

By degrees the Rat began to sit up and to join in. His dull eye brightened, and he lost some of his listless air.

Presently the tactful Mole slipped away and returned with a pencil and a few half-sheets of paper, which he placed on the table at his friend's elbow.

"It's quite a long time since you did any poetry," he remarked. "You might have a try at it this evening, instead of—well, brooding over things so much. I've an idea that you'll feel a lot better when you've got something jotted down—if it's only just the rhymes."

The Rat pushed the paper away from him wearily, but the discreet Mole took occasion to leave the room, and when he peeped in again some time later, the Rat was absorbed and deaf to the world; alternately scribbling and sucking the top of his pencil. It is true that he sucked a good deal more than he scribbled; but it was joy to the Mole to know that the cure had at least begun.

CHAPTER 10

The Further Adventures of Toad

The front door of the hollow tree faced eastwards, so Toad was called at an early hour; partly by the bright sunlight streaming in on him, partly by the exceeding coldness of his toes, which made him dream that he was at home in bed in his own handsome room with the Tudor window, on a cold winter's night, and his bedclothes had got up, grumbling and protesting they couldn't stand the cold any longer, and had run downstairs to the kitchen fire to warm themselves; and he had followed on bare feet, along miles and miles of icy stone-paved passages, arguing and beseeching them to be reasonable. He would probably have been aroused much earlier, had he not slept for some weeks on straw over stone flags, and almost forgotten the friendly feeling of thick blankets pulled well up round the chin.

Sitting up, he rubbed his eyes first and his complaining toes next, wondered for a moment where he was, looking round for familiar stone wall and little barred window; then, with a leap of the heart, remembered everything—his escape, his flight, his pursuit; remembered, first and best thing of all, that he was free!

Free! The word and the thought alone were worth fifty blankets. He was warm from end to end as he thought of the jolly world outside, waiting eagerly for him to make his triumphal entrance, ready to serve him and play up to him, anxious to help him and to keep him company, as it always had been in days of old before misfortune fell upon him. He shook himself and combed the dry leaves out of his hair with his fingers; and, his toilet complete, marched forth into the comfortable morning sun, cold but confident, hungry but hopeful, all nervous terrors of yesterday dispelled by rest and sleep and frank and heartening sunshine.

He had the world all to himself that early summer morning. The dewy woodland, as he threaded it, was solitary and still; the green fields that succeeded the trees were his own to do as he liked with; the road itself, when he reached it, in that loneliness that was everywhere, seemed, like a stray dog, to be looking anxiously for company. Toad, however, was looking for something that could talk, and tell him clearly which way he ought to go. It is all very well, when you have a light heart, and a clear conscience, and money in your pocket, and nobody scouring the country for you to drag you off to prison again, to follow where the road beckons and points, not caring whither. The practical Toad cared very much indeed, and he could have kicked the road for its helpless silence when every minute was of importance to him.

The reserved rustic road was presently joined by a shy little brother in the shape of a canal, which took its hand and ambled along by its side in perfect confidence, but with the same tongue-tied, uncommunicative attitude towards strangers. "Bother them!" said Toad to himself. "But, anyhow, one thing's clear. They must both be coming *from* somewhere, and going *to* somewhere. You can't get over that, Toad, my boy!" So he marched on patiently by the water's edge.

Round a bend in the canal came plodding a solitary horse, stooping forward as if in anxious thought. From rope traces attached to his collar

stretched a long line, taut, but dipping with his stride, the further part of it dripping pearly drops. Toad let the horse pass, and stood waiting for what the fates were sending him.

With a pleasant swirl of quiet water at its blunt bow the barge slid up alongside of him, its gaily painted gunwale level with the towing-path, its sole occupant a big stout woman wearing a linen sun-bonnet, one brawny arm laid along the tiller.

"A nice morning, ma'am!" she remarked to Toad, as she drew up level with him.

"I dare say it is, ma'am!" responded Toad politely, as he walked along the tow-path abreast of her. "I dare say it is a nice morning to them that's not in sore trouble, like what I am. Here's my married daughter, she sends off to me post-haste to come to her at once; so off I comes, not knowing what may be happening or going to happen, but fearing the worst, as you will understand, ma'am, if you're a mother, too. And I've left my business to look after itself—I'm in the washing and laundering line, you must know, ma'am—and I've left my young children to look after themselves, and a more mischievous and troublesome set of young imps doesn't exist, ma'am; and I've lost all my money, and lost my way, and as for what may be happening to my married daughter, why, I don't like to think of it, ma'am!"

"Where might your married daughter be living, ma'am?" asked the barge-woman.

"She lives near to the river, ma'am," replied Toad "Close to a fine house called Toad Hall, that's somewheres hereabouts in these parts. Perhaps you may have heard of it."

"Toad Hall? Why, I'm going that way myself," replied the barge-woman. This canal joins the river some miles further on, a little above Toad Hall; and then it's an easy walk. You come along in the barge with me, and I'll give you a lift."

She steered the barge close to the bank, and Toad, with many humble and grateful acknowledgments, stepped lightly on board and sat down with great satisfaction.

"Toad's luck again!" thought he. "I always come out on top!"

"So you're in the washing business, ma'am?" said the barge-woman politely, as they glided along. "And a very good business you've got too, I dare say, if I'm not making too free in saying so."

"Finest business in the whole county," said Toad airily. "All the gentry come to me—wouldn't go to any one else if they were paid, they know me so well. You see, I understand my work thoroughly, and attend to it all myself. Washing, ironing, clear-starching, making up gents' fine shirts for evening wear—everything's done under my own eye!"

"But surely you don't *do* all that work yourself, ma'am?" asked the barge-woman respectfully.

"O, I have girls," said Toad lightly: "twenty girls or thereabouts, always at work. But you know what *girls* are, ma'am! Nasty little hussies, that's what *I* call 'em!"

"So do I, too," said the barge-woman with great heartiness. "But I dare say you set yours to rights, the idle trollops! And are you *very* fond of washing?"

"I love it," said Toad. "I simply dote on it. Never so happy as when I've got both arms in the washtub. But, then, it comes so easy to me! No trouble at all! A real pleasure, I assure you, ma'am!"

"What a bit of luck, meeting you!" observed the barge-woman thoughtfully. "A regular piece of good fortune for both of us."

"Why, what do you mean?" asked Toad nervously.

"Well, look at me, now," replied the barge-woman. "*I* like washing, too, just the same as you do; and for that matter, whether I like it or not I have got to do all my own, naturally, moving about as I do. Now my husband, he's such a fellow for shirking his work and leaving the barge to me, that never a moment do I get for seeing to my own affairs. By rights he ought to be here now, either steering or attending to the horse, though luckily the horse has sense enough to attend to himself. Instead of which, he's gone off with the dog, to see if they can't pick up a rabbit for dinner somewhere. Says he'll catch me up at the next lock. Well, that's as may be—I don't trust him, once he gets off with that dog, who's worse than he is. But, meantime, how am I to get on with my washing?"

"O, never mind about the washing," said Toad, not liking the subject. "Try and fix your mind on that rabbit. A nice fat young rabbit, I'll be bound. Got any onions?"

"I can't fix my mind on anything but my washing," said the barge-woman, "and I wonder you can be talking of rabbits, with such a joyful prospect before you. There's a heap of things of mine that you'll find in a corner of the cabin. If you'll just take one or two of the most necessary sort—I won't venture to describe them to a lady like you, but you'll recognize 'em at a glance—and put them through the wash-tub as we go along, why, it'll be a pleasure to you, as you rightly say, and a real help to me. You'll find a tub handy, and soap, and a kettle on the stove, and a bucket to haul up water from the canal with. Then I shall know you're enjoying yourself, instead of sitting here idle, looking at the scenery and yawning your head off."

"Here, you let me steer!" said Toad, now thoroughly frightened, "and then you can get on with your washing your own way. I might spoil your things, or not do 'em as you like. I'm more used to gentlemen's things myself. It's my special line."

"Let you steer?" replied the barge-woman, laughing. "It takes some practice to steer a barge properly. Besides, it's dull work, and I want you to be happy. No, you shall do the washing you are so fond of and I'll stick to the steering that I understand. Don't try and deprive me of the pleasure of giving you a treat!"

Toad was fairly cornered. He looked for escape this way and that, saw that he was too far from the bank for a flying leap, and sullenly resigned himself to his fate. "If it comes to that," he thought in desperation, "I suppose any fool can *wash*!"

He fetched tub, soap, and other necessaries from the cabin, selected a few garments at random, tried to recollect what he had seen in casual glances through laundry windows, and set to.

A long half-hour passed, and every minute of it saw Toad getting crosser and crosser. Nothing that he could do to the things seemed to please them or do them good. He tried coaxing, he tried slapping, he tried punching; they smiled back at him out of the tub unconverted, happy in their original sin. Once or twice he looked nervously over his shoulder at the barge-woman, but she appeared to be gazing out in front of her, absorbed in her steering.

His back ached badly, and he noticed with dismay that his paws were beginning to get all crinkly. Now Toad was very proud of his paws. He muttered under his breath words that should never pass the lips of either washerwomen or Toads; and lost the soap, for the fiftieth time.

A burst of laughter made him straighten himself and look round. The barge-woman was leaning back and laughing unrestrainedly, till the tears ran down her cheeks.

"I've been watching you all the time," she gasped. "I thought you must be a humbug all along, from the conceited way you talked. Pretty washer-woman you are! Never washed so much as a dish-clout in your life, I'll lay!"

Toad's temper, which had been simmering viciously for some time, now fairly boiled over, and he lost all control of himself.

"You common, low, *fat* barge-woman!" he shouted; "don't you dare to talk to your betters like that! Washerwoman indeed! I would have you to know that I am a Toad, a very well-known respected, distinguished Toad! I may be under a bit of a cloud at present, but I will *not* be laughed at by a barge-woman!"

The woman moved nearer to him and peered under his bonnet keenly and closely. "Why, so you are!" she cried. "Well, I never! A horrid, nasty, crawly Toad! And in my nice clean barge, too! Now that is a thing that I will *not* have."

She relinquished the tiller for a moment. One big mottled arm shot out and caught Toad by a fore-leg, while the other gripped him fast by a hind-leg. Then the world turned suddenly upside down, the barge seemed to flit lightly across the sky, the wind whistled in his ears, and Toad found himself flying through the air, revolving rapidly as he went.

The water, when he eventually reached it with a loud splash, proved quite cold enough for his taste, though its chill was not sufficient to quell his proud spirit, or slake the heat of his furious temper. He rose to the surface spluttering, and when he had wiped the duckweed out of his eyes the first thing he saw was the fat barge-woman looking back at him over the stern of the retreating barge and laughing; and he vowed, as he coughed and choked, to be even with her.

He struck out for the shore, but the cotton gown greatly impeded his efforts, and when at length he touched land he found it hard to climb up the steep bank unassisted. He had to take a minute or two's rest to recover his breath; then, gathering his wet skirts well over his arms, he started to run after the barge as fast as his legs would carry him, wild with indignation, thirsting for revenge.

The barge-woman was still laughing when he drew up level with her. "Put yourself through your mangle, washerwoman," she called out, "and iron your face and crimp it, and you'll pass for quite a decent-looking Toad!"

Toad never paused to reply. Solid revenge was what he wanted, not cheap, windy, verbal triumphs, though he had a thing or two in his mind that he would have liked to say. He saw what he wanted ahead of him. Running swiftly on he overtook the horse, unfastened the tow-rope and cast off, jumped lightly on the horse's back, and urged it to a gallop by kicking it vigorously in the sides. He steered for the open country, abandoning the tow-path, and swinging his steed down a rutty lane. Once he looked back, and saw that the barge had run aground on the other side of the canal, and the barge-woman was gesticulating wildly and shouting, "Stop, stop, stop!" "I've heard that song before," said Toad, laughing, as he continued to spur his steed onward in its wild career.

The barge-horse was not capable of any very sustained effort, and its gallop soon subsided into a trot, and its trot into an easy walk; but Toad was quite contented with this, knowing that he, at any rate, was moving, and the barge was not. He had quite recovered his temper, now that he had done something he thought really clever; and he was satisfied to jog along quietly in the sun, taking advantage of any by-ways and bridle-paths, and trying to forget how very long it was since he had had a square meal, till the canal had been left very far behind him.

He had travelled some miles, his horse and he, and he was feeling drowsy in the hot sunshine, when the horse stopped, lowered his head, and began to nibble the grass; and Toad, waking up, just saved himself from falling off by an effort. He looked about him and found he was on a wide common, dotted with patches of gorse and bramble as far as he could see. Near him stood a dingy gipsy caravan, and beside it a man was sitting on a bucket turned upside down, very busy smoking and staring into the wide world. A fire of sticks was burning near by, and over the fire hung an iron pot, and out of that pot came forth bubblings and gurglings, and a vague suggestive steaminess. Also smells—warm, rich, and varied smells—that twined and twisted and wreathed themselves at last into one complete, voluptuous, perfect smell that seemed like the very soul of Nature taking form and appearing to her children, a true Goddess, a mother of solace and comfort. Toad now knew well that he had not been really hungry before. What he had felt earlier in the day had been a mere trifling qualm. This was the real thing at last, and no mistake; and it would have to be dealt with speedily, too, or there would be trouble for somebody or something. He looked the gipsy over carefully, wondering vaguely whether it would be easier to fight him or cajole him. So there he sat, and sniffed and sniffed, and looked at the gipsy; and the gipsy sat and smoked, and looked at him.

Presently the gipsy took his pipe out of his mouth and remarked in a careless way, "Want to sell that there horse of yours?"

Toad was completely taken aback. He did not know that gipsies were very fond of horse-dealing, and never missed an opportunity, and he had not reflected that caravans were always on the move and took a deal of drawing. It had not occurred to him to turn the horse into cash, but the gipsy's suggestion seemed to smooth the way towards the two things he wanted so badly—ready money and a solid breakfast.

"What?" he said, "me sell this beautiful young horse of mine? O no; it's out of the question. Who's going to take the washing home to my customers every week? Besides, I'm too fond of him, and he simply dotes on me."

"Try and love a donkey," suggested the gipsy. "Some people do."

"You don't seem to see," continued Toad, "that this fine horse of mine is a cut above you altogether. He's a blood horse, he is, partly; not the part you see, of course—another part. And he's been a Prize Hackney, too, in his time—that was the time before you knew him, but you can still tell it on him at a glance if you understand anything about horses. No, it's not to be thought of for a moment. All the same, how much might you be disposed to offer me for this beautiful young horse of mine?"

The gipsy looked the horse over, and then he looked Toad over with equal care, and looked at the horse again. "Shillin' a leg," he said briefly, and turned away, continuing to smoke and try to stare the wide world out of countenance.

"A shilling a leg?" cried Toad. "If you please, I must take a little time to work that out, and see just what it comes to."

He climbed down off his horse, and left it to graze, and sat down by the gipsy, and did sums on his fingers, and at last he said, "A shilling a leg? Why, that comes to exactly four shillings, and no more. O no; I could not think of accepting four shillings for this beautiful young horse of mine."

"Well," said the gipsy, "I'll tell you what I will do. I'll make it five shillings, and that's three-and-six-pence more than the animal's worth. And that's my last word."

Then Toad sat and pondered long and deeply. For he was hungry and quite penniless, and still some way—he knew not how far—from home, and enemies might still be looking for him. To one in such a situation, five shillings may very well appear a large sum of money. On the other hand, it did not seem very much to get for a horse. But then, again, the horse hadn't cost him anything; so whatever he got was all clear profit. At last he said firmly, "Look here, gipsy! I tell you what we will do; and this is my last word. You shall hand me over six shillings and sixpence, cash down; and further, in addition thereto, you shall give me as much breakfast as I can possibly eat, at one sitting of course, out of that iron pot of yours that keeps sending forth such delicious and exciting smells. In return, I will make over to you my spirited young horse, with all the beautiful harness and trappings that are on him, freely thrown in. If that's not good enough for you, say so, and I'll be getting on. I know a man near here who's wanted this horse of mine for years."

The gipsy grumbled frightfully, and declared if he did a few more deals of that sort he'd be ruined. But in the end he lugged a dirty canvas bag out of the depths of his trouser-pocket, and counted out six shillings and sixpence into Toad's paw. Then he disappeared into the caravan for an instant, and returned with a large iron plate and a knife, fork, and spoon. He tilted up the pot, and a glorious stream of hot rich stew gurgled into the plate. It was, indeed, the most beautiful stew in the world, being made of partridges, and pheasants, and chickens, and hares, and rabbits, and pea-hens, and guinea-fowls, and one or two other things. Toad took the plate on his lap, almost crying, and stuffed, and stuffed, and stuffed, and kept asking for more, and the gipsy never grudged it him. He thought that he had never eaten so good a breakfast in all his life.

When Toad had taken as much stew on board as he thought he could possibly hold, he got up and said good-bye to the gipsy, and took an affectionate farewell of the horse; and the gipsy, who knew the riverside well, gave him directions which way to go, and he set forth on his travels again in the best possible spirits. He was, indeed, a very different Toad from the animal of an hour ago. The sun was shining brightly, his wet clothes were quite dry again, he had money in his pockets once more, he was nearing home and friends and safety, and, most and best of all, he had had a substantial meal, hot and nourishing, and felt big, and strong, and care-less, and self-confident.

As he tramped along gaily, he thought of his adventures and escapes, and how when things seemed at their worst he had always managed to find a way out; and his pride and conceit began to swell within him. "Ho, ho!" he said to himself as he marched along with his chin in the air, "what a clever Toad I am! There is surely no animal equal to me for cleverness in the whole world! My enemies shut me up in prison, encircled by sentries, watched night and day by warders; I walk out through them all, by sheer ability coupled with courage. They pursue me with engines, and policemen, and revolvers; I snap my fingers at them, and vanish, laughing, into space. I am, unfortunately, thrown into a canal by a woman, fat of body and very evil-minded. What of it? I swim ashore, I seize her horse, I ride off in triumph, and I sell the horse for a whole pocketful of money and an excellent breakfast! Ho, ho! I am The Toad, the handsome, the popular, the successful Toad!" He got so puffed up with conceit that he made up a song as he walked in praise of himself, and sang it at the top of his voice, though there was no one to hear it but him. It was perhaps the most conceited song that any animal ever composed:

> *The world has held great Heroes,*
> *As history-books have showed;*
> *But never a name to go down to fame*
> *Compared with that of Toad!*

> *The clever men at Oxford*
> *Know all that there is to be knowed.*
> *But they none of them know one half as much*
> *As intelligent Mr Toad!*

The animals sat in the Ark and cried,
   Their tears in torrents flowed.
Who was it said, "There's land ahead"?
   Encouraging Mr Toad!

The Army all saluted
   As they marched along the road.
Was it the King? Or Kitchener?
   No It was Mr Toad.

The Queen and her Ladies-in-waiting
   Sat at the window and sewed
She cried, "Look! who's that handsome man?"
   They answered, "Mr Toad."

There was a great deal more of the same sort, but too dreadfully conceited to be written down. These are some of the milder verses.

He sang as he walked, and he walked as he sang, and got more inflated every minute. But his pride was shortly to have a severe fall.

After some miles of country lanes he reached the high road, and as he turned into it and glanced along its white length, he saw approaching him a speck that turned into a dot and then into a blob, and then into something very familiar; and a double note of warning, only too well known, fell on his delighted ear.

"This is something like!" said the excited Toad. "This is real life again, this is once more the great world from which I have been missed so long! I will hail them, my brothers of the wheel, and pitch them a yarn, of the sort that has been so successful hitherto; and they will give me a lift, of course, and then I will talk to them some more; and, perhaps, with luck, it may even end in my driving up to Toad Hall in a motor-car! That will be one in the eye for Badger!"

He stepped confidently out into the road to hail the motor-car, which came along at an easy pace, slowing down as it neared the lane; when suddenly he became very pale, his heart turned to water, his knees shook and yielded under him, and he doubled up and collapsed with a sickening pain in his interior. And well he might, the unhappy animal; for the approaching car was the very one he had stolen out of the yard of the Red Lion Hotel on that fatal day when all his troubles began! And the people in it were the very same people he had sat and watched at luncheon in the coffee-room!

He sank down in a shabby, miserable heap in the road, murmuring to himself in his despair, "It's all up! It's all over now! Chains and policemen again! Prison again! Dry bread and water again! O, what a fool I have been! What did I want to go strutting about the country for, singing conceited songs, and hailing people in broad day on the high road, instead of hiding till nightfall and slipping home quietly by back ways! O hapless Toad! O ill-fated animal!"

The terrible motor-car drew slowly nearer and nearer, till at last he heard it stop just short of him. Two gentlemen got out and walked round the trembling heap of crumpled misery lying in the road, and one of them said, "O dear! this is very sad! Here is a poor old thing—a washerwoman apparently—who has fainted in the road! Perhaps she is overcome by the heat, poor creature; or possibly she has not had any food to-day. Let us lift her into the car and take her to the nearest village, where doubtless she has friends."

They tenderly lifted Toad into the motor-car and propped him up with soft cushions, and proceeded on their way.

When Toad heard them talk in so kind and sympathetic a manner, he knew that he was not recognized, his courage began to revive, and he cautiously opened first one eye and then the other.

"Look!" said one of the gentlemen, "she is better already. The fresh air is doing her good. How do you feel now, ma'am?"

"Thank you kindly, sir," said Toad in a feeble voice, "I'm feeling a great deal better!"

"That's right," said the gentleman. "Now keep quite still, and, above all, don't try to talk."

"I won't," said Toad "I was only thinking, if I might sit on the front seat there, beside the driver, where I could get the fresh air full in my face, I should soon be all right again."

"What a very sensible woman!" said the gentleman. "Of course you shall." So they carefully helped Toad into the front seat beside the driver, and on they went once more.

Toad was almost himself again by now. He sat up, looked about him, and tried to beat down the tremors, the yearnings, the old cravings that rose up and beset him and took possession of him entirely.

"It is fate!" he said to himself "Why strive? why struggle?" and he turned to the driver at his side.

"Please, sir," he said, "I wish you would kindly let me try and drive the car for a little. I've been watching you carefully, and it looks so easy and so interesting, and I should like to be able to tell my friends that once I had driven a motor-car!"

The driver laughed at the proposal, so heartily that the gentleman inquired what the matter was. When he heard, he said, to Toad's delight, "Bravo, ma'am! I like your spirit. Let her have a try, and look after her. She won't do any harm."

Toad eagerly scrambled into the seat vacated by the driver, took the steering-wheel in his hands, listened with affected humility to the instructions given him, and set the car in motion, but very slowly and carefully at first, for he was determined to be prudent.

The gentlemen behind clapped their hands and applauded, and Toad heard them saying, "How well she does it! Fancy a washerwoman driving a car as well as that, the first time!"

Toad went a little faster; then faster still, and faster.

He heard the gentlemen call out warningly, "Be careful, washerwoman!" And this annoyed him, and he began to lose his head.

The driver tried to interfere, but he pinned him down in his seat with one elbow, and put on full speed. The rush of air in his face, the hum of the engine, and the light jump of the car beneath him intoxicated his weak brain. "Washerwoman, indeed!" he shouted recklessly. "Ho, ho! I am the Toad, the motor-car snatcher, the prison-breaker, the Toad who always escapes! Sit still, and you shall know what driving really is, for you are in the hands of the famous, the skilful, the entirely fearless Toad!"

With a cry of horror the whole party rose and flung themselves on him. "Seize him!" they cried, "seize the Toad, the wicked animal who stole our motor-car! Bind him, chain him, drag him to the nearest police-station! Down with the desperate and dangerous Toad!"

Alas! they should have thought, they ought to have been more prudent, they should have remembered to stop the motor-car somehow before playing any pranks of that sort. With a half-turn of the wheel the Toad sent the car crashing through the low hedge that ran along the roadside. One mighty bound, a violent shock, and the wheels of the car were churning up the thick mud of a horse-pond.

Toad found himself flying through the air with the strong upward rush and delicate curve of a swallow. He liked the motion, and was just beginning to wonder whether it would go on until he developed wings and turned into a Toad-bird, when he landed on his back with a thump, in the soft rich grass of a meadow. Sitting up, he could just see the motor-car in the pond, nearly submerged; the gentlemen and the driver, encumbered by their long coats, were floundering helplessly in the water.

He picked himself up rapidly and set off running across country as hard as he could, scrambling through hedges, jumping ditches, pounding across fields, till he was breathless and weary, and had to settle down into an easy walk. When he had recovered his breath somewhat, and was able to think calmly, he began to giggle, and from giggling he took to laughing, and he laughed till he had to sit down under a hedge. "Ho, ho!" he cried, in ecstasies of self-admiration. "Toad again! Toad, as usual comes out on the top! Who was it got them to give him a lift? Who managed to get on the front seat for the sake of fresh air? Who persuaded them into letting him see if he could drive? Who landed them all in a horse-pond? Who escaped, flying gaily and unscathed through the air, leaving the narrow-minded, grudging, timid excursionists in the mud where they should rightly be? Why, Toad, of course; clever Toad, great Toad, *good* Toad!"

Then he burst into song again, and chanted with uplifted voice:

> *The motor-car went Poop-poop-poop,*
> *As it raced along the road.*
> *Who was it steered it into a pond?*
> *Ingenious Mr Toad!*

"O, how clever I am! How clever, how clever, how very clev—"

A slight noise at a distance behind him made him turn his head and look. O horror! O misery! O despair!

About two fields off, a chauffeur in his leather gaiters and two large rural policemen were visible, running towards him as hard as they could go!

Poor Toad sprang to his feet and pelted away again, his heart in his mouth. "O my!" he gasped, as he panted along, "what an ass I am! What a *conceited* and heedless ass! Swaggering again! Shouting and singing songs again! Sitting still and gassing again! O my! O my! O my!"

He glanced back, and saw to his dismay that they were gaining on him. On he ran desperately, but kept looking back, and saw that they still gained steadily. He did his best, but he was a fat animal, and his legs were short, and still they gained. He could hear them close behind him now. Ceasing to heed where he was going, he struggled on blindly and wildly, looking back over his shoulder at the now triumphant enemy, when suddenly the earth failed under his feet, he grasped at the air, and, splash! he found himself head over ears in deep water, rapid water, water that bore him along with a force he could not contend with; and he knew that in his blind panic he had run straight into the river!

He rose to the surface and tried to grasp the reeds and the rushes that grew along the water's edge close under the bank, but the stream was so strong that it tore them out of his hands. "O my!" gasped poor Toad, "if ever I steal a motor-car again! If ever I sing another conceited song"—then down he went, and came up breathless and spluttering. Presently he saw that he was approaching a big dark hole in the bank, just above his head, and as the stream bore him past he reached up with a paw and caught hold of the edge and held on. Then slowly

and with difficulty he drew himself up out of the water, till at last he was able to rest his elbows on the edge of the hole. There he remained for some minutes, puffing and panting, for he was quite exhausted.

As he sighed and blew and stared before him into the dark hole, some bright small thing shone and twinkled in its depths, moving towards him. As it approached, a face grew up gradually around it, and it was a familiar face!

Brown and small, with whiskers.

Grave and round, with neat ears and silky hair.

It was the Water Rat!

CHAPTER 11

"Like Summer Tempests came his tears"

The Rat put out a neat little brown paw, gripped Toad firmly by the scruff of the neck, and gave a great hoist and a pull; and the water-logged Toad came up slowly but surely over the edge of the hole, till at last he stood safe and sound in the hall, streaked with mud and weed to be sure, and with the water streaming off him, but happy and high-spirited as of old, now that he found himself once more in the house of a friend, and dodgings and evasions were over, and he could lay aside a disguise that was unworthy of his position and wanted such a lot of living up to.

"O Ratty!" he cried. "I've been through such times since I saw you last, you can't think! Such trials, such sufferings, and all so nobly borne! Then such escapes, such disguises, such subterfuges, and all so cleverly planned and carried out! Been in prison—got out of it, of course! Been thrown into a canal—swam ashore! Stole a horse sold him for a large sum of money! Humbugged everybody—made 'em all do exactly what I wanted! O, I *am* a smart Toad, and no mistake! What do you think my last exploit was? Just hold on till I tell you—"

"Toad," said the Water Rat, gravely and firmly, "you go off upstairs at once, and take off that old cotton rag that looks as if it might formerly have belonged to some washerwoman, and clean yourself thoroughly, and put on some of my clothes, and try and come down looking like a gentleman if you *can*; for a more shabby, bedraggled, disreputable-looking object than you are I never set eyes on in my whole life! Now, stop swaggering and arguing, and be off! I'll have something to say to you later!"

Toad was at first inclined to stop and do some talking back at him. He had had enough of being ordered about when he was in prison, and here was the thing being begun all over again, apparently; and by a Rat, too! However, he caught sight of himself in the looking-glass over the hat-stand with the rusty black bonnet perched rakishly over one eye, and he changed his mind and went very quickly and humbly upstairs to the Rat's dressing-room. There he had a thorough wash and brush-up, changed his clothes, and stood for a long time before the glass, contemplating himself with pride and pleasure, and thinking what utter idiots all the people must have been to have ever mistaken him for one moment for a washerwoman.

By the time he came down again luncheon was on the table, and very glad Toad was to see it, for he had been through some trying experiences and had taken much hard exercise since the excellent breakfast provided for him by the gipsy. While they ate Toad told the Rat all his adventures, dwelling chiefly on his own cleverness, and presence of mind in emergencies, and cunning in tight places; and rather making out that he had been having a gay and highly-coloured experience. But the more he talked and boasted, the more grave and silent the Rat became.

When at last Toad had talked himself to a standstill, there was silence for a while; and then the Rat said, "Now, Toady, I don't want to give you pain, after all you've been through already; but, seriously, don't you see what an awful ass you've been making of yourself? on your own admission you have been handcuffed, imprisoned, starved, chased, terrified out of your life, insulted, jeered at, and ignominiously flung into the water—by a woman, too! Where's the amusement in that? Where does the fun come in? And all because you must needs go and steal a motor-car. You know that you've never had anything but trouble from motor-cars from the moment you first set eyes on one. But if you *will* be mixed up with them—as you generally are, five minutes after you've started—why *steal* them? Be a cripple, if you think it's exciting; be a bankrupt, for a change, if you've set your mind on it; but why choose to be a convict? When are you going to be sensible, and think of your friends, and try and be a credit to them? Do you suppose it's any pleasure to me, for instance, to hear animals saying, as I go about, that I'm the chap that keeps company with gaol-birds?"

Now, it was a very comforting point in Toad's character that he was a thoroughly good-hearted animal, and never minded being jawed by those who were his real friends. And even when most set upon a thing he was always able to see the other side of the question. So although, while the Rat was

talking so seriously, he kept saying to himself muti-
nously, "But it *was* fun, though! Awful fun!" and
making strange suppressed noises inside him, k-i-
ck-ck-ck, and poop-p-p, and other sounds resembling stifled snorts, or the opening of soda-water
bottles, yet when the Rat had quite finished, he
heaved a deep sigh and said, very nicely and
humbly, "Quite right, Ratty! How *sound* you always
are! Yes, I've been a conceited old ass, I can quite
see that; but now I'm going to be a good Toad, and
not do it any more. As for motor-cars, I've not been
at all so keen about them since my last ducking in
that river of yours. The fact is, while I was hanging
on to the edge of your hole and getting my breath, I
had a sudden idea—a really brilliant idea—
connected with motor-boats—there, there! don't
take on so, old chap, and stamp, and upset things,
it was only an idea, and we won't talk any more
about it now. We'll have our coffee, *and* a smoke,
and a quiet chat, and then I'm going to stroll gently
down to Toad Hall, and get into clothes of my own,
and set things going again on the old lines. I've had
enough of adventures. I shall lead a quiet, steady,
respectable life, pottering about my property, and
improving it, and doing a little landscape gardening

at times. There will always be a bit of dinner for my friends when they come to see me; and I shall keep a pony-chaise to jog about the country in, just as I used to in the good old days, before I got restless, and wanted to *do* things."

"Stroll gently down to Toad Hall!" cried the Rat, greatly excited. "What are you talking about? Do you mean to say you haven't *heard*?"

"Heard what?" said Toad, turning rather pale. "Go on, Ratty! Quick! Don't spare me! What haven't I heard?"

"Do you mean to tell me," shouted the Rat, thumping with his little fist upon the table, "that you've heard nothing about the Stoats and Weasels?"

"What, the Wild Wooders?" cried Toad, trembling in every limb. "No, not a word! What have they been doing?"

"—And how they've been and taken Toad Hall?" continued the Rat.

Toad leaned his elbows on the table, and his chin on his paws; and a large tear welled up in each of his eyes, overflowed and splashed on the table, plop! plop!

"Go on, Ratty," he murmured presently; "tell me all. The worst is over. I am an animal again. I can bear it."

"When you—got—into that—that—trouble of yours," said the Rat slowly and impressively; "I mean, when you—disappeared from society for a time, over that misunderstanding about a—a machine, you know—"

Toad merely nodded.

"Well, it was a good deal talked about down here, naturally," continued the Rat, "not only along the riverside, but even in the Wild Wood. Animals took sides, as always happens. The River-Bankers stuck up for you, and said you had been infamously treated, and there was no justice to be had in the land nowadays. But the Wild Wood animals said hard things, and served you right, and it was time this sort of thing was stopped. And they got very cocky, and went about saying you were done for this time! You would never come back again, never, never!"

Toad nodded once more, keeping silence.

"That's the sort of little beasts they are," the Rat went on. "But Mole and Badger, they stuck out, through thick and thin, that you would come back again soon, somehow. They didn't know exactly how, but somehow!"

Toad began to sit up in his chair again, and to smirk a little.

"They argued from history," continued the Rat. "They said that no criminal laws had ever been known to prevail against cheek and plausibility such as yours, combined with the power of a long purse. So they arranged to move their things into Toad Hall, and sleep there, and keep it aired, and have it all ready for you when you turned up. They didn't guess what was going to happen, of course; still, they had their suspicions of the Wild Wood animals. Now I come to the most painful and tragic part of my story. One dark night—it was a *very* dark night, and blowing hard, too, and raining simply cats and dogs—a band of weasels, armed to the teeth, crept silently up the carriage-drive to the front entrance. Simultaneously, a body of desperate ferrets, advancing through the kitchen-garden, possessed themselves of the backyard and offices; while a company of skirmishing stoats who stuck at nothing occupied the conservatory and the billiard-room, and held the French windows opening on to the lawn.

"The Mole and the Badger were sitting by the fire in the smoking-room, telling stories and suspecting nothing, for it wasn't a night for any animals to be out in, when those blood-thirsty villains broke down the doors and rushed in upon them from every side. They made the best fight they could, but what was the good? They were unarmed, and taken by surprise, and what can two animals do against hundreds? They took and beat them severely with sticks, those two poor faithful creatures, and turned them out into the cold and the wet, with many insulting and uncalled-for remarks!"

Here the unfeeling Toad broke into a snigger, and then pulled himself together and tried to look particularly solemn.

"And the Wild Wooders have been living in Toad Hall ever since," continued the Rat; "and going on simply anyhow! Lying in bed half the day, and breakfast at all hours, and the place in such a mess (I'm told) it's not fit to be seen! Eating your grub, and drinking your drink, and making bad jokes about you, and singing vulgar songs, about—well, about prisons, and magistrates, and policemen; horrid personal songs, with no humour in them. And they're telling the tradespeople and everybody that they've come to stay for good."

"O, have they!" said Toad, getting up and seizing a stick. "I'll jolly soon see about that!"

"It's no good, Toad!" called the Rat after him. "You'd better come back and sit down; you'll only get into trouble."

But the Toad was off, and there was no holding him. He marched rapidly down the road, his stick over his shoulder, frowning and muttering to himself in his anger, till he got near his front gate, when suddenly there popped up from behind the palings a long yellow ferret with a gun.

"Who comes there?" said the ferret sharply.

"Stuff and nonsense!" said Toad very angrily. "What do you mean by talking like that to me? Come out of it at once, or I'll—"

The ferret said never a word, but he brought his gun up to his shoulder. Toad prudently dropped flat in the road, and *Bang!* a bullet whistled over his head.

The startled Toad scrambled to his feet and scampered off down the road as hard as he could; and as he ran he heard the ferret laughing, and other horrid thin little laughs taking it up and carrying on the sound.

He went back, very crestfallen and told the Water Rat.

"What did I tell you?" said the Rat. "It's no good.

They've got sentries posted, and they are all armed. You must just wait."

Still, Toad was not inclined to give in all at once. So he got out the boat, and set off rowing up the river to where the garden front of Toad Hall came down to the waterside.

Arriving within sight of his old home, he rested on his oars and surveyed the land cautiously. All seemed very peaceful and deserted and quiet. He could see the whole front of Toad Hall, glowing in the evening sunshine, the pigeons settling by twos and threes along the straight line of the roof; the garden, a blaze of flowers; the creek that led up to the boat-house, the little wooden bridge that crossed it; all tranquil, uninhabited, apparently waiting for his return. He would try the boat-house first, he thought. Very warily he paddled up to the mouth of the creek, and was just passing under the bridge, when... *Crash!*

A great stone, dropped from above, smashed through the bottom of the boat. It filled and sank, and Toad found himself struggling in deep water. Looking up, he saw two stoats leaning over the parapet of the bridge and watching him with great glee. "It will be your head next time, Toady!" they called out to him. The indignant Toad swam to shore, while the stoats laughed and laughed, supporting each other, and laughed again, till they nearly had two fits—that is, one fit each, of course.

The Toad retraced his weary way on foot, and related his disappointing experiences to the Water Rat once more.

"Well, *what* did I tell you?" said the Rat very crossly. "And, now, look here! See what you've been and done! Lost me my boat that I was so fond of, that's what you've done! And simply ruined that nice suit of clothes that I lent you! Really, Toad, of all the trying animals—I wonder you manage to keep any friends at all!"

The Toad saw at once how wrongly and foolishly he had acted. He admitted his errors and wrong-headedness and made a full apology to Rat for losing his boat and spoiling his clothes. And he wound up by saying, with that frank self-surrender which always disarmed his friends' criticism and won them back to his side, "Ratty! I see that I have been a headstrong and a wilful Toad! Henceforth, believe me, I will be humble and submissive, and will take no action without your kind advice and full approval."

"If that is really so," said the good-natured Rat, already appeased, "then my advice to you is, considering the lateness of the hour, to sit down and have your supper, which will be on the table in a minute, and be very patient. For I am convinced that we can do nothing until we have seen the Mole and the Badger, and heard their latest news, and held conference and taken their advice in this difficult matter."

"O, ah, yes, of course, the Mole and the Badger," said Toad lightly. "What's become of them, the dear fellows? I had forgotten all about them."

"Well may you ask!" said the Rat reproachfully. "While you were riding about the country in expensive motor-cars, and galloping proudly on blood-horses, and breakfasting on the fat of the land, those two poor devoted animals have been camping out in the open, in every sort of weather, living very rough by day and lying very hard by night; watching over your house, patrolling your boundaries, keeping a constant eye on the stoats and the weasels, scheming and planning and contriving how to get your property back for you. You don't deserve to have such true and loyal friends, Toad, you don't, really. Some day, when it's too late, you'll be sorry you didn't value them more while you had them!"

"I'm an ungrateful beast, I know," sobbed Toad, shedding bitter tears. "Let me go out and find them, out into the cold, dark night, and share their hardships, and try and prove by—Hold on a bit! Surely I heard the chink of dishes on a tray! Supper's here at last, hooray! Come on, Ratty!"

The Rat remembered that poor Toad had been on prison fare for a considerable time, and that large allowances had therefore to be made. He followed him to the table accordingly, and hospitably encouraged him in his gallant efforts to make up for past privations.

They had just finished their meal and resumed their arm-chairs, when there came a heavy knock at the door.

Toad was nervous, but the Rat, nodding mysteriously at him, went straight up to the door and opened it, and in walked Mr Badger.

He had all the appearance of one who for some nights had been kept away from home and all its little comforts and conveniences. His shoes were covered with mud, and he was looking very rough and tousled; but then he had never been a very smart man, the Badger, at the best of times. He came solemnly up to Toad, shook him by the paw, and said, "Welcome home, Toad! Alas! what am I saying? Home, indeed! This is a poor home-coming. Unhappy Toad!" Then he turned his back on him, sat down to the table, drew his chair up, and helped himself to a large slice of cold pie.

Toad was quite alarmed at this very serious and portentous style of greeting; but the Rat whispered to him, "Never mind; don't take any notice; and don't say anything to him just yet. He's always rather low and despondent when he's wanting his victuals. In half an hour's time he'll be quite a different animal."

So they waited in silence, and presently there came another and a lighter knock. The Rat, with a nod to Toad, went to the door and ushered in the Mole, very shabby and unwashed, with bits of hay and straw sticking in his fur.

"Hooray! Here's old Toad!" cried the Mole, his face beaming. "Fancy having you back again!" And he began to dance round him. "We never dreamt you would turn up so soon! Why, you must have managed to escape, you clever, ingenious, intelligent Toad!"

The Rat, alarmed, pulled him by the elbow; but it was too late. Toad was puffing and swelling already.

"Clever? O no!" he said. "I'm not really clever, according to my friends. I've only broken out of the strongest prison in England, that's all! And captured a railway train and escaped on it, that's all! And disguised myself and gone about the country humbugging everybody, that's all! O no! I'm a stupid ass, I am! I'll tell you one or two of my little adventures, Mole, and you shall judge for yourself!"

"Well, well," said the Mole, moving towards the supper-table; "supposing you talk while I eat. Not a bite since breakfast! O my! O my!" And he sat down and helped himself liberally to cold beef and pickles.

Toad straddled on the hearth-rug, thrust his paw into his trouserpocket and pulled out a handful of silver. "Look at that!" he cried, displaying it. "That's not so bad, is it, for a few minutes' work? And how do you think I done it, Mole? Horse-stealing! That's how I done it!"

"Go on, Toad," said the Mole, immensely interested.

"Toad, do be quiet, please!" said the Rat. "And don't you egg him on, Mole, when you know what he is; but please tell us as soon as possible what the position is, and what's best to be done, now that Toad is back at last."

The position's about as bad as it can be," replied the Mole grumpily; "and as for what's to be done, why, blest if I know! The Badger and I have been round and round the place, by night and by day; always the same thing. Sentries posted everywhere, guns poked out at us, stones thrown at us; always an animal on the lookout, and when they see us, my! how they do laugh! That's what annoys me most!"

"It's a very difficult situation," said the Rat, reflecting deeply. "But I think I see now, in the depths of my mind, what Toad really ought to do. I will tell you. He ought to— "

"No, he oughtn't!" shouted the Mole, with his mouth full. "Nothing of the sort! You don't understand. What he ought to do is, he ought to—"

"Well, I shan't do it, anyway!" cried Toad, getting excited. "I'm not going to be ordered about by you fellows! It's my house we're talking about, and I know exactly what to do, and I'll tell you. I'm going to—"

By this time they were all three talking at once, at the top of their voices, and the noise was simply deafening, when a thin, dry voice made itself heard, saying, "Be quiet at once, all of you!" and instantly every one was silent.

It was the Badger, who, having finished his pie, had turned round in his chair and was looking at them severely. When he saw that he had secured their attention, and that they were evidently waiting for him to address them, he turned back to the table again and reached out for the cheese. And so great was the respect commanded by the solid qualities of that admirable animal, that not another word was uttered until he had quite finished his repast and brushed the crumbs from his knees. The Toad fidgeted a good deal, but the Rat held him firmly down.

When the Badger had quite done, he got up from his seat and stood before the fireplace, reflecting deeply. At last he spoke.

"Toad!" he said severely. "You bad, troublesome little animal! Aren't you ashamed of yourself? What do you think your father, my old friend, would have said if he had been here to-night, and had known of all your goings on?"

Toad, who was on the sofa by this time, with his legs up, rolled over on his face, shaken by sobs of contrition.

"There, there!" went on the Badger more kindly. "Never mind. Stop crying. We're going to let bygones be bygones, and try and turn over a new

THE WIND IN THE WILLOWS 259

leaf. But what the Mole says is quite true. The stoats are on guard, at every point, and they make the best sentinels in the world. It's quite useless to think of attacking the place. They're too strong for us."

"Then it's all over," sobbed the Toad, crying into the sofa cushions. "I shall go and enlist for a soldier, and never see my dear Toad Hall any more!"

"Come, cheer up, Toady!" said the Badger. "There are more ways of getting back a place than taking it by storm. I haven't said my last word yet. Now I'm going to tell you a great secret."

Toad sat up slowly and dried his eyes. Secrets had an immense attraction for him, because he never could keep one, and he enjoyed the sort of unhallowed thrill he experienced when he went and told another animal, after having faithfully promised not to.

"There—is—an—underground—passage," said the Badger impressively, "that leads from the river bank quite near here, right up into the middle of Toad Hall."

"O, nonsense! Badger," said Toad rather airily. "You've been listening to some of the yarns they spin in the public-houses about here. I know every inch of Toad Hall, inside and out. Nothing of the sort, I do assure you!"

"My young friend," said the Badger with great severity, "your father, who was a worthy animal—a lot worthier than some others I know—was a particular friend of mine, and told me a great deal he wouldn't have dreamt of telling you. He discovered that passage—he didn't make it, of course; that was done hundreds of years before he ever came to live there—and he repaired it and cleaned it out, because he thought it might come in useful some day, in case of trouble or danger; and he showed it to me. 'Don't let my son know about it,' he said. 'He's a good boy, but very light and volatile in character, and simply cannot hold his tongue. If he's ever in a real fix, and it would be of use to him, you may tell him about the secret passage; but not before.'"

The other animals looked hard at Toad to see how he would take it. Toad was inclined to be sulky at first; but he brightened up immediately, like the good fellow he was.

"Well, well," he said; "perhaps I am a bit of a talker. A popular fellow such as I am—my friends get round me—we chaff, we sparkle, we tell witty stories—and somehow my tongue gets wagging. I have the gift of conversation. I've been told I ought to have a *salon*, whatever that may be. Never mind.

Go on, Badger. How's this passage of yours going to help us?"

"I've found out a thing or two lately," continued the Badger. "I got Otter to disguise himself as a sweep and call at the back door with brushes over his shoulder, asking for a job. There's going to be a big banquet to-morrow night. It's somebody's birthday—the Chief Weasel's, I believe—and all the weasels will be gathered together in the dining-hall, eating and drinking and laughing and carrying on, suspecting nothing. No guns, no swords, no sticks, no arms of any sort whatever!"

"But the sentinels will be posted as usual," remarked the Rat.

"Exactly," said the Badger; "that is my point. The weasels will trust entirely to their excellent sentinels. And that is where the passage comes in. That very useful tunnel leads right up under the butler's pantry, next to the dining-hall!"

"Aha! that squeaky board in the butler's pantry!" said Toad. "Now I understand it!"

"We shall creep out quietly into the butler's pantry—" cried the Mole.

"—with our pistols and swords and sticks—" shouted the Rat.

"—and rush in upon them," said the Badger.

"—and whack 'em, and whack 'em, and whack 'em!" cried the Toad in ecstasy, running round and round the room, and jumping over the chairs.

"Very well, then," said the Badger, resuming his usual dry manner, "our plan is settled, and there's nothing more for you to argue and squabble about. So, as it's getting very late, all of you go right off to bed at once. We will make all the necessary arrangements in the course of the morning to-morrow."

Toad, of course, went off to bed dutifully with the rest—he knew better than to refuse—though he was feeling much too excited to sleep. But he had had a long day, with many events crowded into it; and sheets and blankets were very friendly and comforting things, after plain straw, and not too much of it, spread on the stone floor of a draughty cell; and his head had not been many seconds on his pillow before he was snoring happily. Naturally, he dreamt a good deal; about roads that ran away from him just when he wanted them, and canals that chased him and caught him, and a barge that sailed into the banqueting-hall with his week's washing, just as he was giving a dinner-party; and he was alone in the secret passage, pushing onwards, but it twisted and turned round and shook itself, and sat up on its end; yet somehow, at the last, he found himself back in Toad Hall, safe and triumphant, with all his friends gathered round about him, earnestly assuring him that he really was a clever Toad.

He slept till a late hour next morning, and by the time he got down he found that the other animals had finished their breakfast some time before. The Mole had slipped off somewhere by himself, without telling any one where he was going. The Badger sat in the arm-chair, reading the paper, and not concerning himself in the slightest about what was going to happen that very evening. The Rat, on the other hand, was running round the room busily, with his arms full of weapons of every kind, distributing them in four little heaps on the floor, and saying excitedly under his breath, as he ran, "Here's-a-sword-for-the-Rat,   here's-a-sword-for-the-Mole,   here's-a-sword-for-the-Toad,   here's-a-sword-for-the-Badger! Here's-a-pistol-for-the-Rat, here's- a-pistol-for-the-Mole,   here's-a-pistol-for-the-Toad, here's-a-pistol-for-the-Badger!" And so on, in a regular, rhythmical way, while the four little heaps gradually grew and grew.

"That's all very well, Rat," said the Badger presently, looking at the busy little animal over the edge of his newspaper; "I'm not blaming you. But just let us once get past the stoats, with those detestable guns of theirs, and I assure you we shan't want any swords or pistols. We four, with our sticks, once we're inside the dining-hall, why, we shall clear the floor of all the lot of them in five minutes. I'd have done the whole thing by myself, only I didn't want to deprive you fellows of the fun!"

"It's as well to be on the safe side," said the Rat reflectively, polishing a pistol-barrel on his sleeve and looking along it.

The Toad, having finished his breakfast, picked up a stout stick and swung it vigorously, belabouring imaginary animals. "I'll learn 'em to steal my house!" he cried. "I'll learn 'em, I'll learn 'em!"

"Don't say 'learn 'em', Toad," said the Rat, greatly shocked. "It's not good English."

"What are you always nagging at Toad for?" inquired the Badger rather peevishly. "What's the matter with his English? It's the same what I use myself, and if it's good enough for me, it ought to be good enough for you!"

"I'm very sorry," said the Rat humbly. "Only I *think* it ought to be 'teach 'em', not 'learn 'em'."

"But we don't *want* to teach 'em," replied the Badger. "We want to *learn* 'em—learn 'em, learn 'em! And what's more, we're going to *do* it, too!"

"O, very well, have it your own way," said the Rat. He was getting rather muddled about it himself, and presently he retired into a corner, where he could be heard muttering, "Learn 'em, teach 'em, teach 'em, learn 'em!" till the Badger told him rather sharply to leave off.

Presently the Mole came tumbling into the room, evidently very pleased with himself "I've been having such fun!" he began at once; "I've been getting a rise out of the stoats!"

"I hope you've been very careful, Mole?" said the Rat anxiously.

"I should hope so, too," said the Mole confidently. "I got the idea when I went into the kitchen, to see about Toad's breakfast being kept hot for him. I found that old washerwoman-dress that he came home in yesterday, hanging on a towel-horse before the fire. So I put it on, and the bonnet as well, and the shawl, and off I went to Toad Hall, as bold as you please. The sentries were on the look-out, of course, with their guns and their 'Who comes there?' and all the rest of their nonsense. 'Good morning, gentlemen!' says I, very respectful 'Want any washing done to-day?'

"They looked at me very proud and stiff and haughty, and said, 'Go away, washerwoman! We don't do any washing on duty.' 'Or any other time?' says I. Ho, ho, ho! Wasn't I *funny,* Toad?"

"Poor, frivolous animal!" said Toad very loftily. The fact is, he felt exceedingly jealous of Mole for what he had just done. It was exactly what he would have liked to have done himself, if only he had thought of it first, and hadn't gone and overslept himself.

"Some of the stoats turned quite pink," continued the Mole, "and the sergeant in charge, he said to me, very short, he said, 'Now run away, my good woman, run away! Don't keep my men idling and talking on their posts.' 'Run away?' says I; 'it won't be me that'll be running away, in a very short time from now!'"

"O, *Moly*, how could you?" said the Rat, dismayed.

The Badger laid down his paper.

"I could see them pricking up their ears and looking at each other," went on the Mole; "and the sergeant said to them, 'Never mind *her;* she doesn't know what she's talking about.'

"'O! don't I?' said I. 'Well, let me tell you this. My daughter, she washes for Mr Badger, and that'll show you whether I know what I'm talking about; and *you'll* know pretty soon, too! A hundred bloodthirsty badgers, armed with rifles, are going to attack Toad Hall this very night, by way of the paddock. Six boat-loads of rats, with pistols and cutlasses, will come up the river and effect a landing in the garden; while a picked body of toads, known as the Diehards, or the Death-or-Glory Toads, will storm the orchard and carry everything before them, yelling for vengeance. There won't be much left of you to wash, by the time they've done with you, unless you clear out while you have the chance!' Then I ran away, and when I was out of sight I hid; and presently I came creeping back along the ditch and took a peep at them through the hedge. They were all as nervous and flustered as could be, running all ways at once, and falling over each other, and everyone giving orders to everybody else and not listening; and the sergeant kept sending off parties of stoats to distant parts of the grounds, and then sending other fellows to fetch 'em back again: and I heard them saying to each other, 'That's *just* like the weasels; they're to stop comfortably in the banqueting-hall, and have feasting and toasts and songs and all sorts of fun, while we must stay on guard in the cold and the dark, and in the end be cut to pieces by blood-thirsty Badgers!'"

"O, you silly ass, Mole!" cried Toad. "You've been and spoilt everything!"

"Mole," said the Badger, in his dry, quiet way, "I perceive you have more sense in your little finger than some other animals have in the whole of their fat bodies. You have managed excellently, and I begin to have great hopes of you. Good Mole! Clever Mole!"

The Toad was simply wild with jealousy, more especially as he couldn't make out for the life of him what the Mole had done that was so particularly clever; but, fortunately for him, before he could show temper or expose himself to the Badger's sarcasm, the bell rang for luncheon.

It was a simple but sustaining meal—bacon and broad beans, and a macaroni pudding; and when they had quite done, the Badger settled himself into an arm-chair, and said, "Well, we've got our work cut out for us to-night, and it will probably be pretty late before we're quite through with it; so I'm just going to take forty winks, while I can." And he drew a handkerchief over his face and was soon snoring.

The anxious and laborious Rat at once resumed his preparations, and started running between his four little heaps, muttering. "Here's-a-belt-for-the-Rat, here's-a-belt-for-the-Mole, here's-a-belt-for-the-Toad, here's-a-belt-for-the-Badger!" and so on, with every fresh accoutrement he produced, to which there seemed really no end; so the Mole drew his arm through Toad's, led him out into the open air, shoved him into a wicker chair, and made him tell him all his adventures from beginning to end, which Toad was only too willing to do. The Mole was a good listener, and Toad, with no one to check his statements or to criticize in an unfriendly spirit, rather let himself go. Indeed, much that he related belonged more properly to the category of what-might-have-happened-had-I-only-thought-of-it-in-time-instead-of-ten-minutes afterwards. Those are always the best and the raciest adventures; and why should they not be truly ours, as much as the some-what inadequate things that really come off?

CHAPTER 12

The Return of Ulysses

When it began to grow dark, the Rat, with an air of excitement and mystery, summoned them back into the parlour, stood each of them up alongside of his little heap, and proceeded to dress them up for the coming expedition. He was very earnest and thorough-going about it, and the affair took quite a long time. First, there was a belt to go round each animal, and then a sword to be stuck into each belt, and then a cutlass on the other side to balance it. Then a pair of pistols, a policeman's truncheon, several sets of handcuffs, some bandages and sticking-plaster, and a flask and a sandwich-case. The Badger laughed good-humouredly and said, "All right, Ratty! It amuses you and it doesn't hurt me. I'm going to do all I've got to do with this here stick." But the Rat only said, "*Please*, Badger! You know I shouldn't like you to blame me afterwards and say I had forgotten *anything*!"

When all was quite ready, the Badger took a dark lantern in one paw, grasped his great stick with the other, and said, "Now then, follow me! Mole first, 'cos I'm very pleased with him; Rat next; Toad last. And look here, Toady! Don't you chatter so much as usual, or you'll be sent back, as sure as fate!"

The Toad was so anxious not to be left out that he took up the inferior position assigned to him without a murmur, and the animals set off. The Badger led them along by the river for a little way, and then suddenly swung himself over the edge into a hole in the river bank, a little above the water. The Mole and the Rat followed silently, swinging themselves successfully into the hole as they had seen the Badger do; but when it came to Toad's turn, of course he managed to slip and fall into the water with a loud splash and a squeal of alarm. He was hauled out by his friends, rubbed down and wrung out hastily, comforted, and set on his legs; but the Badger was seriously angry, and told him that the very next time he made a fool of himself he would most certainly be left behind.

So at last they were in the secret passage, and the cutting-out expedition had really begun!

It was cold, and dark, and damp, and low, and narrow, and poor Toad began to shiver, partly from dread of what might be before him, partly because he was wet through. The lantern was far ahead, and he could not help lagging behind a little in the darkness. Then he heard the Rat call out warningly, "*Come* on, Toad!" and a terror seized him of being left behind, alone in the darkness, and he "came on" with such a rush that he upset the Rat into the Mole and the Mole into the Badger, and for a moment all was confusion. The Badger thought they were being attacked from behind, and, as there was no room to use a stick or a cutlass, drew a pistol, and was on the point of putting a bullet into Toad. When he found out what had really happened he was very angry indeed, and said, "Now this time that tiresome Toad *shall* be left behind!"

But Toad whimpered, and the other two promised that they would be answerable for his good conduct, and at last the Badger was pacified, and the procession moved on; only this time the Rat brought up the rear, with a firm grip on the shoulder of Toad.

So they groped and shuffled along, with their ears pricked up and their paws on their pistols, till at last the Badger said, "We ought by now to be pretty nearly under the Hall."

Then suddenly they heard, far away as it might be, and yet apparently nearly over their heads, a confused murmur of sound, as if people were shouting and cheering and stamping on the floor and hammering on tables. The Toad's nervous terrors all returned, but the Badger only remarked placidly, "They *are* going it, the weasels!"

The passage now began to slope upwards; they groped onward a little further, and then the noise broke out again, quite distinct this time, and very close above them. "Ooo-ray-oo-ray-oo-ray-ooray," they heard, and the stamping of little feet on the floor, and the clinking of glasses as little fists pounded on the table. "*What* a time they're having!" said the Badger. "Come on!" They hurried along the passage till it came to a full stop, and they found themselves standing under the trap-door that led up into the butler's pantry.

Such a tremendous noise was going on in the banqueting-hall that there was little danger of their being overheard. The Badger said, "Now, boys, all

together!" and the four of them put their shoulders to the trap-door and heaved it back. Hoisting each other up, they found themselves standing in the pantry, with only a door between them and the banqueting-hall, where their unconscious enemies were carousing.

The noise, as they emerged from the passage, was simply deafening. At last, as the cheering and hammering slowly subsided, a voice could be made out saying, "Well, I do not propose to detain you much longer"—(great applause)—"but before I resume my seat"—(renewed cheering)—"I should like to say one word about our kind host, Mr Toad. We all know Toad!"—(great laughter)—"*Good* Toad, *modest* Toad, *honest* Toad!"—(shrieks of merriment).

"Only just let me get at him!" muttered Toad, grinding his teeth.

"Hold hard a minute!" said the Badger, restraining him with difficulty. "Get ready, all of you!"

"—Let me sing you a little song," went on the voice, "which I have composed on the subject of Toad"—(prolonged applause).

Then the Chief Weasel—for it was he—began in a high, squeaky voice:

> *Toad he went a-pleasuring*
> *Gaily down the street—*

The Badger drew himself up, took a firm grip of his stick with both paws, glanced round at his comrades, and cried:

"The hour is come! Follow me!"

And flung the door open wide.

My!

What a squealing and a squeaking and a screeching filled the air!

Well might the terrified weasels dive under the tables and spring madly up at the windows! Well might the ferrets rush wildly for the fire-place and get hopelessly jammed in the chimney! Well might tables and chairs be upset, and glass and china be sent crashing on the floor, in the panic of that terrible moment when the four Heroes strode wrathfully into the room! The mighty Badger, his whiskers bristling, his great cudgel whistling through the air; Mole, black and grim, brandishing his stick and shouting his awful war-cry, "A Mole! A Mole!" Rat, desperate and determined, his belt bulging with weapons of every age and every variety; Toad, frenzied with excitement and injured pride, swollen to twice his ordinary size, leaping into the air and emitting Toad-whoops that chilled them to the marrow! "Toad he went a-pleasuring!" he yelled. "*I'll* pleasure 'em!" and he went straight for the Chief Weasel. They were but four in all, but to the panic-stricken weasels the hall seemed full of monstrous animals, grey, black, brown, and yellow, whooping and flourishing enormous cudgels; and they broke and fled with squeals of terror and dismay, this way and that, through the windows, up the chimney, anywhere to get out of reach of those terrible sticks.

The affair was soon over. Up and down, the whole length of the hall, strode the four Friends, whacking with their sticks at every head that showed itself; and in five minutes the room was cleared. Through the broken windows the shrieks of terrified weasels escaping across the lawn were borne faintly to their ears; on the floor lay prostrate some dozen or so of the enemy, on whom the Mole was busily engaged in fitting handcuffs. The Badger, resting from his labours, leant on his stick and wiped his honest brow.

"Mole," he said, "you're the best of fellows! Just cut along outside and look after those stoat-sentries

of yours, and see what they're doing. I've an idea that, thanks to you, we shan't have much trouble from *them* to-night!"

The Mole vanished promptly through a window; and the Badger bade the other two set a table on its legs again, pick up knives and forks and plates and glasses from the debris on the floor, and see if they could find materials for a supper. "I want some grub, I do," he said, in that rather common way he had of speaking. "Stir your stumps, Toad, and look lively! We've got your house back for you, and you don't offer us so much as a sandwich."

Toad felt rather hurt that the Badger didn't say pleasant things to him, as he had to the Mole, and tell him what a fine fellow he was, and how splendidly he had fought; for he was rather particularly pleased with himself and the way he had gone for the Chief Weasel and sent him flying across the table with one blow of his stick. But he bustled about, and so did the Rat, and soon they found some guava jelly in a glass dish, and a cold chicken, a tongue that had hardly been touched, some trifle, and quite a lot of lobster salad; and in the pantry they came upon a basketful of French rolls and any quantity of cheese, butter, and celery. They were just about to sit down when the Mole clambered in through the window, chuckling, with an armful of rifles.

"It's all over," he reported. "From what I can make out, as soon as the stoats, who were very nervous and jumpy already, heard the shrieks and the yells and the uproar inside the hall, some of them threw down their rifles and fled. The others stood fast for a bit, but when the weasels came rushing out upon them they thought they were betrayed; and the stoats grappled with the weasels, and the weasels fought to get away, and they wrestled and wriggled and punched each other, and rolled over and over, till most of 'em rolled into the river! They've all disappeared by now, one way or another; and I've got their rifles. So *that's* all right!"

"Excellent and deserving animal!" said the Badger, his mouth full of chicken and trifle. "Now, there's just one more thing I want you to do, Mole, before you sit down to your supper along of us; and I wouldn't trouble you only I know I can trust you to see a thing done, and I wish I could say the same of every one I know. I'd send Rat, if he wasn't a poet. I want you to take those fellows on the floor there upstairs with you, and have some bedrooms cleaned out and tidied up and made really comfortable. See that they sweep *under* the beds, and put clean sheets and pillow-cases on, and turn down one corner of the bed-clothes, just as you know it ought to be done; and have a can of hot water, and clean towels, and fresh cakes of soap, put in each room. And then you can give them a licking apiece, if it's any satisfaction to you, and put them out by the back door, and we shan't see any more of *them*, I fancy. And then come along and have some of this cold tongue. It's first-rate. I'm very pleased with you, Mole!"

The good-natured Mole picked up a stick, formed his prisoners up in a line on the floor, gave them the order "Quick march!" and led his squad off to the upper floor. After a time, he appeared again, smiling, and said that every room was ready, and as clean as a new pin. "And I didn't have to lick them, either," he added. "I thought, on the whole, they had had licking enough for one night, and the weasels, when I put the point to them, quite agreed with me, and said they wouldn't think of troubling me. They were very penitent, and said they were extremely sorry for what they had done, but it was all the fault of the Chief Weasel and the stoats, and if ever they could do anything for us at any time to make up, we had only got to mention it. So I gave them a roll apiece, and let them out at the back, and off they ran, as hard as they could."

Then the Mole pulled his chair up to the table, and pitched into the cold tongue; and Toad, like the gentleman he was, put all his jealousy from him, and said heartily, thank you kindly, dear Mole, for all your pains and trouble to-night, and especially for your cleverness this morning." The Badger was pleased at that, and said, "There spoke my brave Toad!" So they finished their supper in great joy and contentment, and presently retired to rest between clean sheets, safe in Toad's ancestral home, won back by matchless valour, consummate strategy, and a proper handling of sticks.

The following morning, Toad, who had overslept himself as usual, came down to breakfast disgracefully late, and found on the table a certain quantity of egg-shells, some fragments of cold and leathery toast, a coffee-pot three-fourths empty, and really very little else; which did not tend to improve his temper, considering that, after all, it was his own house. Through the French windows of the breakfast-room he could see the Mole and the Water Rat sitting in wicker chairs out on the lawn, evidently telling each other stories; roaring with laughter and kicking their short legs up in the air. The Badger, who was in an arm-chair and deep in the morning paper, merely looked up and nodded when Toad entered the room. But Toad knew his man, so he sat down and made the best breakfast he could, merely observing to himself that he would get square with the others sooner or later. When he had nearly finished, the Badger looked up and remarked rather shortly: "I'm sorry, Toad, but I'm afraid there's a heavy morning's work in front of you. You see, we really ought to have a Banquet at once, to celebrate this affair. It's expected of you—in fact, it's the rule."

"O, all right!" said the Toad readily. "Anything to oblige. Though why on earth you should want to have a Banquet in the morning I cannot understand. But you know I do not live to please myself but merely to find out what my friends want, and then try and arrange it for 'em, you dear old Badger!"

"Don't pretend to be stupider than you really are," replied the Badger crossly; "and don't chuckle and splutter in your coffee while you're talking; it's not manners. What I mean is, the Banquet will be at night, of course, but the invitations will have to be written and got off at once, and you've got to write 'em. Now, sit down at that table—there's stacks of letter-paper on it, with 'Toad Hall' at the top in blue and gold—and write invitations to all our friends, and if you stick to it we shall get them out before luncheon. And *I'll* bear a hand, too, and take my share of the burden. *I'll* order the Banquet."

"What!" cried Toad, dismayed. "Me stop indoors and write a lot of rotten letters on a jolly morning like this, when I want to go around my property, and set everything and everybody to rights, and swagger about and enjoy myself. Certainly not! I'll be—I'll see you—Stop a minute, though! Why, of course, dear Badger! What is my pleasure or convenience compared with that of others! You wish it done, and it shall be done. Go, Badger, order the Banquet, order what you like; then join our young friends outside in their innocent mirth, oblivious of me and my cares and toils. I sacrifice this fair morning on the altar of duty and friendship!"

The Badger looked at him very suspiciously, but Toad's frank, open countenance made it difficult to suggest any unworthy motive in this change of attitude. He quitted the room, accordingly, in the direction of the kitchen, and as soon as the door had closed behind him, Toad hurried to the writing-table. A fine idea had occurred to him while he was talking. He *would* write the invitations; and he would take care to mention the leading part he had taken in the fight, and how he had laid the Chief Weasel out and he would hint at his adventures, and what a career of triumph he had to tell about; and on the flyleaf he would give a sort of programme of entertainment for the evening—something like this, as he sketched it out in his head:

SPEECH......................................BY TOAD

(There will be other speeches by Toad
during the evening)

ADDRESS...................................BY TOAD

SYNOPSIS—Our   Prison   System—The
Water-ways of Old England—Horse-dealing,
and how to deal—Property, its rights and its
duties—Back to the Land—A Typical English
Squire

(Composed by himself)

OTHER COMPOSITIONS........BY TOAD
will be sung in the course of the evening by
the . . . COMPOSER

The idea pleased him mightily, and he worked
very hard and got all the letters finished by noon, at
which hour it was reported to him that there was a
small and rather bedraggled weasel at the door,
inquiring timidly whether he could be of any
service to the gentlemen. Toad swaggered out and
found it was one of the prisoners of the previous
evening, very respectful and anxious to please. He
patted him on the head, shoved the bundle of invitations into his paw, and told him to cut along
quick and deliver them as fast as he could, and if he
liked to come back again in the evening perhaps
there might be a shilling for him, or, again, perhaps
there mightn't; and the poor weasel seemed really
quite grateful, and hurried off eagerly to do his
mission.

When the other animals came back to luncheon,
very boisterous and breezy after a morning on the
river, the Mole, whose conscience had been pricking him, looked doubtfully at Toad, expecting to
find him sulky or depressed. Instead, he was so

uppish and inflated that the Mole began to suspect something; while the Rat and the Badger exchanged significant glances.

As soon as the meal was over, Toad thrust his paws deep into his trouser-pockets, remarked casually, "Well, look after yourselves, you fellows! Ask for anything you want!" and was swaggering off in the direction of the garden where he wanted to think out an idea or two for his coming speeches, when the Rat caught him by the arm.

Toad rather suspected what he was after, and did his best to get away; but when the Badger took him firmly by the other arm he began to see that the game was up. The two animals conducted him between them into the small smoking-room that opened out of the entrance-hall, shut the door, and put him into a chair. Then they both stood in front of him, while Toad sat silent and regarded them with much suspicion and ill-humour.

"Now, look here, Toad," said the Rat. "It's about this Banquet, and very sorry I am to have to speak to you like this. But we want you to understand clearly, once and for all, that there are going to be no speeches and no songs. Try and grasp the fact that on this occasion we're not arguing with you; we're just telling you."

Toad saw that he was trapped. They understood him, they saw through him, they had got ahead of him. His pleasant dream was shattered.

"Mayn't I sing them just one *little* song" he pleaded piteously.

"No, not *one* little song," replied the Rat firmly, though his heart bled as he noticed the trembling lip of the poor disappointed Toad. "It's no good, Toady; you know well that your songs are all conceit and boasting and vanity; and your speeches are all self-praise and— and—well, and gross exaggeration and—and—"

"And gas," put in the Badger, in his common way.

"It's for your own good, Toady," went on the Rat. "You know you *must* turn over a new leaf sooner or later, and now seems a splendid time to begin; a sort of turning-point in your career. Please don't think that saying all this doesn't hurt me more than it hurts you."

Toad remained a long while plunged in thought. At last he raised his head, and the traces of strong emotion were visible on his features. "You have conquered, my friends," he said in broken accents. "It was, to be sure, but a small thing that I asked— merely leave to blossom and expand for yet one more evening, to let myself go and hear the tumultuous applause that always seems to me—somehow—to bring out my best qualities. However, you are right, I know, and I am wrong. Henceforth I will be a very different Toad. My friends, you shall never have occasion to blush for me again. But, O dear, O dear, this is a hard world!"

And, pressing his handkerchief to his face, he left the room with faltering footsteps.

"Badger," said the Rat. "*I* feel like a brute; I wonder what *you* feel like?"

"O, I know, I know," said the Badger gloomily. "But the thing had to be done. This good fellow has got to live here, and hold his own, and be respected. Would you have him a common laughing-stock, mocked and jeered at by stoats and weasels."

"Of course not," said the Rat. "And, talking of weasels, it's lucky we came upon that little weasel, just as he was setting out with Toad's invitations. I suspected something from what you told me, and had a look at one or two; they were simply disgraceful I confiscated the lot, and the good Mole is now sitting in the blue *boudoir*, filling up plain, simple invitation cards."

At last the hour for the banquet began to draw near, and Toad, who on leaving the others had retired to his bedroom, was still sitting there, melancholy and thoughtful. His brow resting on his paw, he pondered long and deeply. Gradually his countenance cleared, and he began to smile long, slow smiles. Then he took to giggling in a shy, self-conscious manner. At last he got up, locked the door, drew the curtains across the windows, collected all the. chairs in the room and arranged them in a semicircle, and took up his position in front of them, swelling visibly. Then he bowed, coughed twice, and, letting himself go, with uplifted voice he sang, to the enraptured audience that his imagination so clearly saw.

TOAD'S LAST LITTLE SONG!

The Toad—came—home!
There was panic in the parlour and howling in the hall
There was crying in the cow-shed and shrieking in the
*   stall,*
When the Toad—came—home!

When the Toad—came—home!
There was smashing in of window and crashing in of door,
There was chivvying of weasels that fainted on the floor!
When the Toad—came—home!

Bang! go the drums!
The trumpeters are tooting and the soldiers are saluting,
And the cannon they are shooting and the motor-cars are hooting,
As the—Hero—comes!

Shout—Hoo-ray!
And let each one of the crowd try and shout it very loud,
In honour of an animal of whom you're justly proud,
For it's Toad's—great—day!

He sang this very loud, with great unction and expression; and when he had done, he sang it all over again.

Then he heaved a deep sigh; a long, long, long sigh.

Then he dipped his hairbrush in the water-jug, parted his hair in the middle, and plastered it down very straight and sleek on each side of his face; and, unlocking the door, went quietly down the stairs to greet his guests, who he knew must be assembling in the drawing-room.

All the animals cheered when he entered, and crowded round to congratulate him and say nice things about his courage, and his cleverness, and his fighting qualities; but Toad only smiled faintly and murmured, "Not at all!" Or, sometimes, for a change, "On the contrary!" Otter, who was standing on the hearth-rug, describing to an admiring circle of friends exactly how he would have managed things had he been there, came forward with a shout, threw his arm round Toad's neck, and tried to take him round the room in triumphant progress; but Toad, in a mild way, was rather snubby to him, remarking gently, as he disengaged himself, "Badger's was the mastermind; the Mole and the Water Rat bore the brunt of the fighting; I merely served in the ranks and did little or nothing." The animals were evidently puzzled and taken aback by this unexpected attitude of his; and Toad felt, as he moved from one guest to the other, making his modest responses, that he was an object of absorbing interest to everyone.

The Badger had ordered everything of the best, and the banquet was a great success. There was much talking and laughter and chaff among the animals, but through it all Toad, who of course was in the chair, looked down his nose and murmured pleasant nothings to the animals on either side of him. At intervals he stole a glance at the Badger and the Rat, and always when he looked they were staring at each other with their mouths open; and this gave him the greatest satisfaction. Some of the younger and livelier animals, as the evening wore on, got whispering to each other that things were not so amusing as they used to be in the good old days; and there were some knockings on the table and cries of "Toad! Speech! Speech from Toad! Song! Mr Toad's Song!" But Toad only shook his head gently, raised one paw in mild protest, and, by pressing delicacies on his guests, by topical small-talk, and by earnest inquiries after members of their families not yet old enough to appear at social functions, managed to convey to them that this dinner was being run on strictly conventional lines.

He was indeed an altered Toad!

After this climax, the four animals continued to lead their lives, so rudely broken in upon by civil war, in great joy and contentment, undisturbed by further risings or invasions. Toad, after due consultation with his friends, selected a handsome gold chain and locket set with pearls, which he dispatched to the gaoler's daughter with a letter that even the Badger admitted to be modest, grateful, and appreciative; and the engine-driver, in his turn, was properly thanked and compensated for all his pains and trouble. Under severe compulsion from the Badger, even the barge-woman was, with some trouble, sought out and the value of her horse discreetly made good to her; though Toad kicked terribly at this, holding himself to be an instrument of Fate, sent to punish fat women with mottled arms who couldn't tell a real gentleman when they saw one. The amount involved, it was true, was not very burdensome, the gipsy's valuation being admitted by local assessors to be approximately correct.

Sometimes, in the course of long summer evenings, the friends would take a stroll together in the Wild Wood, now successfully tamed so far as they were concerned; and it was pleasing to see how respectfully they were greeted by the inhabitants, and how the mother-weasels would bring their young ones to the mouths of their holes, and say, pointing, "Look, baby! There goes the great Mr

Toad! And that's the gallant Water Rat, a terrible fighter, walking along o' him! And yonder comes the famous Mr Mole, of whom you so often have heard your father tell!" But when their infants were fractious and quite beyond control, they would quiet them by telling how, if they didn't hush them and not fret them, the terrible grey Badger would up and get them. This was a base libel on Badger, who, though he cared little about Society, was rather fond of children; but it never failed to have its full effect.